P9-DGN-752

Women and Religion

*To my mother, Minnie, and my father, James,
whose partnership model of marriage nurtured
a healthy son and daughter.*

Preface

Because most readers of this book will be English speaking and better acquainted with Western religious traditions, more information is directed toward their own life experiences. For instance, the section on language incorporates efforts made at inclusive language using the English language. The female researchers whose works were drawn on for this study are mostly from the Western traditions because this is the area of the author's primary interest and expertise. Western religions are probably the primary interest of most students who will be the readers. Most of the contemporary feminist religious movements as well as feminist scholarship have originated in the West, so more information is presently available on the radical, reconstructionist, and reformist feminine scholars in the Judeo-Christian tradition. Fortunately, more research is being done by feminine scholars in non-Western traditions, but they have not been studied as much by Western scholars. If this book were written twenty years from now, more attention would be given to non-Western feminist movements, but at present little information on them is available in English.

However, I made serious efforts to fulfill the global and diversity requirements suggested by many colleges. Religious writings and practices from Hindu, Buddhist, Chinese, Japanese, traditional African, Native American, Jewish, Christian, and Islamic faith communities are examined mostly from their primary sources.

A chronological approach to the material is used in order to make the content and development more comprehensible to students. By examining their past history, present practices become more intelligible. When students study the original doctrines, scriptures, and practices of a religion, they can recognize the present accretions and their ramifications. One can better apply the practice of critical thinking by examining the primary sources of religious traditions. Therefore, efforts are made to incorporate the original hymns to goddesses, creation and alienation myths, as well as the religious laws that arose at a later date, but claim to be derived from the original scriptures. Students of religion should be able to judge for themselves if these laws and practices are applicable today. By including examples of rituals designed by women, students will gain an opportunity to devise their own prayers and rituals that will be meaningful to them.

This book takes the historical approach beginning with the Goddess religions of Paleolithic and Neolithic times. Female deities from Old Europe and the Near and Far East will be studied. Characteristics of the goddess cultures that appeared to be egalitarian and peaceful will be contrasted with the patriarchal cultures that replaced them. By studying the creation myths extolling the powers of the goddess that were replaced by creation myths praising the creative abilities of the god, students can better understand the demise of the Mother Goddess. Although alienation myths denigrated them in most religious traditions, women were able to recognize and react positively to the stories that treated them with disdain. Creative women learned to bypass the organizational structures and to ignore derogatory statements in order to secure satisfaction from their religions for their sisters and themselves. The creative adaptations that women make worldwide to the unjust situations influenced by their religious culture, hopefully should stimulate the readers to resourceful and critical thinking regarding their own traditions. Whether women create their own rituals, enter into modern goddess religions, practice wicca, or embrace the mystical life, their spirituality has unique characteristics peculiar to them. By studying the aspects of feminine spirituality, one should arrive at a greater understanding of the feminine experience of the divine.

The discussion questions try to apply the knowledge gained in each chapter to contemporary life situations. The beauty of religious studies is its practical application to everyday living. If students can use the information gained through reading to enhance their daily life experience, they find the material both interesting and practical. The content that is read is more likely to be remembered. By considering alternative religious experiences, whether they include prayer, rituals, or other expressions of religious traditions, the creative ability of our students should be enhanced. The glossary at the end was designed to help students understand the concepts of each religious tradition. The students in the author's class who saw the videos responded very enthusiastically to them.

I wish to thank Maggie Barbieri, my editor, for her encouragement and concern that brought the book to completion. Special appreciation is due to Patricia Mumme from the College of Worster, Ohio, for her insightful suggestions as prime reviewer. The efforts of the Reverend John Weimer as copyreader, who tirelessly read all the chapters, gave me greater self-confidence when sending the first drafts to the editor. Thanks also to Jennifer Hense for copyediting the manuscript. Lasting gratitude must be given to Marilyn Coyne, whose many hours typing at the computer made the book a reality.

M. F.

Introduction

According to a survey, Americans are more religious than their European neighbors. A full 90 percent of Americans believe in a personal God, and 79 percent find comfort from their religion. They also attend religious services more often (Gallup International Survey, 1989).

Although 91 percent of Americans are affiliated with a church, women outnumber men in church attendance, 46 percent to 38 percent (Gallup 1988). Sixty-one percent of women agree that religion is an important factor in their lives, versus 47% of men. Women therefore make up the majority of denominational members in the United States, but their progress in gaining positions of influence has not equaled their progress in the work force, politics, or educational areas of life. The U.S. Department of Labor statistics in 1991 showed a 13% increase in the number of female managers over the past decade. Although women only receive $0.73 on the dollar as compared with men, they have increased that rate from $.67 five years ago. More women are entering professions—including law, medicine, college faculty, and other white collar professions—and now equal men in number (*Time*, August 24, 1992). Women are entering politics. They have doubled their number in the Supreme Court and increased their representation in the Senate, House of Representatives, and state executive offices. Colleges have seen an increase in the number of women presidents and professors in the past decade. However, women's leadership in religious organizations has not kept up with their changing roles in American society. This is not only an American phenomenon: Many women across the world find themselves in a similar dilemma.

Women's lives have been affected by religious traditions throughout the world in that religion has played a crucial role in shaping the status and lifestyle of women. Some religions have improved the conditions of women and recognized them as full participants in their faith communities. Most religious traditions teach that women are equal before their deity and that they can receive the promise of salvation. Some women have used the opportunities presented for leadership in their religious communities as springboards to help them further social issues such as abolition of slavery, the right to vote, the establishment of settlement houses, fair housing practices, and child and family protection laws. Other women have become mystics in their own religious traditions, arriving at a spiritual growth marked by union with the divine.

But the institutional religions have not always promoted the welfare of women. Historically, the upper-class hierarchies of Christian churches, Jewish synagogues, Hindu ashrams, Buddhist sanghas, and Islamic ummahs have served men better than women. In traditional religions such as Hinduism, Buddhism, Confucianism, Judaism, Christianity, and Islam, women have usually occupied positions of inferior status and power. They are presently denied positions of cultic leadership in Roman and Orthodox Catholic churches. Hindu and Chinese women are kept in subjection by their male relatives to whom they must give respect and obedience because their religions teach that women are inferior to men. Jewish and Islamic law exempt women from participation in some religious rituals and group prayer because of their monthly discharge, which is considered impure. When discriminatory actions against women are justified by religious scriptures, laws, and practices, they are difficult to change. Usually, the mediators of a religion such as priests, brahmins, and mullahs reflect the gender of the deity. If the deity is male, then his representatives are also male. The deity usually depicts the best characteristics of humans in the religious society. Again, if the deity is male, men are offered many advantages over women in the religious and secular society. Patriarchal religions promote the dominance of men in families as well as in the political, economic, and religious aspects of society.

However, it is important to realize that this has not always been the case in the past and need not be the case in the future. Archaeologists have uncovered evidence of goddess cultures in Paleolithic and Neolithic ages. Female figurines found at sacred places such as temples and burial grounds point to worship of a female deity. Evidence of matrilinear and matrilocal societies has been uncovered recently by male and female researchers. The author hopes that the study of goddesses and their culture will empower students to engage in research that will enhance this knowledge.

Scholarship on the history of religions has tended to ignore the participation of women, most often unintentionally, by focusing on literary sources such as scripture, myths, doctrinal works and the actions of religious institutions that denied women access. The issue of research is critical for students of religion. As in other fields, male researchers have examined evidence from a male perspective and arrived at conclusions that arise from their own male experience. Recently, some female researchers have brought the insights from their own experience to the same evidence, which enhanced, broadened, and in some cases overturned former conclusions. Women researchers look to the original purpose of the sacred writings as well as the early practices in order to understand the spirit behind them before patriarchal cultures made their accretions. For example, female researchers noticed that a number of the female figurines from Neolithic times found by archaeologists contained the remnants of oil and carbon in cups that decorated their headdresses. Male researchers who preceded them at the site had passed these figures off as dolls, but female researchers concluded that they must have been using fire in a religious ritual of offering, probably to a goddess. The work of female researchers should be studied by all students so that religious history can be reconstructed to restore women's stories and reclaim religious culture that belongs to both men and women. We need to expose students to various theological methods of investigation by making available the revisions and reconstructions of religious history that feminist scholarship has achieved.

As female scholars research ancient religious documents, many find that women were accepted in the past as full participating members in their religious traditions. Later changes made by patriarchal cultures have denied women their earlier positions of leadership in their religious communities. If there was a role of prominence for women at one time in a tradition's history, there is a precedent established that should not deny them that role at a later date. Female scholars noticed that women were included in the traditional Jewish male community of the Essenes, who lived by the Dead Sea in the first centuries BCE and CE. For centuries it had been thought that this group of ascetic men had lived in community and practiced Judaism in its purist form. Women scholars recently analyzed the rules of the Essene congregation, which are part of the Dead Sea Scrolls, ancient biblical manuscripts, and commentaries discovered near the Dead Sea in 1947. These scholars found that women were not excluded from the community, even though they might be considered ritually impure because of their monthly discharge. The researchers concluded that Jewish women must have been considered full members of the Essene Jewish community, although women have not been recognized as such by the leaders in later Judaism. Feminine Christian scholars have found mosaics on walls of a third century church in Rome that show a woman bishop. As more women bring their expertise and experience to the field of religious research, they will uncover more evidence to show that women participated more fully in past religious communities than earlier researchers admitted.

Much of the contribution made by women has been in the area of popular religion. It has consisted of the beliefs, myths, rituals, art, and practices of ordinary people, most of whom were illiterate and socially marginal, as opposed to the religious beliefs, art, and practices of the educated and politically powerful. Because most patriarchal cultures have barred women from possessing political power in religious institutions and have neglected the education of women, preventing them from contributing to religious literature, the participation of women in religion has been largely on the popular level. Religion that is associated with the powerful in its tradition such as the clergy, who are educated for their roles, is usually referred to as elite religion. Religion associated with the general populace, whose members are less educated in the formal tenets of their religious beliefs and practices, is usually called popular religion. Michelangelo's Sistine Chapel paintings are elite religious art, whereas the hand-painted Madonna on the wall in an Italian wayside shrine is considered popular religious art. A Catholic Mass in a large cathedral is an elite religious ritual, but a street procession in which people carry statues of Jesus and Mary around town is in the realm of popular religion.

Women, who have been forbidden by patriarchal social structures from participating in elite religions, have made significant contributions to popular religions. By engaging in practices that are meaningful to them, women can enjoy rituals, processions, study groups, and devotional practices that encompass their own experience. In addition to the institutional and popular division, mystical traditions of most religions can offer their followers an opportunity to approach the deity directly without consulting religious structures that might exclude women. Many women find great challenge and consolation with this direct route to the divine. Religious laws, traditions, and scriptures affect women in relation to their own experience. Even though the laws often appear discriminatory toward them, women have adapted creatively, either by ignoring the laws or by circumventing them to approach the divine directly. By recognizing patriarchal traditions for what they are, women can adapt the tradition to their own experience so that they can derive more meaning and satisfaction from the beliefs and practices. With more education women learn to think critically and can recognize the abuses. Thus they can extract from religion the positive experiences of hope, solace, and satisfaction rather than the negative aspects that impede their progress.

We need to investigate the position of women in various major religious traditions in order to make generalizations regarding the use and abuse of religion. Because some tenets of religion are abused by some of its adherents does not mean that women should abandon all religions, but when some women perceive the injustice directed at them by their religious traditions, they may want to leave that community of faith. By exposing students to the contributions of women from various religious traditions, students may see the worth of remaining in their communities of faith in order to improve conditions for everyone. The example of intelligent competent women who brought about change in their faith communities should serve as a stimulus for students to do the same. Women have been influenced by their religious doctrines, scriptures, rituals, symbols, and examples of virtue, but they in turn have shaped the religious experience of these same traditions. Women who understand fully their present condition can do something about it—whether they join the radical feminist movement, look for alternative religious movements such as goddess-centered religions, or stay in their own faith communities. The important issue for students is not whether to be converted to any other movement but to know what factors make them leave or stay in their own religious communities and how they can improve their traditions to become more inclusive.

Contents

CHAPTER 2

Patriarchy and the Shift from Female to Male Deities   *28*

CHAPTER 3

Creation Myths Reflecting the Demise of the Mother Goddess   *56*

CHAPTER 4

Alienation Myths and Other Practices That Affect Women 75

CHAPTER **5**

Competent Women Who Helped Shape Their Religious Traditions   *120*

CHAPTER 6

Language As a Representation of Reality   *157*

CHAPTER 7

Contemporary Feminist Religious Movements   *173*

CHAPTER 8

Reasons for Women to Value Religion   *213*

Women and Religion

CHAPTER 1

Early Goddess Cultures

Contemporary students of Western religions such as Judaism, Christianity, and Islam usually picture their deity as male. Jews may call him Yahweh, Christians address him as God or Christ, and Muslims refer to him as Allah. It was thought until recently that the ancients worshipped primarily male deities or gods. But that is not true! Recent research has uncovered evidence that the female deity, in the form of the goddess, was worshipped in Paleolithic and Neolithic times. Archaeologists and historians have uncovered evidence of goddess religions in southern Europe, in areas now occupied by France, Spain, Italy, and the Balkan countries. Southern Asia—areas in present Turkey as well as Greece and the Islands of Malta and Crete—has yielded many artifacts that point to veneration of the feminine. Even England and Ireland contain remnants of shrines and sacred places that were dedicated to goddesses. Because goddess cultures developed before the discovery of writing, reliable literary evidence is difficult to find. But archaeologists and religious historians have uncovered evidence of goddess religions from female figurines found in areas of sacred significance such as burial grounds and temples. These artifacts give us insights into the religion and customs of the goddess cultures.

Sources of Information Regarding Goddesses

Archaeological Findings

When written historical records are missing, historians must look to archaeological findings to supplement their information. There are no written records from 9,000 years ago, so we must examine pictorial images for messages from the peoples and their cultures. Burial grounds usually provide clues to a civilization's ideas on life after death and to other concepts concerning religion. Items found at sacred places, such as temples or other worship sites, indicate that the mediators of the deity were often women— priestesses—in Paleolithic and Neolithic times.

Pictures painted on cave walls in present-day Spain and France depict dancing priestesses from Paleolithic times, around 7000 BCE. Usually the mediators of a religion would mirror the sex of the deity, so some evidence points to a goddess culture and religion. When digging at the sacred sites, archaeologists in Europe and Asia found many figurines of women. They discovered some figurines of men, but female statues predominated at a rate of 20 to 1. Some historians have tried to dismiss these feminine fig- urines made of clay, stone, marble, and copper as dolls, but the cups found in their headdresses contained remnants of oil and carbon, indicating sacri- ficial offerings of a religious nature. Modern women researchers such as Gimbutas (1982), Condren (1989), Downing (1990), and Dexter (1990) think that these figurines represent goddesses who were the primary deities of their ancient civilizations.

Architecture of buildings usually gives insights into the structures' use and purpose. Similarly, sacred shrines and temples are often built to reflect the prominent symbol of the religion. For instance, Christian churches have been traditionally built in the form of a cross to honor Christ, whose cruci- fixion is remembered with a cross. The remains of a temple excavated in Malta indicate that it was built in the form of a woman. A huge statue of a goddess, erected in the period 3600 to 3000 BCE, stands outside the temple, and the contours of the building match those of her body. If the sacred place was built in the form of a woman, we can deduce that the deity wor- shiped there was likewise female.

Oral Tradition and Myths

Myths are defined by scholars of religion as sacred stories. Whether or not they are true in the historical sense, they are held by their followers to contain symbolic truth. Myths make use of metaphors and images that illus- trate the truth and point to realities beyond the perceived immediate envi- ronment. Since concepts of the deity are beyond immediate human experi- ence, these ideas must often be interpreted through myths and stories. Religious myths help us to interpret the reality of our existence. Most cul- tures have creation myths that explain our origin. Eschatological myths tell us what we might expect in the afterlife. Myths often try to deal with what scholars call the problem of evil—that is, why and how evil and suffering came into the world and what can be done about them. Religions teach that evil is part of our earthly existence but hold out the hope that it can be overcome. One of the methods used by religious traditions to explain the origin of evil in our world is the use of alienation myths. Humans are sepa- rated from their deity or sense of the sacred by the loss of an ideal state of primordial happiness. They endure death, suffering, and deprivation in their alienated state, but humans can hope for salvation or liberation from these evils in this world and the next.

A myth from the Navajo tribe of North America recorded by Jean Savage, a mythologist, deals with the problem of evil by explaining that a coyotes's actions were responsible for introducing death into the world.

> During one long hard winter Coyote saw that there were too many people and not enough food, and he said that Death must be allowed to take away the old ones. Everyone was horrified and said, "This is the worst idea Coyote ever had." But Coyote said the people who died would come back when there was enough food and he explained how to build an arrow path to the sky. So the people agreed. But when some had died and the path of arrows was prepared for their return, cunning Coyote grabbed the last one and pulled all the arrows down out of the sky. That is why there is now no way for the dead to return to earth.
>
> *Savage, 190*

Many societies have originated myths involving goddesses who were responsible for bringing the world into being, aiding its growth, and allowing its regeneration after a period of death. For instance, in some pre-Christian European societies, these goddesses appeared in the triple form of virgin or maiden, mother, and crone. The virgin goddess offered the promise and potential of fertility because she contained within herself the great power of reproduction. The mother goddess shared her power of abundance and nurturance with the faithful, who gratefully received her gifts. The crone, or older woman, did not use her power to reproduce but stored that unused power in the form of wisdom. Her sage advice was diligently sought by her followers. The symbol of the triple goddess is the moon, which waxes, becomes full, and then wanes. The moon's monthly cycle is similar to women's menstrual cycle, which holds such potential for life. It is not surprising that the goddess would be connected to life in all its forms.

Myths are celebrated in rituals. Elinor Gadon, a religious historian, describes the reenactment of the myth of the life of the goddess at a Neolithic shrine in England.

> In the third millennium BCE the life story of the goddess was celebrated at Avebury in a seasonal round of festivals. The major events in her life—puberty, marriage, childbirth, and death—were the themes of dramatic rituals in which the entire community participated. The great monuments were built to symbolize these transformative rites.
>
> *Gadon, 69*

The Avebury henge monument resembled the famous site of Stonehenge with its circular stones, but with the added remnant of two stone streets a mile and a half long. Gadon continues, "The 'architecture' of the entire circle was to be read as a sequence of visual images as the Great Goddess changed from child to maiden, to mother, to crone" (71).

The goddess passed through these stages in her life in a manner similar to the changing seasons. Spring rituals celebrated the youth of the goddess along with the planting season, whose growth continues throughout the summer. Autumn rituals celebrated the rich harvest of the mature goddess. Finally, just as winter allows the vegetation to die so it may grow again, the crone symbolized the death that is necessary for life to come to birth again. A symbol of the three-phased goddess is the triple spiral, which has been found at shrines from Newgrange in Ireland to the temple Ggantia (Giant) in Malta.

Literary Evidence

Some of the myths were committed to writing. Beginning with Sumer, around 3500 BCE, written poems and hymns appear to the mother goddess, addressing her as the queen of heaven. Egyptian creation myths describe the origin of the earth from the body of the mother goddess. The restorative power of the Canaanite goddess is described in the Hebrew scriptures. Greek and Roman myths abound that glorify the mysteries and powers of goddesses. The Celts described the mystic powers of their goddesses until the arrival of Christianity. Numerous written legends and myths extol the virtues and feminine energy of Oriental goddesses even today. The Japanese shrine at Ise holds a sacred mirror that is attributed in a myth to Amaterasu, the sun goddess. Pilgrims visit the shrine annually to pay homage to the goddess. Even the emperor and his household visit the shrine of Ise, Japan, twice a year to perform a ceremony of national purification. The myth of Amaterasu is remembered by rituals performed at her shrine to ensure fertility and abundance of natural gifts.

Devotees of the goddess in various cultures have left hymns and poems that glorify their deity. These hymns or poems usually refer to the goddess as mother and extol her nurturing, protective virtues. An example of a hymn sung to the Egyptian goddess Nut, or Neit, is taken from the early Pyramid Texts. She was credited with the creation of the world and served by priestesses in the third millennium BCE. Reference is made to the priestesses who mediated the deity to her people.

> Most ancient Mother,
> Great Radiant One,
> Lady of the Stars,
> Mistress of the Celestial Ocean,
> Highest Judge,
> Fiery One who rose from the Primordial Floods,
> It is Neit who reaches down from the heavens
> to take the hand of each who dies,
> taking them into Her arms
> to place them as stars of the universe,
> each to light Her perfect body

with an emerald light,
sowing mortals upon Her heavenly self,
as others sow the green plants of the fields.
Though if Her anger was provoked
She might cause the sky to crash upon the ground,
still She was the Mother of All,
broad winged Goddess who protects from evil,
who defends the good with bow and arrow,
as She once defended those ancient priestesses
who took Her name:
Neit Hotep,
Meryet Neit,
Her Neit,
priestess queens who ruled when Egypt was young,
when only women served at Neit's altars,
each knowing throughout her life
that she would one day glisten as a star
upon the measureless body of the Mother of Heaven.

Mercer, 1

Characteristics of Goddess Cultures

Matrilinear Societies

In matrilinear societies children trace their heritage through the mother's line, rather than the father's. Historically, the mother passed down the ancestral goods because she always knew her child as the product of her womb. The father's participation in reproduction of the child was not always understood in ancient cultures, so he was given little consideration for his efforts. Rather, the mother was extolled and her role of motherhood glorified.

Evidence of social position in society is often discovered in burial tombs, because a powerful person may be buried with many possessions that show her or his status. The Etruscan tombs north of Rome, Italy, provide interesting evidence of social position. In them the bed of the mother of the family is larger and more beautifully adorned than the beds of the husband and children that surround her. Researcher E. O. James suggests that such a burial arrangement indicates a matrilinear society. Since the mother would always know her own child, she would pass on property to her offspring and her relatives would be the child's relations.

Condren (1989) says that in the tribal societies of early Ireland in the first millennium BCE the child was identified by the mother's tribe. Also, remnants of matrilinear characteristics can be found in modern Spain, where children bear the surnames of both parents.

The mother goddess in various cultures often embodies the life-giving characteristics women were seen to possess. Many of the early goddess sculptures found in Asia and Europe that date from Paleolithic and Neolithic times accent the reproductive abilities of women. The sculptures' emphasis on breasts, hips, and abdomen stress women's nurturing and creative ability. Women can nurture their children from their own body by their transformative power to make milk. They can give birth out of their bodies, a creative ability that cannot be duplicated by men. Many early societies ascribed life-giving significance to human blood, which causes death upon departing the body in excess. Women who could lose blood periodically without suffering apparent harm appeared to possess a mystical power. Mother goddesses in various cultures would embody the life-giving characteristics that were usually associated with women.

One of the life-giving characteristics of women is their ability to nurture life through their distribution of food in the form of milk. Food nourishes its recipient just as the milk nurtures infants. The nurturing ability of food became associated with the nurturing ability of the mother goddess, who bestowed her gifts in abundance upon her devotees. With the development of agriculture and the domestication of animals, the goddesses associated with human reproduction began to be connected with vegetal and animal fertility. If the goddess would ensure the fertility of humans, she could be petitioned to do the same for vegetation and animals. Woman's ability to reproduce is so awesome that it is not surprising that her offspring would look to their mother to trace their heritage.

Matrilocal Societies

Often matrilinear societies were matrilocal, meaning that the married man left his own society to make his home with his wife in her locale. The Keres Indians from Laguna Pueblo in New Mexico still hold some matrilocal traditions. In tribal culture, the clan is the central kinship group. Among the Keres, clan membership depends on matrilineal descent. The new husband joins the wife's clan and becomes integrated into her kinship relationship system. If he had been a member of the clan before marriage, he simply moves to the locale of his new wife's extended family. Paula Gunn Allen, a professor of ethnic studies from Laguna Pueblo, describes her culture as a peaceful one where men and women work together to provide for the needs of the clan. Clan membership depends not only on physical relationships, but also on the spiritual force that permeates the individual and the group. "'Community' in the American Indian world can mean those who are of a similar clan and Spirit; those who are encompassed by a particular spirit-being are members of a community" (Allen, 252). Both men and women of the clan, imbibed with this spirit, try to transcend the demands of their individual needs to consider the good of the whole kinship clan. Since the gifts of both men and women are needed for this activity, there is no need for one sex to dominate the other.

Excavations from the city of Catal Huyuk in Anatolia (present-day Turkey) from the seventh millennium BCE suggest remnants of a matrilinear and matrilocal society. James Mellaart, an archaeologist, says that the divine family of the goddess is represented in the ordinary family in order of importance as mother, daughter, son, and father (201). He says that the "sleeping platform where the woman's personal possessions and her bed or divan were located is always found in the same place, on the east side of the living quarters. That of the man shifts and is always smaller" (60).

Researchers have found that these matrilinear and matrilocal societies that worshipped a goddess appeared to be very peaceful. Archaeologists have uncovered remains of dishes, bowls, cups, jewelry, and tool designs from the area designated as Old Europe that date from the sixth millennium BCE, but there are very few relics of weapons. Marija Gimbutas, when studying excavations from the area that now is composed of the Balkan countries, claims that these agrarian settlements of 7,000 years ago were built without fortifications, indicating a civilization that saw no need for war. A society that worshipped a nurturing, beneficent mother goddess saw that nurturance in their agrarian fertility. As a result they chose to locate their settlements in lush valleys.

> Old European locations were chosen for their beautiful setting, good water and soil . . . remarkable for their excellent views of the environs, but not for their defensive value. The characteristic absence of heavy fortifications and of thrusting weapons speaks for the peaceful character of most of the art loving people.
>
> *Gimbutas, 1990, 17*

In Sicily, in the area called the Valley of the Goddesses and Gods, a museum holds hundreds of pieces of female figurines and pottery that date f·om the fourth millennium BCE. There are a few (about 30) male figurines that are surrounded by small weapons that were also excavated from the surrounding ruins. Large temples to goddesses dominate the beautiful, lush valley of Agrigento, Sicily, which gently slopes to the blue-green sea. There are no walled cities or fortifications set high on hills like those that characterize the cities whose residents worshipped warrior gods.

These agricultural settlements whose people worshipped the goddess extended from the Indus River Valley in Northwest India through the Tigris and Euphrates river basin to the Adriatic and Mediterranean Sea. Some of the pottery excavated with the female figurines from the sixth millennium BCE was emblazoned with sailing boats, indicating commerce and trade. It is no wonder that during the Neolithic Age, female figurines made from stone, bronze, and copper decorated shrines erected to goddesses from Stonehenge in England to Catal Huyuk, Turkey, and further east to India (Eisler, 22).

Partnership Models of Civilization

Matrilinear and matrilocal societies are not considered matriarchal because women do not dominate men. Researchers noticed very little differences between the graves of men and women, indicating a partnership model of relationship between the sexes. The homes were similar in size and furnishings. The numerous shrines placed between the houses were similar in shape and size to the homes, indicating a communal rather than hierarchical style of religious worship and structure. The editors of a Time–Life series, in citing the excavations from Catal Huyuk, noted that the furnishings of the homes were similar, which indicates a nonhierarchical system (no stratification based on wealth and status) (Time–Life Books). Even the shrines contained both male and female symbols, such as a wall containing a plaster head of a bull flanked by rows of female breasts. Although female figurines predominated, excavators found some male symbols such as horns and bulls. If a peaceful culture is to endure, one might expect a communal or partnership form of civilization to accompany it.

Examples of Goddess-Worshipping Societies

Paleolithic Age (Ca. 30,000 to 7000 BCE) in Europe

New interpretations of older research have produced innovative insights into the goddess culture of old Europe. E. O. James, a religious historian, noticed that corpses found in Paleolithic burial grounds in France were covered with cowrie shells that formed a vaginalike opening. The cowrie, con-

FIGURE 1.1 Earth Mother of Willendorf, 25,000 BCE, Austria. (Courtesy of the American Museum of Natural History, New York.)

sidered a life-giving agent in itself, was painted with a red ocher pigment, which is considered a symbol of the vitalizing power of blood. James thinks that the shells were used in funeral rites aimed at bringing the dead person back to life through physical rebirth. He says they "point to mortuary rituals in the nature of a life-giving ritual closely connected with the female figurines and other symbols of the Goddess cult" (19). The inhabitants of the society evidently hoped that their deceased relatives would be reborn from a mother in a manner similar to their first birth. These burial grounds acknowledge the power attributed to the female by people in the Paleolithic Age to give and restore life.

Stone-carved female figures that date from the Paleolithic age have been found in Austria and France. A famous figurine often referred to as the Venus of Willendorf (Figure 1.1) rests her arms peacefully over her ample breasts. The pubic triangle is emphasized, and the swollen body might indicate pregnancy. Another carving found in France is hewn from the rock in which it is embedded (Figure 1.2). The woman holds a horn, which could be a symbol of regeneration because some animals with horns, such as

FIGURE 1.2 Earth Mother of Loussel, Paleolithic. (Courtesy of Giraudon/Art Resource, New York.)

deer, shed their antlers to be regained later in the season. The horn could also be a male symbol because some gods are portrayed with horns emerging from their heads. Marija Gimbutas, an anthropologist and cultural historian, acknowledges that there were some male deities in polytheistic societies but believes that the female deities predominated from the seventh millennium to the third millennium BCE.

> The primary goddess inherited from the Paleolithic was the Great Goddess, whose functions included the gift of life and increase in material goods, the wielding of death and decrease, and regeneration to new life. She was the absolute ruler of human, animal, and plant life and the controller of lunar cycles and seasons. As giver of all, death wielder, and generatrix, she is one and the same goddess in spite of the multiplicity of forms in which she manifests herself.
> This prehistoric Great Goddess has the ability to appear in the form of other goddesses throughout various cultures in history. She is especially manifested in various goddesses of the Neolithic and later ages.
>
> *Gimbutas, 1980, 511*

Neolithic Age (6500 to 3500 BCE) in Southeast and Central Europe

A woman was highly esteemed in Neolithic times because she was able to reproduce not only her own kind, but also the male child. Although our primal ancestors understood cause and effect in the immediate sense, they did not seem to understand an effect that had a cause nine months earlier. Women contained within themselves an awesome power because their birth-giving powers on a personal level reflected the feminine principle of birth on a cosmic level. Archaeological findings by Marija Gimbutas verify the great devotion to the mother goddess during the Neolithic Age. She reports that "approximately 30,000 miniature sculptures in clay, marble, bone, copper, and gold are presently known from a total of some 3,000 sites in southeastern Europe alone and these testify to the communal worship of the Mother Goddess" (Gimbutas, 1982, 11 and 12). (See Figure 1.3.)

With the increased domestication of plants and animals, village societies developed from agricultural communities. The bone, clay, and stone artifacts from these regions leave insights into the religious attitudes of the inhabitants. The temple or ritual sites contained the more valuable artifacts of marble, gold, or copper, indicating that religion was of central importance to the people. Moreover, the preponderance of female figurines at the Neolithic European sites, 20 times the number of male figurines, strongly indicates goddess worship (Dexter, 4). Recent female researchers such as Gimbutas, Gadon, and Dexter insist that goddesses were more than fertility deities in that they had power over death as well as life. Although she could cause death, the goddess could also bring about rebirth in nature, seasons,

FIGURE 1.3 Sitting Goddess from Pazardzik, Fifth Millenium BCE. (Courtesy of Erich Lessing/Art Resource, New York.)

and humans and so reigned over the whole cycle of life. In her position as the divine mother who bestows life on her people, the goddess continued to nourish that life and finally received it back into her cosmic womb. All of nature reflected this harmonious unity of her person because it came from her creative power and then returned to her in order to be regenerated, or born again.

Often the figurines are represented in the hybrid forms of woman and snake or bird. It is likely that the snake was connected to the regenerative powers of the goddess because it sheds its old skin and miraculously renews itself. The bird goddesses usually had birdlike heads, long necks, breasts, wings, and protruding buttocks that resembled the form of ducks or swans. They were usually associated with the creative energy of a goddess who nourished her people and the earth with water in the form of rain, rivers, and seas.

Great Goddess in India, from Indus Valley, 2500 BCE to the Present

The Maha Devi, or Great Goddess, was a main deity of the highly developed Indus Valley civilization. She was worshipped in the cities of Harappa and Mohenjo-daro, where excavations show homes and large buildings equipped with sewer systems and other technological advances. Many female figurines with headdresses containing smoke-stained cups were found at burial grounds and sacred places such as groves of trees. It is likely that these cups held the oil or incense that was burned in a ritual manner at religious services to honor the Great Goddess. Tree groves or trees alone were sacred places associated with fertility and regeneration. The abundance of the goddess symbolizes fertility, just as the tree grows and extends its branches, which become laden with fruit. The tree sometimes loses its sap and leaves during the cold season, but it regenerates in the growing season. It mirrors the regenerative power of the goddess. Elinor Gadon, a women's studies professor, says, "The association of the sacred female and the Goddess with the tree was a perennial theme in the Indian subcontinent from the earliest surviving artifacts of the Indus Valley civilization to contemporary village worship. The tree, like the Goddess, represents generation" (171).

The worship of the Maha Devi in medieval to modern India appears polytheistic and monotheistic at the same time. It can be called polytheistic because she was worshipped under different names and forms consistent with her functions. For example, under the name *Mother Goddess* she could take the form of the beneficent mother who cared for her devotees or offered them favors. Or, in later times, with the names *Kali* or *Durga*, she assumed the forms of a terrible goddess who was responsible for death and destruction. Worship of the Maha Devi can also be considered monotheistic in that she was the all-powerful deity who transcended all reality. By assuming both forms, the beneficent and the terrible, she could preside over all aspects of life—its creation, growth, and demise. The Vedic scriptures of India, which emerged in the second millennium BCE, refer to the Great Goddess in her benign form as Aditi and identify the fearful death-related aspects of life with her counterpart, Nirriti.

The goddess Aditi was described in the early scriptures of the Aryans, who replaced and absorbed the Indus Valley civilization, as all encompassing and transcending immediate reality.

> II.7.2 Aditi is the heaven, Aditi is the mid-air, Aditi is the mother and the father and the son, Aditi is all gods, Aditi is five-classed men, Aditi is all that has been born and shall be born.
>
> *Rig-veda X. 72, 4; ca. 1200 BCE*

Her terrible counterpart, the goddess Nirriti, was the punisher of transgressors of the laws against nature. She would receive the evil ones and bind them tightly, causing their death.

II.7.8. That cord around your neck, not to
be undone, which Nirriti the goddess bound.

Atharvaveda VI. 63.1; ca. 900 BCE

Statues of the Maha Devi in her various forms decorate shrines in many homes and temples of modern India. Her favor is sought to ward off diseases, to keep the home safe, and to ensure the prosperity of the family. Statues of the goddess are decorated with garlands, perfumed, and carried in processions because she is an integral part of contemporary popular religion. Sometimes the goddess is venerated in the form of Sitala, the small pox goddess who protects the village from disease. The goddess Laksmi is appealed to for her gifts of wealth and prosperity. In the form of Sarasvati, she has guardianship of learning and the arts. Whatever form the Maha Devi takes, her devotees follow her with reverence and enthusiasm.

Ancient Mesopotamia, 3500 to 2000 BCE

Sumeria

The Sumerian culture that inhabited the lower area of the Tigris and Euphrates river basin can trace its origin to about 3500 BCE. One of the earliest goddesses, Ninhursag, was worshipped by Neolithic Mesopotamian society. In the paradise myth of Sumer, she presides over the life and death of goddesses, gods, humans, animals, and vegetation. The origins of agriculture and the healing power of medicinal plants are attributed to this mother goddess.

Another Sumerian goddess, Inanna, the deity of regeneration, was connected with the change of seasons that evokes the cycles of death and rebirth. Inanna was killed after descending into the underworld to visit her sister, Ereshkigal, another goddess. While she was deprived of her vital forces in the underworld, all of nature followed suit. No vegetation grew, and neither humans nor animals produced offspring. After her resurrection to life and return to the upper world, plant, animal, and human life began again.

The goddess Inanna demonstrates the ability of the goddess to incorporate within herself aspects of the woman as virgin and mother. Because she had no significant or equal male consort, but reigned as an independent deity, she was considered a virgin, the first of the triple form of the goddess. A Sumerian fragment recorded around 2000 BCE calls her *Mother Inanna, Goddess and Queen of Heaven*, which indicates the second form of the goddess in her fullness. The poet Enheduanna describes the goddess in her poem *The Exaltation of Inanna* as the "pre-eminent one of heaven and earth Inanna" (1.2.4) (Hallo and Van Dyk, 12, quoting Enheduanna, *The Exaltation of Inanna* 12; ca. 2500 BCE).

Babylonia

Another area of Mesopotamia is Babylonia, where the Babylonian goddess Ishtar assimilated many of the qualities of Inanna. Ishtar was a warrior queen who defended her servants and protected her realm. She was addressed by her worshippers as *All powerful* because she ruled and wore the crown of dominion. She led her people to victory, and they in turn glorified the name of their mistress, who reigns in Heaven according to the following hymn.

> O possessor of all divine power, who reigns
> in Heaven of dominions,
> O Lady, glorious in thy greatness; over all
> the gods it is hailed.
>
> O deity of men, goddess of women, whose
> designs no one can conceive
> Where thou does look, one who is dead lives;
> one who is sick rises up.
>
> *Mendelssohn, 155–159*

In order to secure her favors, petitioners would offer gifts to the goddess Ishtar, often in the form of food, oil, wine, or animal sacrifice. They also offered images of female genitalia, usually carved out of a precious stone. The vulva symbolized not only fertility, but also the sacredness of female sexuality, whose mysterious life-giving power included healing. Ishtar was a virgin goddess who, although protecting her people, also assumed the maternal qualities of giving and restoring life.

Egypt, 2500 BCE

Often gods and goddesses are divided into sky gods and earth goddesses. It is now believed that the primeval Egyptian mother goddess, Nut, was associated with the sky, contrary to the position of most past mythologists, who, in describing other cultures, say that it is more natural for a sky god to inseminate the earth. Nut is often portrayed as stretching across the sky, with her body representing the heavens and her arms and legs, the pillars upon which the sky rests. Her headdress is sometimes encircled by the snake that swallows its tail, called a uraeus. Just as the snake has the power to regenerate itself by shedding its skin, the goddess Nut had power to preside over life, death, and resurrection. The iconography of Nut shows her arching over her lover Geb, the earth. From this union comes a family of gods and goddesses (Figure 1.4.).

Isis, another Egyptian deity, was the daughter of Nut and was deeply involved in her family relationships. She brought back to life her husband/brother Osiris, who was killed by his evil brother Set. Her son Horus, whom Isis conceived in a virginal fashion without the help of a man by using a phallus made of gold, took the throne of Egypt, which Isis pre-

FIGURE 1.4   Goddess Nut, Sarcophagus from the XXX Dynasty, Sakkara. (Courtesy of the Metropolitan Museum of Art, gift of Edward S. Harkness, 1913.)

pared for him. A hymn of praise gives tribute to her powers of creation and establishment of language, laws, justice, wars, religion, and morality. A partial list of the praises of Isis can be found in the *Aretalogy* from Cyme, written in the second century BCE.

> I am Isis, mistress of every land.
> I gave and established laws for humans which
>   no one can change.
> I am the one who finds fruit for humans.
> I am the one who rises in the Dog Star.
> I am the one called goddess by women.
> I divided earth from the heavens.
> I showed the paths of the stars.
> I set up the course of the sun and moon.
> I devised business in the sea.
> I made justice strong.
> I brought women and men together.
> I established that women should bear children
>   after nine months.
> I ordained that parents should be loved by
>   their children.

I and my brother Osiris put an end to
   cannibalism.
I revealed mysteries to humans.
I taught them to honor images of the gods.
I consecrated the temples of the gods.
I broke down governments of tyrants.
I put an end to murders.
I caused men to love women.

The power of Isis is apparent in her relation to all the pharaohs of Egypt who consider themselves the sons of Horus. She is pictured in Egyptian art as the throne upon which Horus and successive pharaohs sit. Some mythologists, such as Joseph Campbell, trace the artistic renditions of Mary the mother of Jesus to the portraits of Isis. Holding her son Horus upon her lap like a throne, Isis appears to be the prototype for the statues of Mary, whose lap becomes the throne for her son Jesus (Figure 1.5 and Figure 1.6).

FIGURE 1.5   Isis Suckling Horus.
(Courtesy of Alinari/Art Resource, New
York.)

FIGURE 1.6 Virgin and Child, Oak Statue, Twelfth Century AD, France. (Courtesy of the Metropolitan Museum of Art, gift of Pierpont Morgan, 1916.)

Canaan

Like Isis the goddesses of Canaan, which was located in the present area of Palestine, involved themselves in their family affairs. Asherath, the creatrix of the gods, was married to the Father God, El. She was praised by her devotees, who recognized her generative ability in hymns: 1, 2.72. "Propitiation to the great lady/ Asherath of the Sea; honor to the Creatrix/ of the Gods. . ." (Mendelssohn, 246–248; *KTU* 1.4; 21, 22; ca. 1300 BCE.

Asherath had a daughter, Anath, who possessed similar qualities to the goddess Isis in that she restored her dead brother to life. Anath's story is told in an ancient myth from about the fourteenth century BCE, written in the Ugaritic language, which was found on clay tablets in an excavation in the early nineteenth century. Anath rose to great prominence as a warrior goddess. She restored to life her brother, the God Baal, by killing his murderer, Mot. Her strong warrior-like qualities intimidated even her father El. When she demanded a favor from him, she threatened him with force, causing him quickly to capitulate.

> 1.2.47 The maiden Anath answered [El] . . .
> I shall cause your gray head
> to flow with blood,
> your gray beard with gore.
>
> *"Hymn to Anath" KTU 1.3. ii v19–25*

Anath, as a warrior goddess, was credited by her devotees for their own success over their enemies. She, like the Mesopotamian goddess Ishtar, displayed a plurality of qualities that appear at times contradictory. Their characteristics of love, beauty, and creativity are paired with the opposing qualities of rage, violence, and destruction. These multifaceted goddesses inspired fear and reverence as well as love and devotion in their followers.

Celtic Goddesses in Ireland, First Millennium BCE

Irish poets, or scribes, were highly esteemed for their portrayal of Irish history through myths, sagas, law codes, and pseudohistorical accounts of the Celtic or Irish peoples. Some of the myths tell of a goddess whose triple form resembled goddesses of Europe. The Irish goddesses represented the cycle of birth, life, and death in the form of the maiden, mother, and crone. Engraved on pre-Christian monuments, such as the Stone Age passage grave at New Grange, is the Triple Spiral, representing the three functions and phases of the goddess as virgin, mother, and crone. Manifested in its mountains, valleys, rivers, and seas, the spirit of the goddess permeated Ireland. Even her name, Eriu, was celebrated by the Irish, who called their island Eire before the eleventh century CE. Many of the rivers were named after goddesses in memory of the womb openings of the Great mother. For example, the goddess Life gave her name to the river Liffey, as did the goddess Sinnann to the river Shannon and the goddess Brigit to the river bearing her name.

Brigit, in the Irish tradition of the triple goddess, was known as Mother Goddess, the daughter and in some instances wife of the Dagda, or Good God. Unlike the previous goddesses, who were considered territorial in that they were tied to a particular land or tribe, Brigit transcended the territorial and clan barriers to become a monotheistic goddess who could unite the various Celtic bands. Her position as law giver enabled the people to live in peace and harmony rather than in perpetual warfare. The law of vengeance had separated the tribes, but the codified laws that she inspired provided a common language for communication and transportation through inhospitable clan territories. Like the goddess Isis, Brigit was known for her wisdom, which helped to unify her people through the heritage of her laws.

Greek Goddesses, First Millennium BCE

Many of the Greek goddesses are connected to their forebears from Neolithic times. Their functions are similar to the earlier goddesses, as are their accoutrements, such as birds and snakes. Besides the figurines, pottery, and oral myths, stories of the goddesses written by Homer, dating from about 800 BCE, testify to their existence.

Demeter was the goddess of vegetation who gave life to the earth. She lost her virgin daughter Persephone to the god of the underworld, Hades, who forcefully abducted her to the underworld and would not let her go. Demeter searched everywhere for her daughter in a manner reminiscent of Isis's search for Osiris. In her sorrow, the goddess of vegetation withdrew her gift from the earth, which grew barren. Zeus, fearing that the human race would starve to death, ordered Hades to give back Persephone to her grieving mother. Because Persephone had eaten food of the underworld, she was forced to spend one third of the year there with her husband Hades but was allowed the other two thirds with her mother in the upper world. While Persephone was in Hades, in winter, the earth would be barren, but it would bloom again in the spring when she returned. Strains of the Inanna myth from Sumer are apparent in the goddess's control of changing seasons and appropriate vegetation.

The origin of Aphrodite, one of the most important goddesses in the Olympian pantheon, was described by Hesiod in the eighth century BCE. The God Kronos (the father of Zeus) had castrated his own father and thrown his genitals into the sea (Figure 1.7).

> 11:10.13 "A white foam arose from the immortal flesh;
> in it there grew a maiden, ...
> There came forth an august and beautiful
> goddess
> Gods and men call her Aphrodite.
>
> *Hesiod Theogony 190–197, ca. 750 BCE*

Aphrodite was given some of the accoutrements of the Neolithic bird and snake goddesses. An early Greek sculptor depicted her with a snake coiled around her arm, and a clay drinking cup that was found portrayed her riding a goose. She was considered a love goddess, but not bound by the rules of chastity. Although Aphrodite was unfaithful to her divine husband, she was not censured by the Gods. Greek men and gods could lust after her beauty, but they could not bind her into a monogamous marriage. She celebrated her power in her autonomy and refused to be bound by the rules of chastity to which the women in Greek society and the rest of the pantheon had to adhere. She was typical of the virgin goddess who could have children, but she was not dominated by or a consort to a god. Aphrodite passed down her love-making ability to her son Eros, who was known for his ability to stir up the passions of his devotees, thus continuing her function as love goddess.

FIGURE 1.7   Birth of Venus, 400 BCE, Greece. (Courtesy of Alinari/Art Resource, New York.)

Roman Goddesses

The Romans incorporated into their own religious belief system many deities from the Greek pantheon, including the forms and functions of some of the goddesses. In the first century BCE, classical Rome borrowed the Greek goddess Cybele, whom the Romans addressed as Great Mother.

> II.ii.3. Bountiful mother of the gods,
> the goddess from Mount Ida . . .
>
> *Virgil, Aeneid X.252, 70–19 BCE*

Isis from Egypt became very popular in Roman Italy. In his story *Metamorphoses,* Apuleius describes her in the following manner.

> II.II.12 I am. . .the mother of all things in
>   nature,
> mistress of all the elements
> the initial offspring of the ages,
> the greatest of all the divine powers . . .
> the uniform face of the gods and
>   goddesses.
>
> *Apuleius, Metamorphoses Xi.2, ca. 123 BCE*

The advent of Christianity in the fourth century CE put an end to the popularity of Isis, but her spirit continued in the form of the Virgin Mary. Isis, often portrayed with her child Horus on her lap, became the model for Mary holding Jesus in Christian iconography. The Romans incorporated the Greek goddess Aphrodite into their love goddess, Venus, but also gave her characteristics of the mother goddess. Ovid called Venus the "founder of the human race." She also took on the law-giving functions of the Egyptian Isis and the Celtic Brigit, but like Aphrodite, passed on her love-giving ability to her son, Cupid. Venus was not married to Jupiter, king of the Gods, but was still addressed as queen. She was more than a consort but a queen in her own right because she exercised her own autonomy and power in the Roman pantheon.

The characteristics of the earlier goddesses from the Neolithic Age continued to pass through the centuries and were assimilated into the Roman goddesses. The triple form of the goddess continued in the virgin phase, where she acted independently from the authority of men. As mother goddess, she was venerated for her vital life-giving abilities. As crone, she not only presided over death, but was credited for her wisdom as law giver and prudent counselor.

Summary

The survey of the goddesses from these various ancient cultures reveals several important insights. Before the development of writing, images of goddesses so extensively outnumbered the images of gods that one can conclude that goddess worship preceded worship of gods by many centuries (Figures 1.8, 1.9, and 1.10).

New research by many women scholars allows interpretation of old findings that give fuller insights into the role and functions of the goddess. Researchers such as Merlin Stone and James Mellaart have found that the worship of goddesses can be traced to early Paleolithic times. Although she assumes different names in various cultures, the goddess retains her triple form of maiden, mother, and crone in Europe. Her energy as maiden appears in the role of warrior goddesses. She assumes the role of mother goddess when creating and nourishing the world and its inhabitants. When she allows the vegetation to diminish or her devotees to suffer, she is able to heal the ailments. If the vegetation should die or her people suffer death, the goddess, or crone, has the power to regenerate life on all levels.

When later pantheons of gods and goddesses developed, the mother goddess could assume the title of virgin goddess, although she often bore children. The virgin goddess retained her autonomy and independence because she was neither the wife nor the consort of a god and was in no way subordinate to a god.

The Cult of the Goddess included women as priestesses as well as men as priests. Women could mediate the deity to the people, which reflected

FIGURE 1.8 Areas of Early Civilization, Old Europe Map. (From Riane Eisler, *The Chalice and the Blade*, New York: HarperCollins, 1988, p. 248).

the esteemed position of women in goddess-centered societies. Excavations and documents from the Neolithic goddess-centered cultures suggest that these societies were matrilinear and matrilocal. Archaeological findings from ancient Europe support a period of peace, prosperity, and technical advancement in many of the goddess-centered societies.

The next chapter will consider the events that caused the diminishment of the influence of the goddess.

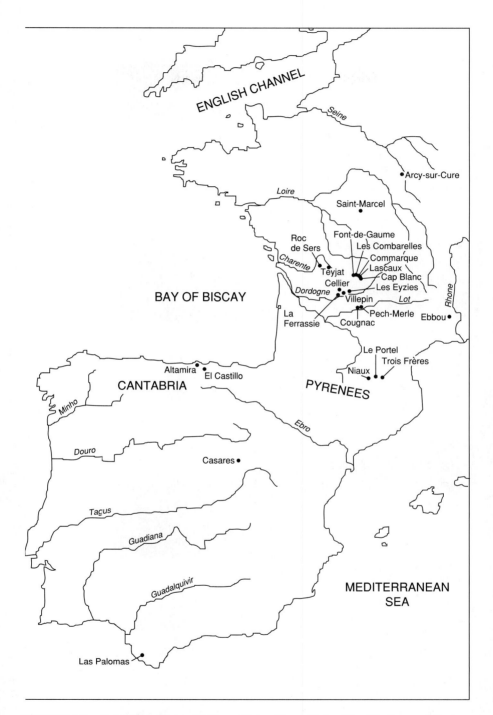

FIGURE 1.9   Paleolithic Cave Art Map. (From Riane Eisler, *The Chalice and the Blade*, New York: HarperCollins, 1988, p. 243.)

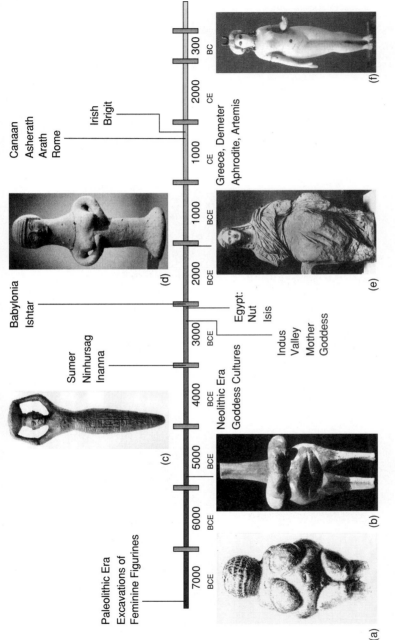

FIGURE 1.10 Time Line by Millennium: (a) Earth Mother of Willendorf, 25,000 BCE, Austria (American Museum of Natural History, New York); (b) Neolithic Female Statuette, from Cernavoda, Romania (Erich Lessing/Art Resource, New York; (c) Bronze Figurine of Ur-Nammu, 2095 BCE, Mesopotamia (Metropolitan Museum of Art, New York, gift of Mrs. William H. Moore, 1947); (d) Ceramic Figure of Asherath/Astarte, 7th Century BCE (Metropolitan Museum of Art, New York, gift of Harris D. Colt and H. Dunscombe Colt, 1934); (e) Demeter, Late Roman Classical (Foto Marburg/Art Resource, New York); and (f) Alabaster Goddess Innana, 3rd Century BCE (RMN/Duplicata, Louvre Museum, Paris).

Questions for Discussion

1. Describe some of the characteristics of the goddess. Explain the significance of each.
2. Compose a two-sentence prayer addressed to the mother goddess. How does it resemble or differ from a prayer addressed to a male deity?
3. How can we say that the later historical goddesses of literate societies bear the imprint of the earlier goddesses in cultures that developed before the discovery of writing?
4. How do the triple forms of the goddess allow her to preside over her different functions?
5. What would you expect the position of women to be in societies that worshipped the mother goddess?
6. Why is archaeological evidence used instead of written evidence in the study of the early goddesses?
7. Why would animals such as birds and snakes be associated with goddesses? What did they symbolize? Give examples.
8. Why would a warrior goddess appeal to her devotees?

Works Cited

Allen, Paula Gunn. *The Sacred Hoop*. Boston: Beacon Press, 1992.

Apuleius, *The Golden Ass*. Trans. Robert Graves. New York: Pocket Library, 1954.

Campbell, Joseph, with Bill Moyers. *The Power of Myth*. New York: Doubleday, 1988.

———. *The Mythic Image*. Princeton, N.J.: Princeton University Press, 1974.

Condren, Mary. *The Serpent and the Goddess*. New York: Harper & Row, 1989.

Dexter, Miriam Robbins. *Whence the Goddess*. Elmsford, N.Y.: Pergamon Press, 1990.

Downing, Christine. *The Goddesses, Mythological Images of the Feminine*. New York: Crossroads, 1990.

Eisler, Riane. *The Chalice and the Blade*. New York: Harper & Row, 1988.

Gadon, Elinor. *The Once and Future Goddess*. New York: Harper & Row, 1989.

Gimbutas, Marija. "The Early Civilizations of Europe." Monograph for *Indo-European Studies* 131 (University of California at Los Angeles, 1980).

———. *The Goddesses and Gods of Old Europe 6500–3500 BC*. Berkeley: University of California Press, 1990.

Grant, Frederick C. "Hellenistic Religions: The Age of Syncretism." In *The Library of Religions*, vol. 2. Liberal Arts Press, 1953.

Hallo, William W., and J. J. Van Dijk. *Exaltation of Inanna*. New Haven: Yale University Press, 1968.

James, Edwin Oliver. *The Cult of the Mother Goddess*. London: Thomas & Hudson, 1959.

Kramer, Samuel Noah. *History Begins at Sumer*. Garden City, N.Y.: Doubleday, 1956.

Lerner, Gerda. *The Creation of Patriarchy*. New York: Oxford University Press, 1986.

Mellaart, James. *Catal Huyuk*. New York: McGraw-Hill, 1967.

Mendelssohn, Isaac, ed. "Prayer of Lamentation to Ishtar." In *Religions in the Ancient Near East Sumero Akkadian Religious Texts and Ugaritic Epics*, ed. I. Mendelssohn. New York: Liberal Arts Press, 1955.

Mercer, Samuel. *The Pyramid Texts in Translation and Commentary,* vol. 2; 4 vols. New York: Longmans, Greene, 1952.

Ruether, Rosemary. *Womanguides.* Boston: Beacon Press, 1985.

Savage, Jean. "Theme and Variations on the Trickster Myth." In *Exploring Religion,* ed. Rodger Schmidt. Belmont, Calif.: Wadsworth, 1988.

Time–Life Books, ed. *The Human Dawn.*: Time–Life Books, 1985.

Suggested Readings

Agrawala, Vasudeva S. *The Glorification of the Great Goddess.* Varanasi: All-India Kashiraj Trust, 1963.

Albenda, Pauline. "Western Asiatic Women in the Stone Age: Their Image Revealed." *Biblical Archaeologist* 46, no. 2 (Spring 1983): 82–88.

Barstow, Anne. "The Prehistoric Goddess." In *The Book of the Goddess Past and Present: An Introduction to Her Religion,* ed. Carl Olson. New York: Crossroads, 1983.

———. "The Uses of Archeology for Women's History: James Mellaart's Work on the Neolithic Goddess at Catal Huyuk." *Feminist Studies* 4, no. 3 (October 1978): 7–18.

Cameron, Dorothy. *Symbols of Birth and Death in the Neolithic Era.* London: Kenyan–Dean, 1981.

Casuto, U. *The Goddess Anath.* Jerusalem: Magnes Press, 1951.

Christ, Carol P. *The Laughter of Aphrodite.* New York: Harper & Row, 1987.

Coburn, Thomas. *Encountering the Goddess.* Albany N.Y.: State University Press, 1991.

Dhal, Upendra Nath. *Goddess Laksmi: Origin and Development.* New Delhi: Oriental Publishers, 1978.

Downing, Christine. *The Goddess: Mythological Images of the Feminine.* New York: Crossroads, 1981.

Ferguson, John P. "The Great Goddess Today in Burma and Thailand: An Exploration of Her Symbolic Relevance to Monastic and Female Roles." In *Mother Worship: Theme and Variations,* ed. James J. Preston. Chapel Hill: University of North Carolina Press, 1982.

Gadon, Elinor W. *The Once and Future Goddess: A Symbol for Our Time.* New York: Harper & Row, 1989.

Gleason, Judith Oya. *In Praise of the Goddess.* Boston: Shambhala Publications, 1987.

Gray, John. *The Canaanites.* London: Thames & Hudson, 1964.

Grigson, Geoffrey. *The Goddess of Love: The Birth, Triumph, Death and Return of Aphrodite.* London: Constable & Co., 1976.

Hall, Nor. *The Moon and the Virgin.* New York: Harper & Row, 1980.

Hardin, M. Esther. *Woman's Mysteries: Ancient and Modern.* New York: Harper & Row, 1971.

———. *Theogony.* Tr. with commentary by M. L. West. Oxford: Oxford University Press, 1966.

———. *Works and Days.* Ed. T. A. Sinclair. Hildesheim: George Olms, 1966.

James, E. O. *The Cult of the Mother-Goddess: An Archaeological and Documentary Study.* New York: Frederick A. Praeger, 1959.

Keller, Mara Lynn. "Eleusinian Mysteries: Ancient Nature Religion of Demeter and Persephone," *The Journal of Feminist Studies in Religion* 1 (1987).

Kinsley, David. *The Sword and the Flute: Kali and Drsna: Dark Visions of the Terrible and the Sublime in Hindu Mythology*. Berkeley: University of California Press, 1975.

Kramrisch, Stella. "The Indian Great Goddess," *History of Religions* 14, no. 4 (May 1975): 235–65.

Lambert, W. G. *Babylonian Wisdom Literature*. Oxford: Clarendon Press, 1960.

Lloyd, Seton. *Early Anatolia*. London: Thames & Hudson, 1961.

———. *Early Highland Peoples of Anatolia*. London: Thames & Hudson, 1967.

Long, Aspholdel. "Goddesses of Wisdom," *Arachne* 6 (1987).

———. "Lilith-Night-Hag or Mother Goddess," *Arachne* 2 (1985).

Luke, Helen M. *The Way of Women, Ancient and Modern*. Three Rivers, Mich.: Apple Farm, 1975.

Maity, Pradyot Kumar. *Historical Studies in the Cult of the Goddess Manasa*. Calcutta: Punthi Pustak, 1966.

———. "Anatolian Chronology in Early Middle and Bronze Age," *Anatolian Studies Journal* (1957).

———. *Catal Huyuk*. London: Thames & Hudson, 1967.

———. *Catal Huyuk: A Neolithic Town in Anatolia*. New York: McGraw-Hill, 1967.

———. "Excavations at Catal Huyuk," *Anatolian Studies Journal* (1964).

———. "Excavations at Hacilar," *Anatolian Studies Journal* (1961).

Miller, Patrick. "Ishtar and Her Cult." In *Book of the Goddess Past and Present*, ed. Carl Olson. New York: Crossroads, 1983.

Monoghan, Patricia. *The Book of Goddesses and Heroines*. New York: E. P. Dutton, 1981.

Mullins, J. *The Goddess Pele*. Hawaii: Tong Publishing, 1977.

Neumann, Erich. *The Great Mother*. Princeton, N.J.: Princeton/Bollingen, 1955.

Oda, Mayumi. *Goddesses*. Berkeley: Lancaster–Miller, 1981.

Olson, Carl, ed. *The Book of the Goddess, Past and Present*. New York: Crossroads, 1985.

Saggs, H. W. F. *The Greatness That Was Babylon*. London: Sidgwick & Jackson, 1962.

Sargent, T., trans. *Homerick Hymns*. New York: W. W. Norton, 1973.

Schmandt-Besserat, Denise, and S. M. Alexander. *The First Civilization: The Legacy of Sumer*. Austin: University of Texas Press, 1975.

Schneider, David M., and Kathleen Gough, eds. *Matrilineal Kinship*. Berkeley: University of California Press, 1962.

Stone, Merlin. *When God Was a Woman*. New York: Harcourt Brace, 1976.

Wolkstein, D., and S. N. Kramer. *Innana*. New York: Harper & Row, 1983.

CHAPTER 2

Patriarchy and the Shift from Female to Male Deities

Students may wonder why so few cultures in the world today venerate goddesses. We are hard pressed to find goddess cultures in the Western world. Male gods and patriarchal cultures have replaced the goddesses and matrilinear and matrilocal societies in most areas of Europe, the Near East, and the Americas. *Patriarchy* refers to men's dominance over women and children in the family and male dominance over women in society. Gerta Lerner says "it implies that men hold power in all the important institutions of society and that women are deprived of access to such power" (239). She points out that women are neither totally powerless nor totally deprived of their rights and resources but that they do remain in a secondary position in their social, political, economic, and religious institutions.

Patriarchy is manifested in paternalism, whereby the father of the family dominates his wife and children in exchange for economic support and protection. Governments that are controlled by men, businesses that impede the growth of women workers, and religious organizations that forbid women leadership roles are other examples of patriarchal institutions.

The establishment of patriarchy was a gradual process extending over 2,500 years, from approximately 3100 to 600 BCE in Europe and Asia. This chapter examines the causes of the rise of patriarchy and its influence on the mother goddess cultures of Asia Minor, the Near East, and "Old Europe," an area designated by Marija Gimbutas that extended from the Adriatic to the Aegean Seas, including the islands.

Sources of Information Regarding Patriarchy

Archaeological Findings

The most concrete evidence of the rise of patriarchy is archaeological. James Mellaart, using a sophisticated method of correlating radiocarbon dates with dendrochronology (tracing time through rings on trees), found a pattern of disruption, invasion, and natural catastrophes of the Neolithic cultures of the Near East. The areas of Old Europe, Asia Minor, the Mediterranean, and India were marked by cultural regression and stagnation, as evidenced by the dislocation of peoples, disappearance of towns, and destruction of shrines to the mother goddess. Metals such as copper and gold, which had been used for jewelry, statues, and tools, were used to make implements of destruction by 3500 BCE. The nomadic hordes from northern Europe converted these metals, especially bronze, into weapons such as daggers, maceheads, arrowheads, and battle-axes.

Archaeologists have also found that graves differed considerably from those in the mother goddess societies in that some of the more important men, such as chiefs, were buried in large, decorated burial places. Wealth seemed to influence burial rites in that an abundance of weapons, ornaments, sacrificed animals, and even remains of human sacrifices were found. "Among these contents, for the first time in European graves, we find along with an exceptionally tall or large boned male skeleton the skeletons of sacrificed women—the wives, concubines, or slaves of the men who died" (Eisler, 50). Archaeologists investigate burial grounds to discover clues to a civilization's beliefs regarding the afterlife and also look for insights into the status of its members.

It appears that most of the peaceful and egalitarian societies of the mother goddess cultures were replaced by male warriors who worshipped male warrior gods. V. Gordon Childe, a historian, notes the change in the location of the settlements that had previously flourished near fertile river basins in unprotected valleys. He says that settlements were often planted on hill tops and that the valleys were often fortified. "Competition for land assumed a bellicose character, and weapons such as battle axes became specialized for warfare" (119).

Oral Traditions and Myths

Like archaeological findings, oral traditions and myths reveal customs and ideologies of previous cultures. The new patriarchal societies developed or brought with them the oral tradition and myths that support and explain their beliefs and practices.

Some myths are written down and transmitted to the followers in forms of stories, legends, folklore, or scriptures. Others are passed down orally from generation to generation, usually with serious attempts at precision and reliability.

Joseph Campbell assigns certain functions to religious myths. Myths address the basic realities of life, such as the questions about where we come from, why we are here, and where we are going. Humans question the mysteries of their existence and seek answers regarding the beginning of life and the cosmos. Alienation myths try to explain reasons for evil in the world, for separation from the divine, and for strained relations between humans. Future or eschatological myths try to imagine life after death. Myths also present an organized image of the universe that supersedes chaos and disorder. Images of the sacred, such as gods, goddesses, and symbols, are often used to delineate sacred boundaries of the sky, water, and earth.

Myths help integrate the members of the faith community into the social order with a designation of appropriate roles for each person. The psychological function of myths helps the members of a faith community negotiate the different crises in their lives in a smooth and integrated manner. Heroes of the myths present an example of how to cope with these crises successfully. The heroes often appear to possess the most desirable qualities of the originators of the myths. For instance, the warlike nomads, Aryans from northern Europe, sang and told stories of their gods, who personified the characteristics they most admired. Troy Wilson Organ suggests that the Aryans' most prominent god, Indra, was a projection or a personification of their own sense of character (51). Indra was the god of war who helped them in their conquering endeavors, and he was often portrayed with weapons and thunderbolts. Some gods were given the credit for creation, such as Marduk in Babylonia, Yahweh in Israel, Ra in Egypt, and Prajapati in India. Even the heroes present the ideals that are cherished by the group consciousness of the community. Odysseus became the Greek ideal of manly courage, cleverness, and endurance. King Arthur brought to new heights the Norman-English ideals of chivalry, and Sigrid became the personification of the Norse Code of heroism.

In the later myths of the city states and kingdoms, in Mesopotamia and Greece, myths arose that patterned or reflected the form of government that was established. For example, if the area was ruled by a king, there was a king of the gods, such as Zeus of the Greeks and Jupiter of the Romans. Many of these archaic states made use of provincial councils in their authority system. Likewise, the myths of Greece and Rome contained a council of gods and goddesses, usually called a pantheon. Each member of the pantheon had specific duties, such as presiding over war, thunder, wind, the sea, the sky, or the underworld.

Literary Evidence

Priests and scribes wrote down the sacred myths that extolled the powers and deeds of the gods. These documents were sometimes referred to as charter documents or scriptures, because they became the foundation of the religious belief systems. The poets of Ireland and the writers of the Hebrew Bible and New Testament were all held in high esteem because their revelations helped to form the religious identities of their people. Whether their writings reflected the patriarchal focus of their societies or whether their writings helped to form their patriarchal societies is a question that has not been fully settled. Most historians will admit that both aspects, the recording and initiating, were integral to the solidification of patriarchy.

The priests and scribes became the representatives of the divinity, who mediated the will of the god through the written word. These sacred words demanded obedience from devotees, whose salvation and happiness would be determined by their compliance. The patriarchal leader of the religious community could sanctify his authority by declaring that his power was a sacred mandate given by the god. Obedience to the ruler or patriarch would become a practical application of obedience to the god. Male rulers could appeal to such gods as the Greek Zeus, Roman Jupiter, Egyptian Ra, or Hebrew Yahweh to legitimate their actions, whether they involved war, murder, or rape or concerned care and protection for their people. Often this power was used for good, but abuses of authority also occurred.

The Hebrew Bible presents a good example of the relationship between the patriarch Abraham and the Hebrew god Yahweh. Rosemary Ruether says that the sense of the deity among the Hebrews was built on the experience of desert patriarchy (3).

> The Lord of the sky speaks to the chieftain of the small tented world as patriarch to patriarch. He (Abraham) is his humble son and servant, who is thereby also empowered to rule his clan as god rules the tent of the cosmos.
>
> *Ruether, 4*

Yahweh makes a covenant, or agreement, with Abraham that signifies the conditions of their relationship. Yahweh will care for Abraham, give him land, and give him descendants who will form a nation if Abraham will show his loyalty to God through his obedience. These children, or descendants, do not seem to need the contribution of a mother, because of the words of Yahweh (Gen. 15:4): "Your heir will be issue of your own body."

The covenant became more formalized in Gen. 17:5, in which Yahweh, or God, promises Abraham that he will be the father of a multitude of nations. "I will keep my promise to you and your descendants in future generations as an everlasting covenant" (Gen. 17:7). The translators of the *Interpreter's Dictionary of the Bible* use the word *seed* for the word *issue* in Gen. 15:4 and *seed* for *descendants* in Gen. 17:7. *Seed* seems more consistent with the original Hebrew wording, which underscores the predominance of the father in generation. The covenant is sealed with the symbol of circumcision, which divinely defines the Hebrew community as male.

Characteristics of Patriarchal Cultures

Nomadic Herding Societies

A group of pastoral people inhabited the steppes of northern Europe and Asia in Neolithic times. They raised horses, sheep, and cattle. Marija

Gimbutas suggests that they were likely nomadic or seminomadic pastoral-ists because there is evidence of wheeled vehicles, which the people proba-bly used to transport household goods and families seeking new pasture ground (1977, 27). It is likely that this nomadic group migrated in several waves from the fifth millennium through the third millennium BCE. They have been referred to by some archaeologists as Proto-Indo-Europeans that moved from the steppes of northern Europe to central, southern, and west-ern Europe and into the British Isles. A similar group moved south from northern Russia to the Balkan area, Turkey, and Iran. Close to this time peri-od, a group of nomadic Hebrews migrated from the fringes of the southern civilizations into Canaan.

Archaeologists have traced the travels of these groups through the remains of their weapons. Weapons made of copper and copper-tin alloys can be traced to about 3500 BCE. These weapons were not essential to the farmers of the Neolithic age, who were more interested in using metal for hoes and agricultural implements. "But for the warlike hordes that came pouring down from the north, as well as up from the deserts of the south, they were" (Eisler, 46). Dexter says that these "Proto-Indo-Europeans lived in small patrilinear units, socially stratified according to the functions per-formed by the males in society" (34–35). The most important function was that of a warrior, a necessary role for groups that were constantly encroach-ing on one another's lands. The invaders brought physical and cultural dev-astation. Cities and villages were destroyed, as were the pottery and female figurines. Many people were massacred, as evidenced by the remains of skeletons of entire families buried in corners of their homes, where they were killed in siege. Referring to archaeological remains in Old Europe that date to the third millennium, Gimbutas says, "The diminished size of com-munities—no larger than 30 to 40 individuals—indicates a restructured social system of small herding units" (1977, 289).

The strong male warriors needed horses. The horse (which some historians claim was the first war machine) was often offered in sacrifice in India to ensure continued success in battle (Kinsley, 28). The priest knew the correct words to say to make the sacrifice acceptable to the gods. Soon a class system developed in most patriarchal societies that placed the priests, lawgivers, and judges at the highest level. The warriors were the second class because of their importance to the pastoral community. The third class, or nurturing class, which served the higher class, was composed of farmers, herdsmen, artisans, and women. The place of women and motherhood had so degenerated in the nomadic societies that the greatest insult that a warrior could hurl at a coward-ly Celtic warrior was to say he was as weak as a woman giving birth to a child.

Patrilinear and Patrilocal Societies

In patriarchal societies, lineage is traced through the father. When men began to realize their role in reproduction, they were anxious to establish their paternity because they could not be certain of their fatherhood in the same way that women could be secure in their motherhood. Humans often perceive that their quest for immortality will be achieved through their children, who will bear their names. Nomadic people wanted their flocks to be passed down to their own children, and agriculturists wanted their descendants to inherit their land.

The Hebrew Bible illustrates the concentrated effort to protect patrilinear custom by its reference to Isaac, son of Abraham; Jacob, son of Isaac; and so on, ignoring the names of their wives. The genealogy of Jesus in the New Testament is traced through all his earthly male ancestors, even though Joseph was not designated as the father of Jesus (Luke 3:23–38). Regarding Mary, designated as the only human parent of Jesus, the book of Matthew says "Jacob fathered Joseph the husband of Mary: of her was born Jesus, who is called the Christ" (Matt. 1:16).

The spread of private property made it more urgent to designate the blood relationship of children so the estate could be passed down to them by their fathers. This in turn called for more control of the sexuality of women, so the father could be certain that the child was his own. The child who would bear his name and inherit his property must have no questions regarding its origin. Monogamy, or marriage between one man and one woman, would ensure this arrangement. There would be no doubts regarding the paternity of the child, which was often questioned in matrilinear societies, in which the mother always knew her child, even though the father did not. Even today, modern civilizations usually identify children through their father's surnames.

Perhaps the ultimate justification for patriliny in Indo-European culture can be made by the Greek playwright Aeschylus in his play *The Furies*. After the hero, Orestes, kills his mother, he is hounded by the Furies, feminine prophetic personages or goddesses, for killing the one who gave him birth. Orestes asks, "But am I of my mother's?" The Furies answer, "Vile wretch, she nourished you in her womb. Do you disown your mother's blood?" Aeschylus had the god Apollo assert the claim of patriliny by saying, "The mother is not the parent of the child which is called hers. She is the nurse who tends the growth of young seed planted by its true parent the male" (Aeschylus, "Eumenides" 658:59).

In the fourth century BCE Aristotle gave scientific credence to this belief by stating that the mother has little to do with the birth of a child because she contributes only the matter, which is inferior to the spirit bestowed by the father. Overturn of matriliny was thus accomplished by the Greeks, to whom the West has turned for the birth of civilization. The patriarchal societies were designated as patrilocal in that the new bride left her family and took residence at the locale of her husband, often to live with his family.

Many theories have been examined to explain this development of patrilocality, which seems to coincide with the subordination of women. One of the theories suggested by feminist scholars Riane Eisler and Gerta Lerner connects patrilocality with slavery. When the warriors defeated their enemies, they killed the men but took the unmarried women as slaves and concubines to their own locale. "During long periods, perhaps centuries, while enemy males were being killed by their captors or severely mutilated or transported to isolated and distant areas, females and children were made captives and incorporated into the households of their captors" (Lerner, 78). Moses told the victorious Israelites to take the unmarried women of the defeated Midianites for their wives.

> So kill all male children and all the women who have ever slept with a man;
> but spare the lives of the young girls who have never slept with a man, and
> keep them for yourselves.
>
> *Numbers 31: 17, 18*

Women would develop loyalty to the new tribe because of their bond to their children. They would be less likely than male captives to lead insurrections that might endanger their children. Some of these slave women would become concubines for their masters or fill the brothels and harems of their captors.

In later neolithic times, agricultural settlements fostered the growth of patrilocality to halt tribal warfare. Lerner suggests that "the development of agriculture in the Neolithic period fostered inter-tribal exchange of women" (212). The tribes could foster better relations and less warfare if they were related by marriage. The women were expected to go live with the groom's tribe and bear his children. Sometimes the women were sold, and their future husbands paid a bride price. Poor families could better their economic situation by selling off their daughters so their sons could amass enough wealth to buy into an economically satisfying marriage.

Mary Condren, a feminist theologian, interprets a story in the Hebrew Bible about the punishment for trying to return to matrilocality (19). A concubine leaves her marriage and home of her master and returns to the home of her father. Her master/husband, a Levite of high caste, goes to her father's house to force her to return to his house. On their way back to his house, they seek hospitality at a house in a town of Gilead. A group of men gather outside the host's house and demand that the host surrender the Levite so they can abuse him. The householder offers the townsmen his own virgin daughter, saying, "Ill treat her, do as you please with her, but do not commit such an infamy against this man." But the men will not listen to him. The Levite then takes hold of his concubine and brings her out to them. "They had intercourse with her and abused her all night" (Judges 19:23–26). The Levite finds his concubine dead at the doorstep after her torture and gang rape. She has paid with her life for her attempt to return to her home and family.

Matrilocality had given way to patrilocality with the development of patriarchy. As the tribal culture developed into states with centralized government headed by kings, a more pronounced hierarchy evolved. Some of the caste societies evolved into hierarchical class societies with men and

women composing all classes, but with the power residing with the dominant men.

Hierarchy and Class Society Based on Religious Traditions

The constant fear of attack by marauding warriors caused the small settlements and villages in Old Europe and the Near East to unite for protection. They had to build fortifications, raise armies, and initiate an organized
structure to maintain them both. A strong centralized authority seemed to
be the most appropriate structure to protect the people. The new gods
seemed best represented by a sacred king, who topped the hierarchical
structure and demanded obedience from his underlings. The propertied
and wealthy classes followed in order of importance, constituting the upper
classes. The military elite and priestly class contributed to the hierarchy,
which had its basis in the patriarchal family in which the father dominated
the economic, political, and social life of the family members.

Historians refer to these hierarchical organizations—which characterized
this change from neolithic villages to urban centers—as archaic states.
These states appeared in the ancient Near East, southern Europe, and
northern Africa around the second millennium BCE. Although some of the
goddesses remained, they failed to retain their power. Most of the ancient
mother goddesses were transformed into goddesses of war or became part
of the pantheon of gods and goddesses who ruled in the same way as the
governing boards of the archaic states. The king of the pantheon was similar to the king of the state. Although the goddesses remained, most of them
were reduced to wives or consorts of the king god.

A mark of the king's power and wealth, along with property, armies, and
precious objects, was his harem. Men found it easy to control the sexuality
of women when they were slaves or concubines. Control of women's sexuality became necessary if men were to dominate the social structure of society, and laws regulating sexual behavior become more prominent in archaic
states than in goddess cultures. "Of the 282 laws in the Code of
Hammurabi, 73 cover subjects pertaining to marriage and sexual matters"
(Lerner, 102). In most archaic states, as in Greece, a woman was punished
more severely than a man for adultery because she was considered the
property of her husband, so it was he who was violated by her adultery.
This led to double standards regarding divorce. In the Hebrew sacred law,
for example, a husband could divorce his wife, but a woman could not seek
a divorce under any circumstances.

In ancient Greece and other archaic states, the practice of dividing
women into acceptable and nonacceptable classes impeded the bonding
between women. The acceptable women were under the protection of a
man, whereas the unacceptable class was composed of prostitutes, servants,
and slaves. The sharp division between the two groups of upper-class and

lower-class women blocked cross-class relationships. Women could not col-laborate, which in turn prevented their bonding.

Religious as well as social roles were transferred from women to men in archaic states. Priestesses were stripped of their rank, and the ritual prac-tices passed into the hands of the priests when male gods replaced the god-desses. Men took over other functions, such as the role of recorder, or scribe. "When the patron of the scribes changed from goddess to a god, only male scribes were employed in the temples and palaces, and his-tory began to be written from an androcentric perspective" (Rohrlich-Leavitt, 55).

Male gods who glorified war, death, and power replaced the goddesses who represented peace, life, and nurturance. By appealing to the authority of the gods, male authorities of the religious traditions instituted customs that subjugated women. Female subordination within the family became codified by law in Mesopotamia by the second millennium BCE.

Whereas the most powerful men gained their status by achieving control over land or the means of production, women gained their status through their connection to a powerful man, usually a father or husband. Women kept the benefits of this man's protection by submitting to his wishes. Those who were not under the protection of a man were doomed to the lower-class activities of servant, slave, or prostitute. Women were excluded from schooling and most professions, which limited the majority of their activities to the home.

Societies That Replaced Goddess Worship with Male Gods

Kurgan and Indo-European Invasions of Old Europe and Asia Minor, 4300 to 3000 BCE

Scholars describe the Kurgans as part of the Indo-European group because of their language, which linked them to the Aryans who invaded India and to the Achaeans and to the Dorians who later settled in Greece and Crete. They appeared to be a class society, with warriors and priests at the top of the hierarchy. The Kurgans worshipped gods of war and of mountains, to whom they offered sacrifices of their most prized posses-sion—the horse.

The first wave of the Kurgan invasions occurred between 4300 and 4200 BCE. The invaders came from the present area of Russia and attacked the Balkan area of eastern Europe. The second wave, around 3000 BCE, was much more extensive and covered northern Europe, hit southern Scandinavia, and probably reached through Britain to Ireland. The first wave swept into the area that had been inhabited by the civilization of Old Europe.

The tribes were ruled by chieftains, who often dwelled in a hill fort. The male child was prized as a potential warrior, and the Kurgan culture was patriarchal, patrilinear, and patrilocal. Their small villages or seasonal settlements replaced the larger villages and townships of the sedentary agricultural economy of the mother goddess cultures of Old Europe. Weapons of destruction were so important to the Kurgans that engravings on Kurgan caves indicated that they worshipped them (Gimbutas, 1977, 281). The invaders replaced the mother goddess—who presided over the agricultural cycle of birth, death, and regeneration—with heroic warrior gods. Often these powerful gods appeared from the sky carrying thunderbolts, a symbol of their virility and might. Sometimes just the weapons of the god prepared on Kurgan caves were enough to identify him. There is some indication that the origins of female slavery began with the Kurgans, because the graves in Kurgan camps contained skeletons of women whose remains indicated that they came from the Old European civilization.

Perhaps the greatest evidence of the overthrow of goddess worship can be detected from the graves of the Kurgan chieftains. The female figurines and artistic pottery that had decorated the graves of the goddess cultures were left out: Instead, a tribal chieftain was buried with his weapons and pig or boar tusks, along with wives, concubines, and female slaves. The chieftain's graves were larger and more imposing than others, indicating just how stratified the society had become. The Kurgan war gods evidently did not place the value on life that a mother creatrix was expected to, because the graves point to human sacrifice of women and children.

As they swept through the areas of Old European civilization, the Kurgans left a trail of destruction. They destroyed the shrines to the mother goddesses, demolished art and pottery, and devastated the houses that demonstrated the egalitarian dimension of a peaceful and more technologically advanced society.

Aryan Invasions from Northern Eurasia, 2000 BCE

As we described in Chapter 1, the mother goddess reigned in the Indus Valley of present-day Pakistan from 3500 to 1500 BCE. In the technologically advanced cities of Harappa and Mohenjo-daro, archaeologists have found that all the houses were similar, indicating a democratic or egalitarian type of society, because there was no evidence of concentrated wealth. There were no fortifications built around these cities, which lay in grid fashion in the lush valley of the Indus River. Agricultural communities surrounded the cities, suggesting that farmers exchanged food with city inhabitants in return for merchandise.

All this changed when some of the Aryan cattle herders left central Asia in search of new grazing land about 1500 BCE and overran the Indus Valley. The Indus Valley civilization declined as camps, villages, and eventually cities were settled by the very different Aryan peoples. The tribal organization of the Indo-Aryans was based on a hierarchical model: The highest class included the priests, or Brahmins. The warriors, or kshatriyas, were next, and artisans, merchants, women, herders, and other common folk made up the third class. A fourth group of people, called shudras, was composed of slaves or servants who came from conquered peoples.

The Aryans brought with them the various gods of their polytheistic religion. The diverse gods worshipped by the Aryans appear to be projections or personifications of nature, such as the sun, moon, storms, thunder, and earth. The chief rituals of the Aryans were sacrifices, which they offered on open altars because their nomadic lifestyle prevented them from building shrines or temples. Aryans believed that sacrifices to the gods were necessary to keep the forces of the cosmos in action, so some of their rituals were very lavish. They sacrificed many animals, particularly their most prized possession, the horse. The Aryans looked down on the Dravidians, or Dasas, whom they conquered in the Indus Valley, because they perceived that the latter had no religious rituals. The Aryans referred to their conquered people in derogatory language by calling them "the riteless ones."

The most outstanding god, Indra, has been glorified in the Aryan scriptures: "Now I tell the heroic deeds of Indra, which he performed first with his thunderbolt. He smote the serpent and released the waters; the bellies of the cloud-mountains split open" (*Rig-veda* 1:32.1–3). Another hymn to Indra asks him to defeat their enemies, the Dasas. "With trust in his prowess, he roams the cities of the Dasas with his bolt. A wielder of the bolt, O wise one, throw your weapons at the Dasas, our enemies, and increase the might and glory of the Aryans" (*Rig-veda* 1:103).

The Aryans also honored two sky gods, Varuna and Mitra, who seemed to be more kingly than warriorlike. They were expected to uphold the cosmic law. The goddesses appear more peripheral in that they represented the dawn and dusk, not the sun or the moon or the vibrant activity of the male gods.

Because the sacrifices were so important to the Aryans, the priests ascended in importance. Only they knew the sacred words that would make the sacrifices effective. The priestess who mediated the goddesses disappeared in favor of the priest who interceded to the gods for his people. The Aryans began to settle in, to assimilate some of the features of the Indus Valley civilization. The mother goddess did reappear in later times in various forms with specific functions or as consorts to the gods.

The newer goddesses seemed to support and affirm patriarchal values that assign subservient roles to women. One of the goddesses who appeared 1,000 years after the Aryan invasion is the Hindu goddess Sita, who appears subservient to her husband, the god Rama. She is still honored as the ideal wife who serves her husband faithfully during trials and sufferings. Rama is considered an incarnation of the great god Visnu, preserver of the world. His wife Sita receives prominence because of her relation to him, not for any creative endeavor of her own. Devotees address prayers to her in order to have her intercede for them to her husband. She is not likely to grant favors on her own because her power rests in her relation to the god Rama.

Rama is the hero in the great Hindu epic, *The Ramayana*, written in the first century BCE. Although Rama is heir to the throne in the story, his father, the king, sends him to the forest for a period of preparation. Sita, his wife, begs to accompany him, but he refuses because the hardships will be too great for her. Even though she protests that she does not care to live without him because her love for him is so strong, she obeys her husband in the behavior expected of a dutiful wife. While Rama is away, Sita is kidnapped by the demon Ravana, who is enamored of her beauty and wishes to marry her. Sita remains chaste and loving toward her husband because she is always thinking of him. The austerity of her chastity protects her from the advances of Ravana. Rama finally rescues her, but he is reticent to take her back because he thinks she has been touched by another man. Sita protests her innocence and offers to undergo an ordeal of fire to prove her chastity and love for Rama. She appeals to the fire god, Agni, who refuses to allow the flames to touch her. Rama is impressed with her proof of innocence and accepts her back, offering to protect her in the future. Despite Sita's proven innocence, the people of Rama's kingdom begin to complain that Rama has accepted Sita back although she has spent time in the presence of Ravana. Fearing his reputation, Rama decides to banish Sita from his kingdom, even though she is pregnant. Sita does not blame Rama when she hears of his plans, but thinks she must have done something in a past life to deserve such ill treatment. She shows great understanding and subservience to her husband, whom she calls Gadhava:

> O Gadhava, thou knowest I am truly pure and that I have been bound to thee in supreme love, yet thou has renounced me in fear of dishonour, because thy subjects have reproached and censured thee. . . . As for me, I am not distressed on mine own account, O Prince of Raghu, it is for thee to keep thy fair name untarnished! The husband is as a god to the woman, he is her family, and her spiritual preceptor, therefore, even at the price of her life, she must seek to please her lord.
>
> *Ramayana 7.48*

After the birth of her twins, Sita willingly accepts the banishment and enters the embrace of the goddess Earth, who offers her a throne and then swallows her. Rama is sorry for his behavior and spends the rest of his life lamenting the loss of his beloved and loyal wife. Sita is honored for her steadfast innocence and loyalty to her husband. She becomes the epic's model for wives, who always have the good of their husbands as their highest priority.

The patriarchal culture of India emphasizes goddesses who are the models of the behavior that men desire from their wives. Because Sita represents the qualities of a good wife, she is the most popular goddess for women hoping to live up to her ideals of wifely chastity and long suffering.

Sita is no longer connected to the creative function of the mother goddess or to the nurturing characteristics that endeared a mother goddess to her people. She is reduced to a powerless consort of a powerful god king who is the model for his male followers, once again affirming patriarchal values that stress the submission of women.

The Hebrews and Their Warrior God, 1800 to 1000 BCE

The ancient Hebrews were a Semitic people on the fringes of the major Semitic civilization of Mesopotamia. The book of Genesis tells us that the great patriarch Abraham and his entourage led his flocks of followers out of the land of Ur near the Tigris and Euphrates rivers. Being nomads, they worshipped their god, Yahweh, wherever the tribe wandered rather than in large temples or shrines in the way that the other Semitic people in Mesopotamia worshipped their goddesses. Yahweh seemed to prefer ritual sacrifice of animals from the herds over the agricultural sacrifice offered by their more sedentary neighbors, who worshipped fertility goddesses and gods.

The book of Genesis (4:3–16) tells the story of the farmer Cain, whose sacrificial gift of the produce of the soil was not acceptable to Yahweh. The god received with favor the gifts of Cain's brother, the shepherd Abel, who took his sacrificial offerings from his flocks. When Cain killed his brother, Yahweh punished him by forcing the tiller of the ground to leave the area.

The migratory nature of the Hebrews led to the elevation of the warrior as the people sought new grazing lands, which usually belonged to others. Some of these others were their neighbors from Canaan and Phoenicia, who worshipped many different gods and goddesses. The goddesses Asherath and Astarte were very popular among agriculturalists, who often celebrated using sexual rituals to ensure the fertility of the crops. The priestess who represented the goddess would have ritual intercourse with a priest, who represented the god of fertility, in hopes of securing blessings upon the fertility of humans, animals, and the land. These priestesses exercised sexual autonomy over their lives in that they were not required to be virgins, yet did not belong to a father, husband, or brother.

The priestesses caused the Hebrews concern because, in the Hebrew's strong patriarchal society, patrilinear descent was mandatory. They not only had to know to whom to pass down their flocks but also had to fulfill the covenant that Yahweh had promised to their descendants. The polytheism of the neighboring countries also challenged the Hebrews, who, according to Mosaic law in the Bible, were monotheistic and dedicated to their one god.

Some of the hymns addressed to Yahweh resemble the hymns to Indra, in that both gods use implements of war that were modeled on the fury of nature.

> Yahweh thundered in the heavens,
>> and Elyon gave forth his thunder,
>> hailstones and coals of fire.
> And he sent forth his arrows and scattered them,
>> and lightnings he flashed, and routed them.
> And then were seen the channels of the waters,
>> and there were revealed the foundations of the world,
>> at your rebuke, O Yahweh,
>> at the blast of the wind of your nostrils.
>
> *Psalm 18:13–15*

Yahweh was said to destroy the enemies of the Hebrews, who were termed "wicked": "You rebuked nations/ you destroyed (the) wicked,/ their name you wiped out forever and ever" (Psalm 9:5).

Although the Hebrews were linguistically and racially unrelated to the Indo-Europeans invaders discussed previously, they had a similar lifestyle and social organization. Their widespread influence on Western civilization has been recognized by serious scholars of religion. Eisler points out that the ancient Hebrews resembled the Indo-European invaders in that "the way they characteristically acquired material wealth was not by developing technologies of production, but through ever more effective technologies of destruction" (45). The book of Numbers in the Hebrew Bible depicts the scenes of neighboring cities being burnt to the ground by the Hebrews. They melted the gold from the artwork of their conquered people, which they called heathen idols of goddesses.

Like the Aryans, the tribal society of the Hebrews was ruled by a group of priestly elites. The tribes of Aaron and Moses, the Levites, held that their authority came directly from Yahweh and therefore demanded complete obedience from their followers. The priestly class acted not only as mediator to Yahweh but also as the vehicle of communication from Yahweh to his people. The priests did much of the writing of the Hebrew Bible and appeared to rewrite some of the myths in order to uphold their powerful positions.

Although biblical evidence supports the ancient Hebrews' strong monotheistic views of the worship of Yahweh alone, archaeological evidence suggests a more polytheistic worship of goddesses and other gods. Hundreds of female figurines have been found all over Palestine, dated from all ages of the Israelite period. Many of the figurines resemble the Canaanite goddess Asherath, whose hands offer her protruding breasts in a nurturing fashion. Her torso resembles a pillar, whose flaring base enables her to stand alone. During the monarchy period beginning in the tenth century BCE, the non-Hebrew wives of Solomon brought with them to the palace their images and devotions to their own goddesses. The image of Asherath even made her way into and out of the temple in Jerusalem for a period of 300 years. Even though the prophets denounced the idols, Raphael Patai, a Hebrew scholar, says, "The Hebrew people, by and large, clung to her for six centuries in spite of the increasing vigor of Yahwist monotheism" (52). (See Figure 2.1.)

The prophets Isaiah (17:8) and Micah (5:11–15) denounced devotion to the goddess and demanded the removal of her representations. They placed worship of the Asherath pillar in the same category as the ritual sins of witchcraft, soothsaying, and graven images that would cause Yahweh to "wreak vengeance on the nations who disobey me." Yahweh becomes more precise in Deut. 7:5–6, in which he says that his wrath will blaze out and destroy them unless they tear down the altars of their enemies, smash their standing-stones, cut down their sacred pillars [Asherath?] and burn their idols. "For you are a people consecrated to Yahweh your God, of all the peoples of the earth, you have been chosen by Yahweh your God to be his own people."

FIGURE 2.1   Ceramic Figure of Asherath/Astarte, Seventh Century BCE. (Courtesy of the Metropolitan Museum of Art, gift of Harris D. Colt and H. Dunscombe Colt, 1934.)

King Josiah eliminated the image of Asherath from the temple.

> He brought out the image of Asherath herself from the Temple, had it burned in the Kidron Valley, ground it up into powder, and cast the dust over the graves of those who had worshipped her. Next he demolished the quarters of the Qudeshim, the sacred male prostitutes, which were in the Temple, and in which the women wove "houses" for the Asherath.
>   Finally, he turned his attention to the countryside and cut down the Asheraths wherever they were found.
>
> *Patai, 37*

The monotheistic god, Yahweh, was not ever to be embodied in iconoclastic form. The ten commandments of Moses made this injunction very clear. From prehistoric times, however, images of the goddesses had represented their worship. Forbidding icons and destroying the images of the goddess suppressed the very religion of the goddess.

Crete, Mesopotamia, Greece, Ireland, and Rome

Crete

Before the Indo-Aryan invasion, ancient Minoan Crete was known for its highly developed civilization and religious inclinations in the third millennium BCE. Gimbutas describes the religiousness of the people. "Shrines of one kind or another are so numerous that there is every reason to believe that not only every palace, but every private house was put to some such use. . . . To judge by the frequency of shrines, the whole palace of Knossos must have resembled a sanctuary. Wherever you turn, pillars and symbols remind one of the presence of the Great Goddess" (1982, 80).

Recent excavation by Nicolas Platon has revealed "vast multi-storied cities, harbor installations, networks of roads, organized places of worship and burial grounds." Goddess worship still reigned in Crete until the eleventh century BCE, as evidenced by the frescoes of the goddess and her priestesses on recently unearthed walls. The wealth seemed to be shared in that the homes were similar, and public works provided "extensive drainage systems, sanitary installations, and domestic conveniences" (Platon, 147). The treatment of Cretan women seemed to reflect the view of the goddess in that women were accepted politically, socially, and economically on an equal basis with men. For example, wall frescoes portray young men and women bull-leaping together. Bull-leapers must trust their lives to each other's expertise and agility because their partner must catch them as they somersault over the back of the charging bull.

This spirit of egalitarianism ended when the Dorians and Achaeans invaded from Greece with iron weapons and destroyed the art, culture, and civilization of Crete around 1200 BCE. Both invading groups worshipped a war god, Ares, who represented their ideal. A large, fortified settlement supplanted the peaceful towns, whose beauty, culture, and art were dedicated to their female deity.

One of the methods used by patriarchal societies to subdue another group is rape and plunder. When the Greeks took over the island of Crete, they wrote the myth that had their god Zeus rape the great goddess Europa. Her symbol was the moon-cow, and Zeus, changing himself into the sun-bull, triumphed over her by raping her. Elinor Gadon, a religious historian, claims that "rape metaphorically describes the actual plunder and suppression of the goddess and her culture, as well as the changing attitude toward women with the onset of patriarchy" (106).

The Cretan palace of Knossos contains a huge labyrinth whose convoluted passageways end in a cave that resembles the womb of the mother goddess. It appears to be in the center of the earth. The Greeks used the myth surrounding the cavern and labyrinth of Knossos Palace to explain their suppression of the Cretans. According to Greek myth, the Cretan king Minos receives the gift of a beautiful white bull from the god of the sea, Poseidon. Minos's queen, Pasiphae, develops a lust for the bull and mates with it. Their union produces Minotaur, half man and half bull, whose rapacious appetite can be satisfied only by seven maidens and seven young men sent to him from Athens each year. The monster is hidden in the cavern at the end of the labyrinth, from which no one can find the way out. Theseus, the son of the Athenian king, volunteers to kill the monster, and aided by a Minoan princess who gives him a ball of string, he accomplishes his mission and finds his way out of the labyrinth.

Gadon describes Theseus's victory as the metaphoric death blow to the way of the goddess. Theseus kills the bull-headed monster at the center of the labyrinth, which is the symbol of the body of the goddess, and thus usurps her power. "The Labyrinth, her sacred space deep within, her 'holy of holies,' was transformed into the dreaded kingdom of the dead, a complete reversal of goddess values. Death was no longer viewed as rebirth in the body of the mother" (Gadon, 105). Patriarchy transformed death into something to be dreaded because it eliminated the belief in the return to life that had been recorded in goddess cultures.

Mesopotamia

Powerful kings find that patriarchy favors their political prestige. By the eighteenth century BCE, King Hammurabi had united Babylonia, consisting of Sumer and Akkad, into one state. The country was composed of independent city-states headed by a king or priest king. The pantheon of gods reflected this political division, with each city-state contributing its own god to the assembly. The gods usually symbolized natural phenomena, and together under the leadership of the sky god, Anu, they resembled the hierarchical organization of the king and local rulers.

The gods were grouped in hierarchical fashion similar to a family. The father god was most powerful, then the mother goddess, and finally the brothers and sisters. Sometimes they resembled the city-state governmental structure, with a strong god accompanied by ministers, warriors, and slaves. Although Inanna/Ishtar was present, she was one in a pantheon of the male deities such as the god of the wind, Enlil; the god of the water, Eriki; the god of the moon, Nanna; the rain god, Adad; and the vegetation god, Tammuz. There was a national god, Marduk, and personal gods who cared for the people, cured their sicknesses, and brought them good fortune.

The mythology of the gods and goddesses in the pantheon reflects the power struggles of the city-states. In later mythology, the Babylonian god Marduk defeats a goddess and uses her body to construct the universe.

Greece

The Mycenaeans—Indo-Europeans who invaded Greece and Crete from the north in the second millennium BCE—assimilated into their society much of the culture and social systems of the earlier Minoans. But instead of venerating the mother goddess, they, like the archaic Mesopotamian states, erected a pantheon of gods and goddesses. Although the goddesses were included in the pantheon, they were outnumbered in prominence by the male deities, who held the more active roles.

Zeus was the king of the gods, reflecting the powers of the archaic state. Zeus was married to Hera, a goddess who lost much of her prestige after she became his wife. She seems to have spent much of her time reprimanding Zeus for his extramarital escapades. Zeus and Hera are mentioned in the oldest extant Greek writings, the Mycenaean Greek Linear B texts: II:10.1 "For Zeus: one gold bowl/And one male [attendant]. For Hera, one gold bowl and one female [attendant]" (Mycenaean Tablet PY 172, ca. 1200 BCE). As king, Zeus was endowed with great creative powers. One of his adulterous affairs produced the goddess Athena, the patroness of Athens. She was associated with war and wore the garb of the war goddess: helmet, spear, and shield. It was she who cast the deciding vote in favor of Orestes for the murder of his mother in Aeschylus' play. David Leeming, a mythologist, says that her paradoxical nature is reflected in the story of her remarkable birth. "In the classical version of her story, as told by Hesiod, Pindar, and Apollodorus, Athena sprang fully armed from the head of her father, Zeus. Thus stripped of her feminine origin and nature, she reflects the patriarchal value system that enables the man to create a child from his own body" (Leeming, 104).

The Greeks modeled their pantheon on human families. The family of gods and goddesses resided on Mt. Olympus and contained in their personalities many human qualities such as pride and lust; at the same time, however, some of these deities showed concern for mortals and their well-being. The Greek gods represented the irrational forces of human nature and therefore had to be approached by mortals with hesitation and fear. The gods' power and capricious natures did not often lend themselves to mercy and compassion. For instance, Zeus, the leader of the pantheon, punished the god Prometheus for trying to make life easier for mortals by giving them the gift of fire. Zeus displayed his sexual prowess by impregnating human women and populating his pantheon with the offspring. Poseidon, the god of the seas, reflected his tempestuous nature in the fury of the waters. His vengeful nature is recorded in Homer's *Odyssey*, in which he causes much trouble for Odysseus. Hades ruled over the underworld and is known in the myth of Demeter for his abduction of her daughter Persephone. Ares was the god of war who aided the Greeks in their numerous martial adventures.

The goddesses were subsumed in the pantheon by becoming lesser members of the Olympic family. Aphrodite lost her nurturing abilities and became an erotic love goddess, known for her beauty and extramarital affairs with the war god, Ares. Artemis, the great mother goddess of Ephesus, was demoted by the Greek pantheon to huntress and was associated with wild animals. Her huge temple at Ephesus glorified her role as nurturer and creatrix in the statues that portrayed her with many egglike breasts. When subsumed in the male-dominated Greek pantheon, she, like Athena, lost her feminine and motherly qualities to take on more masculine attributes. Even Demeter, the goddess of vegetation, became subservient to Dionysus, the god of the vine, when she was brought into the pantheon of powerful gods.

The Celts in Northern Ireland, First Millennium BCE

The indigenous people of northern Ireland worshipped the mother goddess Macha, who was venerated at harvest festivals. She delighted in providing fruits, nuts, and grains to her people, who wore on their waists pieces of food as a badge of honor. These products of the harvest were known as the "masts of Macha." She is remembered today by the inhabitants of Armagh, to whom she gave her name, Ard Macha.

One of the many stories told about Macha depicts her transition from the benevolent mother goddess of the ancient Irish to a war goddess of the invading Celts. The following story is recorded in the preamble to Ireland's epic saga, the *Tain*. Macha goes to the house of a lonely widower and helps him with household tasks. She does not reveal her identity but always turns to the right, in the same manner as the sun travels over the earth. They live happily as husband and wife, and Macha becomes pregnant. One day, the man, Crunnchu, leaves for an assembly of Ulstermen that features a horse race. The king and queen's horse wins the race, and the people gather to praise the swiftness of the royal steeds. Crunnchu begins to brag about the swiftness and talents of his wife, who can outrun any horse. The king angrily makes him a prisoner until he can produce this outstanding woman for a match against his royal horses. Macha responds reluctantly to the messengers sent by the king because she is in her last stages of pregnancy for twins. But she goes to the new assembly in order to rescue her husband. She asks to delay the race until her delivery, but the king forced her to compete immediately. Macha calls out to the bystanders for help, asking them to "remember the mother who bore you." Childbirth was then considered a sacred activity, and the activity of a woman in labor was kept private. She appeals to the crowd to remember their relationships to their mothers and to free her from her plight, but no one comes to her aid. The race begins, and Macha so quickly outruns the horses that she has time to give birth to her twins before the royal steeds arrive at the gate.

According to Mary Condren, "for men to look upon the act of giving birth would be a sacrilege and in this case a sacrilege that also wrested power from the goddess by exposing her ultimate act of creativity to the world" (34). She could be changed from a mother goddess into a goddess of war by the warriors who now wore around their waists a belt of the severed heads of the enemies they had felled in battle. The warriors referred to this belt as the masts of Macha "as though Macha delighted in making a head collection just as she had once delighted in providing fruits and grains for a hungry people" (Condren, 34). Condren explains that Macha's transition from mother goddess to war goddess reflected the new concerns of patriarchal consciousness because the head, rather than the body, became the location of creativity. "The overthrow of Macha could be described as the foundation myths of Irish patriarchal culture" (30). Macha is an example of the change that occurred from the supreme mother goddess to one of many goddesses whose devotees would petition her for help in their supreme activity—war.

Rome

The Romans, after defeating Greece in the first century BCE and becoming a world power, simply assimilated or borrowed the Greek gods. The Romans changed the names of the gods in the Greek pantheon but did not change their functions. Jupiter replaced Zeus as king of the gods, and Juno became his consort. The god of war, Ares, was renamed Mars and was still highly revered. The god of the waters was called Neptune, and Bacchus became the name for the Greek Dionysus. The Greek sun god, Apollo, kept his name in Rome.

The Roman pantheon of gods still reflected the political organization of the archaic Greek city-states, with their hierarchical and male-dominant pattern. Female goddesses appeared as wives, consorts, or goddesses of war in a subservient position to the powerful male gods. Rome was typical of the patriarchal culture that replaced or demoted the female deity to a lesser position in its pantheon.

Native American Societies

Native American tribal groups represent a wide variety of social forms. Some tribes appear to be patriarchal, but others are more egalitarian and female centered. Paula Gunn Allen describes the transition in the Native American tradition of the Cherokee, Navajo, Hopi, Keres Pueblo, and

Iroquois tribes from what she describes as gynocracy, or female-centered society, to patriarchy. A member of the Keres Laguna tribe and a professor of languages, Allen has the advantage of a Western education with inside knowledge of the Native American tradition. She says "the coming of the white man created chaos in the old (gynocratic) systems, which were for the most part superbly healthy, simultaneously cooperative and autonomous, peace-centered, and ritual oriented" (31). Women were acknowledged as leaders, both as heads of clans and performers of rituals. The religious rituals that acted out the myths were led by men and women in turn. When men dominated the rituals, women took helping roles, and when women dominated the rituals, men were helpers. The Great Spirit was thought to speak through the head of the Council of the Cherokees, who was called Beloved Woman of the Nation. Until the nineteenth century "the Iroquois were a mother-centered, mother-right people whose political organization was based on the central authority of the Matrons, the Mothers of the Longhouses (clans)" (Allen, 33).

After the American revolution, the Iroquois living in New York state were considered a defeated nation. The Americans burned their homes, salted their fields, and ridiculed the power of the Matrons, whom they said led a "petticoat government." Christian missionaries sent to the Iroquois tried to convert them to their patriarchal religion, and, with the help of an Indian convert, Handsome Lake, they met with some success. "Under the Code of Handsome Lake, which was the tribal version of the white man's way, the Longhouse declined in importance, and eventually the Iroquois women were firmly under the thumb of the Christian patriarchy" (Allen, 33). The Christian missionaries brought their male God and hierarchical organization to the Cherokee nation as well. By sending some of the male Christians to England for education, the missionaries were able to implant the patriarchal culture upon the men's return. The once-powerful women had to retire to sewing circles and Bible study groups and lost all voice in the future direction of the Cherokee Nation.

Other Native American tribes have fallen under the influence of patriarchy. Their clan structure, with its egalitarian features and religious rituals, has been replaced by the nuclear family. Elected officials, mostly male, have replaced the women as clan and religious leaders. Some Native American tribes, such as the Keres Pueblo, Hopi, Iroquois, Seneca, Cherokee, and Abanaki, have myths that suggest a previous goddess-worshipping stage. The Hopi goddess, Spider Woman, has been transformed into the male god called Maseo or Tawa. The Navajo goddess Changing Woman is challenged by male gods, and Thought Woman of the Keres is succumbing to the male god Utset. The Cherokee river goddess has been replaced by the god of thunder, and the Iroquois sky woman presently secures her powers from her dead father or monstrous grandson. In order to ensure the effects of patriarchy, male gods must dominate the religious systems, most often at the expense of the goddesses.

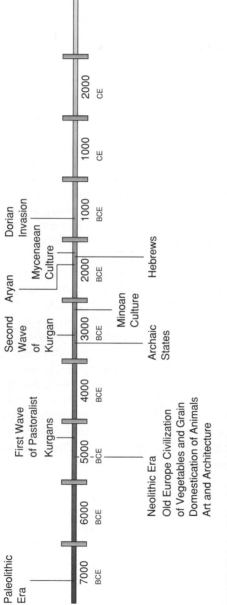

FIGURE 2.2 Time Line by Millennium.

49

Summary

The preeminence of the goddess disappeared with the arrival of the patriarchal period during the third millennium BCE. Patrilinear replaced matrilinear descent, and patrilocality supplanted matrilocality. Patriarchy appeared after goddess worship, which gives the scholar more archaeological and literary evidence of patriarchal societies than of the earlier goddess cultures. In Europe the evidence shows an incursion upon the Old European civilization of the mother goddess by patriarchal nomadic herders who came from the geographical fringes of the well-established goddess culture. In their search for pasture land, the Indo-Europeans, Kurgans, Indo-Aryans, Mycenaeans, Dorians, Greeks, and Celts as well as the Semitic Hebrews used force and implements of war to conquer the people who worshipped the mother goddess. These warriors replaced the goddess with gods who glorified war, and they supplanted the peaceful egalitarian societies with stratified hierarchical divisions that left women and slaves at the bottom of the structure. The priests supplanted the priestesses in religious rituals that mediated the power of the god to the people.

The new patriarchal society was based on the family unit in which the father held for himself the power, wealth, and status. The role of women in reproduction was undermined by ascribing the spirit of life to the father's seed. Private property became a characteristic of patriarchy, in which women, children, and slaves were included as part of the paternal estate. The king modeled the behavior for patriarchs in that he amassed great wealth, power, and concubines and wives in exchange for protecting his people from warlike enemies. The political organization of the archaic states was reflected in their pantheons of gods and goddesses. Gods held the prominent positions, whereas the goddesses were relegated to minor positions or became goddesses of war or consorts of the gods. As Hebrews developed monotheism, they worshipped only a male god, Yahweh, and slowly marked the complete disappearance of the goddess from their scriptures and religious observances.

Just as the finding of female figurines, similarity in housing, and lack of fortifications and weapons is insufficient reason to argue for the widespread existence of mother goddess worship in Europe and Asia, archaeological findings lack sufficient evidence that universal patriarchal societies mistreated women. It has not been proved that all matrilinear and matrilocal societies were peaceful and egalitarian, nor that all patriarchal societies were warlike, cruel, and destructive, although the gods worshipped by the patriarchal cultures were gods of war.

Questions for Discussion

1. Why do you think that the establishment of patriarchy was a gradual one, transpiring over many years?

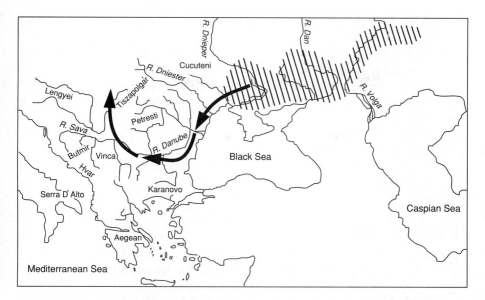

FIGURE 2.3 Kurgan Wave One Map, 4300 to 4200 BCE. (From Riane Eisler, *The Chalice and the Blade*, New York: HarperCollins, 1988, p. 243.)

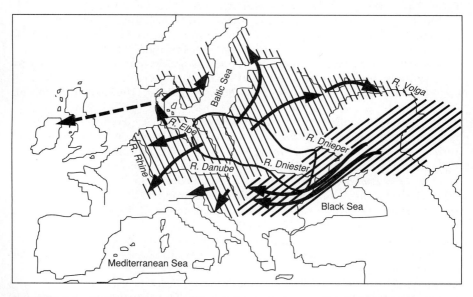

FIGURE 2.4 Kurgan Wave Two Map, 3000 to 2800 BCE. (From Riane Eisler, *The Chalice and the Blade*, New York: HarperCollins, 1988, p. 248.)

2. How do a nation's myths establish the values, aspirations, and heroes of its society?
3. Why was the position of warrior, a role not defined by mother goddess culture, so important in patriarchal societies?
4. How does private property contribute to the institution of patriarchy?
5. Why was it important for men to control the sexual behavior of women? Are there any remnants of this ideology today?
6. What is the relation of the sacred king to patriarchy?
7. Why were the priestesses replaced by priests?
8. What methods were used to replace goddesses with gods in nomadic and archaic state societies?

Works Cited

Allen, Paula Gunn. *The Sacred Hoop*. Boston: Brown Press, 1992.

Campbell, Joseph. *Myths to Live By*. New York: Bantam Books, 1972.

Childe, V. Gordon. *The Dawn of European Civilization*, 6th ed. New York: Alfred Knopf, 1958.

Condren, Mary. *The Serpent and the Goddess*. New York: Harper & Row, 1989.

Crim, K. R., ed. *The Interpreter's Dictionary of the Bible*, supp. vol. Nashville: Abingdon, 1976.

Dever, William G. "The Contribution of Archaeology to the Study of Canaanite and Early Israelite Religion." In *Ancient Israelite Religion*, ed. Patrick Miller, Paul D. Hanson, and S. Dean McBride. Philadelphia: Fortress Press, 1987.

Dexter, Miriam Robbins. *Whence the Goddesses*. New York: Pergamon, 1990.

Eisler, Riane. *The Chalice and the Blade*. New York: Harper & Row, 1987.

Gadon, Elinor. *The Once and Future Goddess*. New York: Harper & Row, 1989.

Gimbutas, Marija. "The Beginnings of the Bronze Age in Europe and the Indo Europeans: 3500–2500 BC," *Journal of European Studies* 1 (1973): 201.

———. "The First Wave of Eurasian Steppe Pastoralists into the Copper Age of Europe," *Journal of Indo-European Studies* 5 (Winter 1977).

———. *The Goddesses and Gods of Old Europe*. Berkeley: University of California Press, 1982.

Kinsley, David. *Hinduism: A Cultural Perspective*. New Jersey: Prentice Hall, 1993.

Leeming, David Adams. *The World of Myth*. New York: Oxford University Press, 1990.

Lerner, Gerta. *The Creation of Patriarchy*. New York: Oxford University Press, 1986.

Mellaart, James. *Neolithic of the Near East*. New York: Scribner, 1975.

The New Jerusalem Bible. Garden City, N.Y.: Doubleday, 1985.

Organ, Troy Wilson. *Hinduism*. Woodbury, N.Y.: Barrons, 1974.

Patai, Raphael. *The Hebrew Goddess*. New York: Avon Books, 1978.

Platon, Nicolas. *Crete*. Geneva: Nagel, 1966.

Rohrlich-Leavitt, Ruby. "Women in Transition Crete and Sumer." In *Becoming Visible*, ed. Renate Bridenthal and Claudia Koonz. Boston: Houghton Mifflin, 1975.

Ruether, Rosemary Radford. *Womanguides*. Boston: Beacon Press, 1985.

Shastri, Hari Prosad, trans. *The Ramayana of Valmiki*, vol 1. London: Shantisoden, 1957.

Suggested Readings

Adams, Robert McCormick. *The Evolution of Urban Society*. Chicago: Aldine, 1966.

————. *Heartland of the Cities: Surveys of Ancient Settlement and Land Use on the Central Flood Plain of the Euphrates*. Chicago: University of Chicago Press, 1981.

Alexiou, Stylianos. *Ancient Crete*. London: Thames and Hudson, 1967.

Angel, Lawrence. "Neolithic Skeletons from Catal Huyuk," *Anatolian Studies* 21 (1971): 77–98.

Bachofen, J. J. *Myth, Religion and Mother Right*. Trans. Ralph Manheim. New Jersey: Princeton University Press, 1967.

Bakan, David. *And They Took Themselves Wives: The Emergence of Patriarchy in Western Civilization*. New York: Harper & Row, 1979.

Bamberger, Joan. "The Myth of Matriarchy: Why Men Rule in Primitive Society." In *Women, Culture, and Society*, ed. Michelle Zimbalist Rosaldo and Louise Lamphere. Stanford, Calif.: Stanford University Press, 1974.

Burland, C. A. *The Gods of Mexico*. New York: Putnam, 1967.

Carneiro, Robert. "A Theory of the Origin of the State," *Science* 169, no. 3947 (August 1970): 733–35.

Cassuto, Umberto. *The Goddess Anath*. Jerusalem: Hebrew University Press, 1971.

Childe, Gordon. *New Light on the Most Ancient East*. New York: Norton, 1969.

Cirrigan, Robert W., trans. *Euripides*. New York: Dell, 1965.

Clements, R. E. *Prophecy and Tradition*. Oxford: Blackwell, 1978.

Coe, Michael D. *The Maya*. London: Thames and Hudson, 1966.

Cross, Frank Moore. *Canaanite Myth and Hebrew Epic*. Cambridge, Mass: Harvard University Press, 1973.

Danielou, Alain. *Hindu Polytheism*. London: Routledge and Kegan Paul, 1963.

Davies, Steve. "The Canaanite-Hebrew Goddess." In *The Book of the Goddess, Past and Present*, ed. Carl Olson. New York: Crossroads, 1983.

Dever, William G. "Asherah, Consort of Yahweh? New Evidence from Kuntillet Ajrud." *Basor* 255 (1954).

Dimmitt, Cornelia. "Sita: Mother Goddess and *Sakti*." In *The Divine Consort: Radha and the Goddesses of India*, ed. John Stratton Hawley and Donna Marie Wulff. Berkeley: Berkeley Religious Studies Series, 1982.

Dodson Gray, Elizabeth. *Patriarchy as a Conceptual Trap*. Wellesley, Mass.: Roundtable Press, 1982.

Dover, K. J. "Classical Greek Attitudes to Sexual Behavior," *Arethusa* 6, no. 1 (1973): 59–73.

Eliade, Mircea, ed. *The Encyclopedia of Religion*. New York: Macmillan, 1987.

Erndl, Kathleen M. "The Absorption of Santoshi Ma into the Panjabi goddess Cult." Paper presented at the meeting of the American Academy of Religion, Chicago, 1984.

————. "Worshipping the goddess: Women's Leadership Roles in the Cult of Seranvali." In *Women's Rites, Women's Desires*, ed. Mary McGee, forthcoming.

Farnell, Lewis R. *The Cults of the Greek States*. Oxford: Oxford University Press, 1907.

Figes, Eva. *Patriarchal Attitudes*. New York: Stein and Day, 1970.

Frymer-Kensky, Tikva. "Patriarchal Family Relationships and Near Eastern Law," *Biblical Archaeologist* 44, no. 4 (Fall 1981): 209–14.

Geertz, Clifford. *The Interpretation of Cultures*. New York: Basic Books, 1973.

Glubok, Shirley, ed. *Discovering the Royal Tombs at Ur*. London: Macmillan, 1969.

Gordon, Cyrus H. *Ugarit and Minoan Crete*. New York: W. W. Norton, 1966.

Gottwald, Norman K. *The Tribes of Yahweh: A Sociology of the Religion of Liberated Israel 1250–1050 B.C.* Maryknoll, N.Y.: Orbis Books, 1979.

Graves, Robert, and Raphael Patai. *Hebrew Myths: The Book of Genesis*. New York: Greenwich House, 1983.

Griffith, Ralph T. M., trans. *The Hymns of the Rgveda*, 4th ed. 2 vols. Banaras: Chowkhamba Sanskrit Series Office, 1963.

Harris, Marvin. "Why Men Dominate Women," *Columbia* 21 (Summer 1978): 9–13, 39.

Harris, Rivkah. "Women in the Ancient Near East." In *The Interpreter's Dictionary of the Bible*, supp. vol., ed. K. R. Crim. Nashville: Abingdon, 1976.

Hawkes, Jacquetta, and Sir Leonard Woolley. *History of Mankind. Vol. I: Prehistory and the Beginnings of Civilization*. New York: Harper & Row, 1963.

Jacobsen, Thorkild. *The Treasures of Darkness: A History of Mesopotamian Religion*. New Haven: Yale University Press, 1976.

Janssen-Jurreit, Marielouise. *Sexism: The Male Monopoly on History and Thought*. New York: Farrar, Straus and Giroux, 1980.

Kapelrud, A. S. *The Ras Shamra Discoveries and the Old Testament*. Norman: University of Oklahoma Press, 1963.

Kinsley, David. *The Goddesses*. Albany, N.Y.: Mirror State University Press, 1989.

Lemaire, Andre. "Mari, the Bible and the Northwest Semitic World." *Biblical Archaeologist* 47, no. 2 (June 1984): 101–8.

———. "Who or What Was Yahweh's Asherath?" *Biblical Archeology Review* 10, no. 6 (1984): 42–51.

Lichtheim, Miriam. *Ancient Egyptian Literature II*. Berkeley: University of California Press, 1976.

Long, Asphodel. "Canaanite Goddesses," *Arachne* 5 (1986).

Maier, Walter A., III. *Aserah: Extrabiblical Evidence*. Atlanta: Scholars Press, 1986.

Marshak, Alexander. *The Roots of Civilization: The Cognitive Beginnings of Man's First Art, Symbol and Notation*. New York: McGraw-Hill, 1971.

Martin, M. Kay, and Barbara Voorhies. *Female of the Species*. New York: Columbia University Press, 1975.

Matthews, Caitlin. *Sophia—Goddess of Wisdom*. London: Mandala, 1990.

Millard, Alan R. "In Praise of Ancient Scribes," *Biblical Archaeologist* 45, no. 3 (Summer 1982).

Millett, Kate. *Sexual Politics*. Garden City, N.Y.: Doubleday, 1969.

O'Brien, Mary. *The Politics of Reproduction*. London: Routledge & Kegan Paul, 1981.

Oldenburg, Ulf. *The Conflict Between El and Ba'al in Canaanite Religion*. Leiden: J. Brill, 1969.

Polome, Edgar. *The Indo-Europeans in the Fourth and Third Millennia*. Ann Arbor: Karoma, 1982.

Redman, Charles. *The Rise of Civilization: From Early Farmers to Urban Society in the Ancient Near East*. San Francisco: W. H. Freeman, 1978.

Reed, Evelyn. *Woman's Evolution: From Matriarchal Clan to Patriarchal Family*. New York: Pathfinder, 1975.

Reed, W. L. *The Asherah in the Old Testament*. Fort Worth: Texas Christian University, 1949.

Rohrlich-Leavitt, Ruby. "Women in Transition: Crete and Sumer." In *Becoming Visible*, ed. Renate Bridenthal and Claudia Koonz. Boston: Houghton Mifflin, 1977.

Rowbotham, Sheila. *Woman's Consciousness, Man's World*. New York: Penguin, 1973.

Saggs, H. W. F. *The Encounter with the Divine in Mesopotamia and Israel*. London: Athlone Press, 1978.

Sanday, Peggy Reeves. *Female Power and Male Dominance: On the Origins of Sexual Inequality*. New York: Cambridge University Press, 1981.

Saporetti, Claudio. "The Status of Women in the Middle Assyrian Period." *Monographs on the Ancient Near East* 2, no. 1. Malibu, Calif.: Undena Publishing, 1979.

Schlegel, A. *Male Dominance and Female Autonomy: Domestic Authority in Matrilineal Societies*. New Haven, Conn.: Human Relations Area Files Press, 1972.

Scully, Vincent. *The Earth, the Temple and the Gods*. New Haven, Conn.: Yale University Press, 1962.

Steinberg, N. "Gender Roles in the Monarchy." Sociology of the Monarchy Seminar Paper, Society of Biblical Literature Annual Meeting, Atlanta, 1986.

Swerdlow, Amy, and Hanna Lessinger, eds. *Class, Race and Sex: The Dynamics of Control*. Boston: G. K. Hall, 1983.

Teubal, Savina J. *Sarah the Priestess*. Athens, Ohio: Swallow Press, 1984.

Trible, Phyllis. *Texts of Terror: Literary-Feminist Readings of Biblical Narratives*. Philadelphia: Fortress Press, 1984.

Watterson, Barbara. *The Gods of Ancient Egypt*. London: B. T. Batsford, 1984.

Whitmont, Edward. *Return of the Goddess*. New York: Crossroads, 1982.

Wright, Henry T., and Gregory A. Johnson. "Population, Exchange and Early State Formation in Southwestern Iran." *American Anthropologist* 77, no. 2 (Spring 1975): 267–89.

Wulff, David M. "Prolegomenon to a Psychology of the Goddess." In *The Divine Consort: Radha and the Goddesses of India*, ed. John Straton Hawley and Donna Marie Wulff. Berkeley: Religious Studies Series, 1982.

CHAPTER 3

Creation Myths Reflecting the Demise of the Mother Goddess

The rise of patriarchy from 4000–1000 BCE made for the gradual demise of the mother goddess. As seen in the previous chapter, the patriarchal nomads from northern Europe and central Asia brought their own gods to Europe, Greece, Crete, Rome, and India, and the equally patriarchal Hebrews brought theirs to the Near East. The new pantheon of gods in each case reflected the patriarchal political organization of these new societies. Naturally, this new religious and political order was reflected in new myths, as oral religious traditions were written down by new generations of male scribes and priests. The male scribes of patriarchal religions were able not only to rewrite the myths in a patriarchal form, but to fix their version of the myth for later generations.

Creation myths often reflect the origin of power and order in a society. As anthropologist Peggy Reeves Sanday explains, "By articulating how things were in the beginning, people . . . make a basic statement about their relationship with nature and about their perception of the source of power in the universe" (57). In the earlier matrilinear and matrilocal societies, the source of power resided in the goddess, as demonstrated by archaeological findings. The new patriarchal cultures emphasized their male gods at the expense of the mother goddess, whom they demoted from creatrix to consort of son/brother or to lesser partner in the pantheon, until she completely disappeared. Since most of the new patriarchal societies now had writing, the male scribes of patriarchal religions could document in written creation myths the ascendancy of their gods. This chapter describes the demise of the mother goddess, as illustrated in creation stories or myths that explain where we come from.

Understanding the Meaning and Function of Myths

The myths, or sacred stories, of a society often highlight and affirm the meaning and values of that society. When the myths are written down, they become part of the sacred corpus of the society's literature, often considered sacred scripture.

Sacred myths form the unity and identity of a group by recounting its origins through creation myths. Leonard Biallas, a theologian, claims that creation myths are the most universal kind of myths because "they portray human attempts to discover or provide some cosmic order or meaning" (39). Most cultures, past and present, possess creation myths. These stories describe not only the cosmic origin of the universe, but also the formation of the first human beings. The cosmos is often portrayed in a chaotic state until the creatrix/creator imposes order, thereby ensuring its fruitfulness. Sometimes the cosmos is brought about by a mother goddess who spontaneously generates the life force that creates the universe. Some myths recount the origin of the universe through the act of intercourse between a god and goddess. Some of the later myths advocate creation by a single male god who creates through his thoughts or words. Humans are usually created from the earth, in the form of clay, dirt, or dust. Bodies of primeval gods and goddesses also provide the creative matter for the first humans.

The earliest myths from the Near East, Old Europe, and Greece depict the creation of the cosmos from the body of the mother goddesses, who, through spontaneous generation, or parthenogenesis, gives birth to the universe, gods and goddesses, and humans. When the more recent myths were committed to writing, they assumed a sacredness that the preliterate mother goddess myths lacked. Because the later myths were written in a patriarchal society, it would follow that male scribes and priests recorded them. When the authors of the myths designated them as sacred scriptures revealed by gods, these myths assumed a seriousness that bore the imprint of "truth." One is hesitant to question revealed truths that are disclosed by a deity to a special person, who then writes it down. Judaism, Christianity, and Islam all have such revealed myths.

As we trace the writing and rewriting of myths, we notice a change in the status and function of the mother goddess. A common theme is that the creatrix of the universe, earth, heavens, gods, goddesses, and eventually humans bears a son, who becomes her lover. She, who has no need for a consort, finds this son/lover elevated to the position of consort. Isis of Egypt and Inanna of Mesopotamia lose power and status to their consorts. The consort then usurps the goddess's power, and she finds herself relegated to a subordinate position in the pantheon of gods and goddesses. In some cultures, she retains her birth-giving qualities by creating the cosmos and humans through intercourse with a god, in what often is referred to as divine pairing.

By the time the creation myths were written as part of sacred scripture in later Judaism, Christianity, and Islam, the mother goddess had completely disappeared and had been replaced by a god who, in the myths, creates alone.

Creation by Spontaneous Generation of the Mother Goddess—Sumer, Babylonia, India, China, Egypt, and North America

Sumer

It is no wonder that the early myth makers would look to a mother as a source of fecundity for creation. If a mother could bring forth a child, why could she not also create the cosmos and then populate it with gods and goddesses? In logical order, gods and goddesses together would produce the first humans. Although there is not much written material describing this process, some tablets from ancient Sumer (third to fourth millennia BCE) address the goddess Nanna as "The Mighty Lady, the Creatress." Merlin Stone, an art historian, reports that another tablet refers to the goddess Nammu as "the Mother who gave birth to heaven and earth" (82). Nammu had the ability to create virginally and generated from her own body the male sky god, An, and the female earth goddess, Ki. They in turn created other gods and goddesses of the elements, who then gave birth to plants and humans.

E. O. James, a mythologist, claims that although there is no single myth that describes the origin of the universe in Sumer, the introductory passages from a Sumerian poem, "Gilgamesh, Enkidu and the Nether World," ascribe creation to the goddess Nammu. "The Goddess Nammu was the primeval ocean who gave birth to the universe in the form of a giant cosmic mountain" (157). James Pritchard describes an Assyrian version of an older Sumerian myth in which the goddess Maimi, who is also referred to as Nintu, is called "the mother womb, the one who creates humankind. The Mother-Womb, the creatress of destiny, in pairs she completed them" (100).

Babylonia

An early Babylonian myth ascribes the creation of the universe to the goddess Tiamat, who, as in the Sumerian myth, is identified with the primal sea. Rosemary Ruether depicts Tiamat as "the idea of a primal mother described like a watery womb that contains within herself the male principle of fertilization" (39). The waters of this primal sea are a mixture of sweet and salty but are mingled together as in one body. These waters can also be considered the primary parents in that the gods and goddesses are begotten and born from this primal body called the goddess Tiamat.

India

The Hindus have a variety of myths to explain the creation of the world. One of them is contained in the *Rig-veda* 10.72. It credits the goddess Aditi with creation, not only of the cosmos but also of gods, which she appears to create without the help of a god.

> In the first age of the gods, existence was born from nonexistence. After this the quarters of the sky were born from her who crouched with legs spread. The earth was born from her who crouched with legs spread, and from the earth the quarters of the sky were born. From Aditi, Daksa was born, and from Daksa, Aditi was born. For Aditi was born as your daughter, O Daksa, and after her were born the blessed gods, the kinsmen of immortality. When you gods took your places there in the water with your hands joined together, a thick cloud of mist arose from you like dust from dancers. When you gods like magicians caused the worlds to swell, you drew forth the sun that was hidden in the ocean. Eight sons are there of Aditi, who were born of her body. With seven she went forth among the gods, but she threw Martanda, the sun, aside. With seven sons Aditi went forth into the earliest age.

In saying that existence was born from nonexistence, we get the idea that Aditi created from nothing but herself. She appears to be the first cause of creation from which all of nature and the cosmos were born.

China

In describing the nature of the Tao, which is the essential concept of the Chinese philosophy of Taoism, one detects the necessity of the feminine. The Tao is the force or energy behind all Chinese creation as well as its destiny. The Tao becomes the parent of yin and yang, the masculine and feminine forces that keep the world in balance. The Tao is described as female and mother of heaven in the *Tao Te Ching*, ascribed to the great Chinese philosopher Lao Tzu in the third century BCE. In trying to name the nameless and formless Tao, the author says in Chapter 1, "The named is the mother of the ten thousand things." The term *ten thousand things* is a common Chinese expression for all the forms of living things in the world. Again in Chapter 25, the *Tao Te Ching* emphasizes the feminine element of this creation force.

> There was something formed out of chaos,
> That was born before Heaven and Earth.
> Quiet and still! Pure and deep!
> It stands on its own and doesn't change.
> It can be regarded as the mother of Heaven and Earth.

> I do not yet know its name:
> I "style" it "the Way."
> Were I forced to give it a name, I would call it "the Great."

Again this mother element does not seem to have a parent, but is the primal force responsible for all creation. The existence of chaos is mentioned, and order seems to be placed on the chaos by the mother of heaven and earth.

Egypt

Egyptian mythology includes a version of creation by the goddess Nun. She is called the "primeval ocean that filled the universe," similar to a cosmic egg. Nun gave birth to the sun god Atum, whose children became the gods and goddesses of sky and earth. The sky goddess, Nut, daughter of Atum, appeared to have creative power in that she was the mother of Ra, the god from whom the pharaohs traced their heritage.

Veronica Ions, an Egyptian mythologist, describes the position of the mother goddess. "Like many primitive peoples, the ancient Egyptians seem early on to have worshipped a universal mother-goddess. She took many forms, and her tradition can be traced in a number of goddesses who survived into the pantheon of historical times" (38).

North America—Native American Cultures

The Keres of the Pueblo tribe from North America do not say that their mother goddess, Thought Woman, gave birth to creation from her own body. Rather, through her intelligence, she imagined all things into being. Behind everything that is, there is the thought that formed it. Anthony Purley, a Keres member, recounts from the creation myth that "in the beginning, Tse che nako, Thought Woman, finished everything, thoughts, and the names of all things. She finished also all the languages" (29). As the necessary precondition for all of creation, Thought Woman is the responsible agent for it. She is considered a supreme spirit whose gifts to her people include agriculture, weaving, religion, rituals, memory, and intuition. Purley says that she is both mother and father to all people and all creatures because she is "the only creator of thought and thought precedes creation" (31). In the Keres myth Thought Woman then sings two daughters, who are sometimes referred to as her sisters, into existence. They carry bundles from which humans and other creatures emerge. They are considered goddesses, one of whom gives birth to twin boys. One of the boys marries the other sister, and the Pueblo tribe members trace their origins to this union.

These myths picture a mother goddess who can create parthenogenetically, or virginally, the universe, gods and goddesses, and sometimes humans. According to myth she could spontaneously generate from her own body all of creation, a symbol of her great power over life. As patriarchy became established, however, the position of the creatrix goddess diminished as she was subsumed into the position of a consort of the god. When men became more aware of their contribution to reproduction, the origin myths ascribed the work of creation to the combined work of gods and goddesses in a term usually described as a divine pair.

Creation Through the Activity of a Divine Pair— Babylonia, Egypt, Japan, Greece, Rome, and America

Babylonia

One of the ways that patriarchal societies appropriated the power of the goddess was to pair her with a powerful god. Inanna, Queen of Heaven and Earth from Mesopotamia, became a faithful daughter of the Sun god, Utu, who advised her to sleep with the mortal shepherd Dumuzi. Their courtship is remembered in love songs that culminate in their marriage. Inanna promised to give her husband the strength to provide leadership, guidance, and fertility to others in his role as king. He, in turn, after the marriage, left her alone while he prepared for his kingly duties.

The Sumerian love songs are repeated in a sacred marriage rite between each king and the goddess Inanna. The king symbolically weds the goddess, who is represented by a priestess, in order to secure fertility for himself, the plants, the flocks, and his people. Inanna has turned from Queen of Heaven into the goddess of love who will ensure the king's powers of leadership.

Egypt

The goddess Isis became a consort to her brother Osiris and gained prominence through the birth of their son, the father of the pharaohs, Horus. After 2500 BCE, she was no longer venerated as the powerful mother goddess who presided over life and death, but as the ancestor of the powerful pharaohs of Egypt. Isis, who needed no husband to conceive her son, lost her independence to become the model of the faithful wife.

Gerda Lerner makes the connection between the displacement of the goddess in Egypt with the rise of patriarchy.

> The fact that in Egyptian belief generativity was embodied in the male god Osiris as early as the third millennium BC supports the thesis that religious beliefs reflected societal conditions. Here, the early establishment of a strong kingship, in which the Pharaohs reigned as gods incarnate, was reflected in the power and dominance of the male gods in creation myths.
>
> *Lerner, 152*

Japan

The Japanese creation story of their islands and of later humans depicts the work of a pair of deities in the *Kojiki*, completed around 712 CE.

At this time the heavenly deities, all with one command,
said to the two deities Izanagi-no-mikoto and Izanami-no-
mikoto:
  "Complete and solidify this drifting land!"
  Giving them the Heavenly Jeweled Spear, they entrusted
  the mission to them.
Thereupon the two deities stood on the Heavenly
Floating Bridge and, lowering the jeweled spear, stirred
with it. They stirred the brine with a churning-churning
sound; and when they lifted up [the spear] again, the brine
dripping down from the tip of the spear piled up and became
an island. This was the island Onogoro.

Kojiki, Chapter 3

This process continued until all the islands of Japan were formed. Descending from the heavens to the island, they erected a pillar around which they walked in a circle. Meeting and recognizing their several differences, they had conjugal intercourse that resulted in three noble children. One of the children, the sun goddess Amaterasu, was regarded as the ancestor of the Japanese royal family. Because the emperor had a divine ancestor he too was considered divine and possessed the goddess's symbol of the rising sun.

Greece

The Greek pantheon ruled by Zeus, especially in the accounts by Homer, clearly subordinates the goddesses. The goddess Aphrodite, born long before Zeus in the story by Hesiod, becomes the daughter of Zeus in the *Iliad*. Homer changes Hera, the wife of Zeus, into his younger sibling. Athena, the proud and independent goddess, becomes the daughter of Zeus that he produces by himself from his own body.

But in Homer's story Zeus owes his existence to the primal parents: Gaea, the earth mother, and Ouranus, the sky father. Their marital union had produced the Titans and the Giants, the youngest of whom, Kronos, had married his sister Rhea. Kronos had castrated his father, Ouranus, who then returned to wander the sky. Fearing reprisal from his own children, Kronos swallows each baby at birth. Rhea hides Zeus, the youngest child, who grows up to attack his father and forces him to disgorge his children. Each of Zeus' siblings takes a position in the pantheon of which Zeus becomes king. He marries his sister, the goddess Hera, who is demoted to the position of the jealous wife. Together and apart, they produce gods and goddesses who rule such areas of life as war, love, and prophecy. Although the ancient writers consider Zeus and Hera a divine pair, the goddess Hera is less important in status and function than her husband.

Rome

As in Greece, the powerful ruler of the pantheon is the Roman version of Zeus, called Jupiter. His wife, Juno, is like Hera in that she spends her time in jealous rage at Jupiter's infidelities. Juno is often obscured by the power of Jupiter in Virgil's epic poem, the *Aeneid*, in which he refers to Jupiter as the omnipotent king of Olympus and to Juno simply as "wife." Jupiter and Juno's children, however, are assigned to various positions as gods and goddesses who rule over natural phenomena, love and war. Juno is an example of a goddess who becomes less significant as her husband, the god, rises to prominence in the Roman pantheon.

North America—Native American Cultures

The Luiseno tribe from California tell a creation story that starts with a divine pair, Kyuvish, space, and Atahvish, emptiness. This pair creates a man—Tukomit, the sky—and a woman—Tamayowut, the earth. The new pair gives birth to mountains, rocks, stone and flint, grasses, trees, birds, animals, and, finally, humans.

The Hopi Indians' creation story invokes a divine pair: the goddess Mother Earth and the god Sky Father. They lie close together, and with the rain as the fertilizing agent, they give birth to the natural forces such as the wind, sun, moon, and all of the living creatures, including humans.

It is only natural for humans who have watched the reproductive activity of plants, animals, and their own people to project upon the cosmos this same action. Because everything in existence had two parents, it was easy for the Native Americans to imagine that the universe emerged in the same manner. However, as we discuss in the next section, patriarchal societies produced patriarchal religions that attributed the process of creation to one male god. Sometimes he produced creation from parts of his own separated body, as Purusha in India, or virginally from his own body, as Zeus in Greece, or outside himself through his word, as Yahweh in Judaism or Allah in Islam.

Creation Through the Single Activity of a Sky God— India, Greece, Hebrew, and Islam

India

The cosmos was formed from the body of the man Purusha according to one myth of creation in the earliest of the Hindu scriptures, the *Rig-veda*. The gods divided up the man Purusha in a sacrificial manner, and from his pieces the gods, such as Indra, Vayu, and Agni, were born. The parts of his body also provided material for the creation of humans, who appeared to fall along caste lines. His most noble part (i.e., his head) went to create the highest castes in India, the Brahmins. The next class, the warriors and nobles, came from his arms; the merchant class or workers came from either his stomach or his thighs; and the lowest class, the servants or shudras, emerged from his feet. This creation story claims that the Hindu caste system was divinely ordained and therefore must be accepted by all the populace. Because the Brahmins, or priests, were most likely the writers of this story, we would expect them to attribute the most important parts to themselves. Not only is this passage a description of the physical world, but it is also a justification of the caste system that was prevalent in India in the first millennium BCE.

> When they divided the Man, into how many parts did they disperse him? What became of his mouth, what of his arms, what were his two thighs and his two feet called? His mouth was the Brahmin, his arms were made into the nobles, his two thighs were the populace, and from his feet the servants were born. The moon was born from his mind; the sun was born from his eye. From his mouth came Indra and Agni, and from his vital breath the wind [Vayu] was born. From his navel the atmosphere was born; from his head the heaven appeared. From his two feet came the earth, and the regions of the sky from his ear. Thus they fashioned the worlds.
>
> *Rig-veda, X.90*

Indra was the war god and Agni the god of fire. The wind was called the god Vayu, who blew Purusha's body pieces to populate the heavens as well as the earth. Although India has other creation stories, the origin story of creation from the dismembered body of the huge man Purusha is one of the favorites.

Greece

Although the Greek gods did not produce the universe by themselves in the creation myths, they did not always need a female partner to create human offspring. Two gods, Ouranos and Zeus, produced daughters without the aid of a mother. Ouranus was the sky god whose genitals were severed by his son, Kronos. When Kronos cast the genitals into the sea, a white foam formed from the semen, out of which arose the goddess Aphrodite.

Zeus did impregnate a goddess, Metis, but swallowed her because he feared her offspring. He was warned that their child, a warrior god, would dethrone him in the way that he had ousted his own father. Several months later, according to one version of the myth, Athena sprang from Zeus' head fully grown and armed as a warrior goddess: "Now [Zeus] himself/[bore] sparkling-eyed [Athena] Tritogeneia/out of his own head" (Hesiod, *Theogony* 924, II.10.37, ca. 750 BCE). Another myth has her emerge from his thigh.

In his play *The Eumenides*, Aeschylus extols the ability of Zeus to produce an offspring virginally.

> There can be a father without any mother
> There she stands, a living witness, daughter
>   of Olympian Zeus, she who was never fostered
>   in the dark womb, yet such a child as no
>   goddess could bring to birth.
>
> *Aeschylus, 158*

It is interesting that in the male-dominated pantheon of Greece, the two children born of men were women. In the Egyptian goddess culture, Isis conceived her son Horus virginally; later, Mary the mother of the male Jesus was considered a virgin mother. Just as the early goddess cultures thought that women brought forth children without the help of men, the patriarchal cultures wrote myths about gods who could bear children without the cooperation of women.

Hebrew Culture

The six-day creation story told in the Genesis book of the Hebrew Bible climaxes the process of the trend in creation stories from spontaneous generation by the mother goddess, to a watery mass containing the primal parents who bear the gods and goddesses, to a male god who creates from his body. The Genesis myth goes one step further: Yahweh creates outside of himself through his word. The Hebrew creation story of the cosmos and humans, which both Jews and Christians revere, ignores any roles of gods or goddesses. It gives all the credit to Yahweh in the account written by priests in about 500 BCE. In a series of six days, God, or Yahweh, created the earth, night and day, heavens, seas and dry land, plants, the planetary system, animals, and finally humans. In this account, the man and woman were created simultaneously in the image of God. The words "let us create humans in our image" has led to much speculation regarding the sex of God and the relationship of the one or ones who are referred to as *our*. Most feminine theologians consider God beyond either sex, or possibly encompassing or reflecting both male and female characteristics. The *our* has been interpreted by some Jewish theologians as possibly including the goddess Sophia, or other heavenly beings. Others have considered the likelihood of using an editorial *we*. Being strictly monotheistic, the presence of these words have challenged Jews and Christians over the centuries.

The creation story in Genesis 1:1–31

In the beginning God created heaven and earth. Now the earth was a formless void, there was darkness over the deep, with a divine wind sweeping over the waters.

God said, "Let there be light," and there was light. God saw light was good, and God divided light from darkness. God called light "day," and darkness he called "night." Evening came and morning came: the first day.

God said, "Let there be a vault through the middle of the waters to divide the waters in two." And so it was. God made the vault, and it divided the waters under the vault from the waters above the vault. God called the vault "heaven." Evening came and morning came: the second day.

God said, "Let the waters under heaven come together into a single mass, and let dry land appear." And so it was. God called the dry land "earth" and the mass of waters "seas," and God saw that it was good.

God said, "Let the earth produce vegetation: seed-bearing plants, and fruit trees on earth, bearing fruit with their seed inside, each corresponding to its own species." And so it was. The earth produced vegetation: the various kinds of seed-bearing plants and the fruit trees with seed inside, each corresponding to its own species. God saw that it was good. Evening came and morning came: the third day.

God said, "Let there be lights in the vault of heaven to divide day from night, and let them indicate festivals, days and years. Let them be lights in the vault of heaven to shine on the earth." And so it was. God made the two great lights: the greater light to govern the day, the smaller light to govern the night, and the stars. God set them in the vault of heaven to shine on the earth, to govern the day and the night and to divide light from darkness. God saw that it was good. Evening came and morning came: the fourth day.

God said, "Let the waters be alive with a swarm of living creatures, and let birds wing their way above the earth across the vault of heaven." And so it was. God created great sea-monsters and all the creatures that glide and teem in the waters in their own species, and winged birds in their own species. God saw that it was good. God blessed them, saying, "Be fruitful, multiply, and fill the waters of the seas; and let the birds multiply on land." Evening came and morning came: the fifth day.

God said, "Let the earth produce every kind of living creature in its own species: cattle, creeping things and wild animals of all kinds." And so it was. God made wild animals in their own species, and cattle in theirs, and every creature that crawls along the earth in its own species. God saw that it was good.

God said, "Let us make man in our own image, in the likeness of ourselves, and let them be masters of the fish of the sea, the birds of heaven, the cattle, all the wild animals and all the creatures that creep along the ground."

> God created man in the image of himself,
> in the image of God he created him,
> male and female he created them.

God blessed them, saying to them, "Be fruitful, multiply, fill the earth and subdue it. Be masters of the fish of the sea, the birds of heaven and all the living creatures that move on earth." God also said, "Look, to you I give all the seed-bearing plants everywhere on the surface of the earth, and all the trees with seed-bearing fruit; this will be your food. And to all the wild animals, all the birds of heaven and all the living creatures that creep along the ground, I give all the foliage of the plants as their food." And so it was. God saw all he had made, and indeed it was very good. Evening came and morning came: the sixth day.

Thus heaven and earth were completed with all their array. On the seventh day God had completed the work he had been doing. He rested on the seventh day after all the work he had been doing. God blessed the seventh day and made it holy, because on that day he rested after all his work of creating.

Such was the story of heaven and earth as they were created.

Genesis 1:26.

This first account of the origin of humans created together as equals is thought by some to be from the priestly tradition written about 500 BCE. Another account of the creation story in Gen. 2:5 depicts the man as created first and the woman afterward, created from the man's rib. Adam, the man, names the animals and the birds, indicating through the naming process that he has power over them. He also names the woman who is produced from his side. This second account, written by the Yahwist tradition in about 900 BCE, reflects the hierarchical situation of a patriarchal society in which the man has power over the woman.

Gen 2:5–24

At the time when Yahweh God made earth and heaven there was as yet no wild bush on the earth nor had any wild plant yet sprung up, for Yahweh God had not sent rain on the earth, nor was there any man to till the soil. Instead, water flowed out of the ground and watered all the surface of the soil. Yahweh God shaped man from the soil of the ground and blew the breath of life into his nostrils, and man became a living being.

Yahweh God planted a garden in Eden, which is in the east, and there he put the man he had fashioned. From the soil, Yahweh God caused to grow every kind of tree, enticing to look at and good to eat, with the tree of life in the middle of the garden, and the tree of the knowledge of good and evil.

Yahweh God took the man and settled him in the garden of Eden to cultivate and take care of it. Then Yahweh God gave the man this command, "You are free to eat of all the trees in the garden. But of the tree of the knowledge of good and evil you are not to eat; for, the day you eat of that, you are doomed to die."

Yahweh God said, "It is not right that the man should be alone. I shall make him a helper. So from the soil Yahweh God fashioned all the wild animals and all the birds of heaven. These he brought to the man to see what he would call them; each one was to bear the name the man would give it. The man gave names to all the cattle, all the birds of heaven and all the wild animals. But no helper suitable for the man was found for him. Then, Yahweh God made the man fall into a deep sleep. And, while he was asleep, he took one of his ribs and closed the flesh up again forthwith. Yahweh God fashioned the rib he had taken from the man into a woman, and brought her to the man. And the man said:

> This one at last is bone of my bones
>   and flesh of my flesh!
> She is to be called Woman.
>   because she was taken from Man.

This is why a man leaves his father and mother and becomes attached to his wife, and they become one flesh.

Now, both of them were naked, the man and his wife, but they felt no shame before each other.

In neither creation story do the Hebrew writers mention the work of a goddess in the creation of the universe or humans. There are no divine pairs of goddesses and gods; rather, humans are appointed by God to rule the earth. Humanity appears to be the crown of creation, with the plants and animals given to them for their use by the single male deity, Yahweh.

Islam Culture

The Quran of Islam furthers the idea of creation by a single all-powerful god, Allah. To Muslims the Quran holds the same sacredness that the Hebrew Bible holds for Jews and Christians. They believe it was given to

Muhammad in the seventh century CE. Surah (meaning chapter) 6 in the Quran stresses the oneness of the creator who brought the universe into existence by himself without the need of a woman.

> He is the Creator of the heavens and the
> earth. How should He have a son when He had no
> consort? He created all things and has
> knowledge of all things.
>   Such is God, your Lord. There is no god but
> Him, the Creator of all things. Therefore serve
> Him. He is the Guardian of all things.
>   No mortal eyes can see Him, though he sees
> all eyes. He is benignant and all-knowing.
>
> *Surah 6:101–3*

Surah 59 stresses again the unity of God, who creates alone without the help of anyone. There are no other gods or goddesses: Allah is the sole reality upon which all else depends. Not only does God create the cosmos and humans, but he also sustains it. The order and balance in the universe is a sign of God's unity and creative power. Animals and humans are endowed with qualities that enable them to function in an ordered manner.

> He is God, besides whom there is no other
> deity. He knows the unknown and the manifest. He
> is the Compassionate, the Merciful.
>   He is God, besides whom there is no other
> deity. He is the Sovereign Lord, the Holy One,
> the Giver of Peace, the Keeper of Faith; the
> Guardian, the Mighty One, the All-powerful, the
> Most High! Exalted by God above their idols!
>   He is God, the Creator, the Originator, the
> Modeler. His are the most gracious names. All
> that is in heaven and earth gives glory to Him.
>
> *Surah 59:22–24; Medinah*

The names Creator, Originator, Modeler, Holy One, and Mighty One give insights into a concept of a god that stresses the transcendence or otherness of divine reality. Muslims attribute to Allah other characteristics that stress compassion, mercy, and justice, as "One who no vision can grasp" yet "He who is ever near." By combining characteristics of transcendence and immanence, Allah does not need a goddess as wife, daughter, or consort.

Examination of creation myths in various cultures gives insights into the beliefs and values of the civilization that produced them. As patriarchal societies developed, the sacred writings point to a culture that extolled men more than women. When the mythological work of creation is moved from the mother goddess to a single male god, we would expect the societal position of women to reflect this development. This is not to say that all cultures that worship male gods discriminate against women, nor that all cultures in which goddesses are central are egalitarian. Hinduism, for example, with its great variety of goddesses, is a strongly patriarchal society;

Western feminists do not envy the position of Hindu women. However, if the supreme beings are male, it is unlikely that men will be oppressed in that society. We would expect the same to be true for women in cultures that worship a goddess as the primary deity.

Defeat of the Goddess by Destruction of Her Symbols

One of the methods used by patriarchal society to overcome the influence of the goddess was destruction of her symbols. In Crete and elsewhere in Greece, the goddess was often pictured with her symbol of the snake, which was considered the vehicle of immortality because it could shed its skin and replenish it again. The serpent was considered to be the stimulator of life's energy. Karen Joines, a mythologist, says that in Egypt the serpent was called "life of the earth," "full of years," the "life of the gods," and the "life of forms and of nutritious substances" (20). Because serpents hibernate in winter and reemerge in the spring, they were ideal symbols of rebirth and regeneration. Serpents were also associated with wisdom, as was the goddess, because they were believed to be in touch with the earth from which they came (Figure 3.1).

FIGURE 3.1 Minoan Snake Goddess, Earthenware, 1700 BCE. (Courtesy of Erich Lessing/Art Resource, New York.)

By destroying the symbol of the goddess, the patriarchal culture destroyed the political, social, and religious power traditionally associated with women. The snake was often associated with water, and in the Babylonian myth, Marduk cuts it in half and forms the heavens and earth from its body. The Hebrews refer to the serpent as a dragon called Leviathan, whom Yahweh slays. In Greece, Zeus conquers and kills the giant serpent Syphon, and the snake-haired Medusa has her head cut off. St. Patrick drives out the snakes from Ireland and replaces the goddess religion with Christianity. Even St. George of England defeats the dragon who has become the symbol of evil.

Not only does the goddess disappear from creation myths, but so does her symbol of the snake. When a good symbol is turned into an evil one, attacks against it seem justified. In the next chapter on alienation myths, we will see that the snake became a cause of evil in the fall story of Adam and Eve, thereby validating the banishment of the goddess.

Summary

Societies legitimate or justify their social patterns by attributing their origins to the time of creation. When creation myths are considered sacred scripture, as in monotheistic religions, the present social conditions appear justified because they are dictated by an all-powerful deity. The writers of the sacred scriptures in patriarchal societies were usually male scribes or priests who benefitted from the presentation of creation myths that presented a hierarchical structure that favored the action of male gods. The creation stories that depict creation through the generation of a mother goddess were usually passed on orally, so they are more difficult to document. Even the creation stories that describe the origin of the universe by the intercourse of a divine pair do not have the lasting effects of the story of creation accomplished by a single male god. Judaism, Christianity, and Islam have been the primary religions to influence the Western world and spread their creation myths with their religious cultures.

The scribes ensured the triumph of the single male deity by attributing the power of creation to him at the expense of the mother goddess and divine pairs of gods and goddesses. Subordination of the goddess was accomplished by demoting her to the role of a consort in a pantheon of gods and goddesses, by destroying her symbol of the snake, or by transforming the serpent into an evil entity.

Questions for Discussion

1. How do creation myths influence the position of women in society?
2. What is the significance of the fact that scriptures were written by

male writers, such as the Brahmins in India, the priests in Judaism, and male authors in Christianity?

3. Why could it be said that it is natural to think of creation in terms of the activity of a divine pair?
4. How do the present social structures in a society become justified by their creation myths?
5. Why are religious symbols so important to both followers and enemies of the religious tradition?

Works Cited

Aeschylus. "Eumenides." In *The Complete Greek Tragedies*, vol. I, ed. David Grene and Richmond Lattimore. Chicago: University of Chicago Press, 1959.

Biallas, Leonard. *Myths, Gods, Heroes, and Saviors*. Mystic, Conn.: Twenty-Third Publications, 1986.

Griffith, Ralph, trans. *Hymns of the Rig Veda*. 2 vols. Varanasi, India: The Chowkhamba Sanskrit Series Office, 1963.

Hesiod, *Theogony* 924, II.10.37.

Ions, Veronica. *Egyptian Mythology*, rev. ed. New York: Peter Bedrick Books, 1983.

James, E. O. *Myth and Ritual in the Ancient Near East*. London: Thames and Hudson, 1958.

Joines, Karen. *Serpent Symbolism in the Old Testament*. Haddonfield, N.J.: Haddonfield House, 1974.

Phillipi, Donald L., trans. *Kojiki*. Princeton, N.J.: Princeton University Press, 1969.

Lao, D. C. *Lao Tzu: Tao Te Ching*. New York: Penguin, 1982.

Leach, Maria. *The Beginning Creation Myths Around the World*. New York: Funk & Wagnalls, 1956.

Lerner, Gerda. *The Creation of Patriarchy*. New York: Oxford University Press, 1986.

Pritchard, James. "Myth of Atrahosis." In *Ancient Near Eastern Texts Relating to the Old Testament*, ed. James Pritchard. Princeton, N.J.: Princeton University Press, 1950.

Purley, Anthony. "Keres Pueblo Concepts of Deity," *American Indian Culture and Research Journal* 1 (Fall 1974).

Ruether, Rosemary Radford. *Womanguides*. Boston: Beacon Press, 1985.

Sanday, Peggy Reeves. *Female Power and Male Dominance. On the Origins of Sexual Inequality*. Cambridge: Cambridge University Press, 1981.

Stone, Merlin. *When God Was a Woman*. New York: Harcourt Brace Jovanovich, 1976.

Wolkstein, Diane, and Samuel Noah Kramer. *Inanna*. New York: Harper & Row, 1983.

Suggested Readings

Barr, James. "The Meaning of 'Mythology' in Relation to the Old Testament," *Vetus Testamentum* 9 (1959): 1–10.

Bausch, William J. *Storytelling: Imagination and Faith*. Mystic, Conn.: Twenty-Third Publications, 1984.

Boedeker, Deborah Dickmann. *Aphrodite's Entry into Greek Epic*. Leiden: Brill, 1974.

Bratton, Fred G. *Myths and Legends of the Ancient Near East*. New York: Thomas Y. Crowell, 1970.

Briffault, Robert. *The Mothers*. Abridged Gordon Rottray Taylor. New York: Atheneum, 1977.

Bruhl, Odette. "Japanese Mythology." *Larousse Encyclopedia of Mythology*, ed. Robert Graves. New York: Prometheus Press, 1960.

Bynum, Caroline Walker, Stevan Aareel, and Paula Richman, eds. *Gender and Religion*. Boston: Beacon Press, 1986.

Campbell, Joseph. *The Hero with a Thousand Faces*. New York: World, 1956.

––––––. *The Masks of God: Creative Mythology*. London: Secker & Warburg, 1968.

––––––. *The Masks of God: Occidental Mythology*. London: Secker & Warburg, 1965.

––––––. *Myths, Dreams and Religion*. New York: Dutton, 1970.

––––––. *Myths to Live By*. New York: Viking, 1972.

Ceram, C. W. *The Secret of the Hittites*. New York: Knopf, 1956.

Childs, Brevard S. *Myth and Reality in the Old Testament*. London: S.C.M. Press, 1960.

Clark, R. T. Rundle. *Myth and Symbol in Ancient Egypt*. New York: Grove Press, 1960.

Clay, Jenny Strauss. *The Wrath of Athena*. Princeton: Princeton University Press, 1983.

Coburn, Thomas B. "Consort of None, *Sakti* of All: The Vision of the *Devi Mahatmya*." In *The Divine Consort: Radha and the Goddesses of India,* ed. John Stratton Hawley and Donna Marie Wulff. Berkeley: Religious Studies Series, 1982.

––––––. *Devi-Mahatmya: The Crystallization of the Goddess Tradition*. Columbia, Mo.: South Asia Books, 1985.

Curtin, Jeremiah. *Myths and Folktales of Ireland*. New York: Dover, 1975.

Detienne, Marcel, and Jean-Pierre Vernant. *Cunning Intelligence in Greek Culture and Society*. Trans. J. Lloyd. Atlantic Highlands, N.J.: Humanities Press, 1978.

Diel, Paul. *Symbolism in Greek Mythology*. Trans. V. Stuart, M. Stuart, and R. Folkman. Boulder, Colo.: Shambhala, 1980.

Driver, G. R. *Canaanite Myths and Legends*. Edinburgh: T & T Clark, 1956.

Eliade, Mircea. *Cosmos and History*. Trans. W. R. Trask. New York: Harper & Row (Harper Torchbook), 1959. First published by Pantheon Books, 1954.

––––––. *Cosmos and History, The Myth of the Eternal Return*. New York: Bollingen Foundation, 1954.

––––––. *The History of Religion: Essays in Methodology*. Chicago: University of Chicago Press, 1959.

––––––. *The Quest: History and Meanings in Religion*. Chicago: University of Chicago Press, 1968.

––––––. *The Sacred and the Profane*. Trans. W. R. Trask. New York: Harcourt Brace Jovanovich, 1959.

Emery, W. B. *Archaic Egypt*. Baltimore: Penguin, 1961.

Erndl, Kathleen. *Victory to the Mother*. New York: Oxford University Press, 1993.

Evelyn-White, Hugh G., trans. *Hesiod, the Homeric Hymns and Homerica*. New York: G. P. Putnam's Sons, 1920.

Fairservis, Walter A., Jr. *The Ancient Kingdoms of the Nile*. New York: Thomas Y. Crowell, 1962.

Falk, Marcia. *The Song of Songs: Love Poems from the Bible*. New York: Harcourt Brace Jovanovich, 1977.

Feifel, Herman, ed. *The Meaning of Death*. New York: McGraw Hill, 1959.

Ferguson, John. *Moral Values in the Ancient World*. London: Methuen, 1958.

Forsyth, Neil. *The Old Enemy: Satan and the Combat Myth*. Princeton, N.J.: Princeton University Press, 1987.

Friedrich, Paul. *The Meaning of Aphrodite*. Chicago: University of Chicago Press, 1978.

Gardiner, Alan. *Egypt of the Pharaohs*. New York: Oxford University Press, 1961.

Gimbutas, Marija. *Achilleion, Neolithic Site in Thessaly*. Institute of Archaeology, UCLA, Monomenta Archaeological Monograph Series, 1987.

Graves, Robert. *The White Goddess: A Historical Grammar of Poetic Myth*. New York: Farrar, Straus and Giroux, 1973.

Graves, Robert, and Raphael Patai. *Hebrew Myths: The Book of Genesis*. New York: McGraw-Hill, 1966.

Habel, Norman C. *Yahweh Versus Baal: A Conflict of Religious Cultures*. New York: Bookman Associates, 1964.

Hawley, John, and Donna Wulff, eds. *The Divine Consort: Radha and the Goddesses of India*. Berkeley: Berkeley Religious Studies Series, 1902.

Herzberg, Max John. *Myths and Their Meaning*. Boston: Allyn and Bacon, 1961.

I Ching. Trans. R. Wilhelm. London: Routledge & Kegan Paul, 1983.

Jaffe, Anicia. *The Myth of Meaning*. Trans. R. F. C. Hull. New York: Putnam, 1971.

James, E. O. *The Ancient Gods*. London: Weidenfeld & Nicolson, 1960.

———. *Seasonal Feasts and Festivals*. New York: Barnes & Noble, 1961.

James, T. R. *Myths and Legends of Ancient Egypt*. New York: Grosset & Dunlap, 1971.

Kapera, Constance. *The Worship of Kali in Banaras: An Inquiry*. Delhi: Motilal Banarsidass, n.d.

Keleman, Stanley. *The Human Ground: Sexuality, Self and Survival*. Palo Alto, Calif.: Science and Behavior Books, 1975.

Kitagawa, Joseph M., and Charles H. Long, eds. *Myths and Symbols*. Chicago: University of Chicago Press, 1969.

Kramer, S. N. *History Begins at Sumer*. New York: Doubleday, 1958.

———. *Sumerian Mythology*. Philadelphia: University of Pennsylvania Press, 1944.

———. *Sumerian Myths, Epics and Tales*. Princeton, N.J.: Princeton University Press, 1957.

———. *The Sumerians: Their History, Culture and Character*. Chicago: University of Chicago, 1963.

Lang, Mabeb L. "Reverberation and Mythology in the *Iliad*." In *Approaches to Homer*, ed. C. A. Rubino and C. W. Schelmerdine. Austin: University of Texas Press, 1983.

Lannoy, Richard. *The Speaking Tree: A Study of Indian Culture and Society*. New York: Oxford University Press, 1971.

Larue, Gerald A. *Old Testament Life and Literature*. Boston, Mass.: Allyn & Bacon, 1968.

Layton, Lynne, and Barbara Ann Shapiro, eds. *Narcissism and the Text: Studies in Literature and the Psychology of the Self*. New York and London: New York University Press, 1986.

Loew, Cornelius. *Myth, Sacred History and Philosophy*. New York: Harcourt Brace Jovanovich, 1967.

MacKenzie, Donald. *Myths of China and Japan*. London: Gresham, n.d.

May, Rollo, ed. *Symbolism in Religion and Literature*. New York: Braziller, 1960.

Merrill, James. *The Inner Room*. New York: Alfred A. Knopf, 1988.

Miller, P. D. "The Absence of the Goddess in Israelite Religion," *Hebrew Annual Review* 10 (1986): 239–48.

Mueller, Martin. "Knowledge and Delusion in the *Iliad*," *Mosaic* 3.2 (1970): 86–103.

Murray, Henry A., ed. *Myth and Mythmaking*. Boston: Beacon Press, 1968.

Nagy, Gregory. *The Best of the Achaeans*. Baltimore: Johns Hopkins University Press, 1979.

Nakamura, Kyoko Motomochi. "The Significance of Amaterasu in Japanese Religious History." In *The Book of the Goddess Past and Present: An Introduction to Her Religion*, ed. Carl Olson. New York: Crossroads, 1983.

O'Brien, Joan, and Wilfred Major. *In the Beginning: Creation Myths From Ancient Mesopotamia, Israel and Greece*. Chico, Calif.: Scholars Press, 1982.

Pagels, Elain. *Adam and Eve and the Serpent*. New York: Random House, 1988.

Patai, Raphael, and Robert Graves. *Hebrew Myths: The Book of Genesis*. Garden City, N.Y.: Doubleday & Co., 1963.

Pettazoni, R. *The All-Knowing God: Researches into Early Religion and Culture*. Trans. H. J. Rose. London: Methuen, 1978.

Pfeiffer, C. F. *Ras Shamra and the Bible*. Grand Rapids, Mich.: Baker Book House, 1962.

Pharr, Clyde. *Homeric Greek*. Rev. J. Wright. Norman: University of Oklahoma Press, 1985.

Pucci, Pietro. *Hesiod and the Language of Poetry*. Baltimore: Johns Hopkins University Press, 1977.

Radin, Paul. *The Trickster: A Study in American Indian Mythology*. New York: Schocken Books, 1972.

Sagan, Carl. *The Dragons of Eden*. New York: Random House, 1977.

Sahtouris, Elizabeth. *Gaia: Humanity's Bridge from Chaos to Cosmos*. New York: Asian, 1989.

Segal, Charles. "Sophocles' *Trachiniae*: Myth, Poetry, and Heroic Values," *Yale Classical Studies* 25 (1977): 99–158.

Senior, Michael. *Greece and Its Myths*. London: Victor Gollancz, 1978.

Slater, Philip. *The Glory of Hera*. Boston: Beacon Press, 1968.

Solmsen, Friedrich. *Isis Among the Greeks and Romans*. Cambridge: Harvard University Press, 1979.

Sproul, B. C. *Primal Myths: Creating the World*. New York: Harper & Row, 1979.

Srivastava, M. C. P. *Mother Goddess in Indian Art, Archaeology and Literature*. Delhi: Agam Kala Prakashan, 1979.

Telley, Terrence W. *Story Theology*. Wilmington, Del.: Michael Glazier, 1985.

Thompson, William Irwin. *The Time Falling Bodies Take to Light: Mythology, Sexuality, and the Origins of Culture*. New York: St. Martin's Press, 1981.

Vernant, Jean-Paul. "The Myth of Prometheus in Hesiod." In *Myth and Society in Ancient Greece*, trans. J. Lloyd. Atlantic Highlands, N.J.: Humanities Press, 1980.

———. "Sacrificial and Alimentary Codes in Hesiod's Myth of Prometheus." In *Myth, Religion and Society*, ed. R. L. Gordon. Cambridge; Cambridge University Press, 1981.

Vivante, Paolo. *The Epithets in Homer*. New Haven and London: Yale University Press, 1982.

———. *The Homeric Imagination*. Bloomington: Indiana University Press, 1970.

Young, Katherine. *Hinduism*. Ed. Sharma Arind. Albany: State University of New York Press, 1987.

CHAPTER 4

Alienation Myths and Other Practices That Affect Women

One of the fundamental questions asked of religion is how evil originated and how it affects humanity. Most paradisiacal religions look back on a happy state in which the deity or deities and humans experienced a happy, congenial relationship. The divine provided humans with the necessities of life, immortality, and a blissful, peace-filled existence on earth. Something happened to disrupt this perfect state of affairs and caused suffering, disease, hard work, and death to burden humans, and it usually disrupted their relationship with the divine, who withdrew from their presence. In monotheistic religions, alienation myths usually describe this rupture in the relationship with the god and the sorry effects it has on the humans who instigated the disaster. Just as humans try to understand their origins with creation myths, they look to alienation myths to explain the cause of evils that bring them unhappiness.

Many of the alienation myths advocated by patriarchal religions blame women for the introduction of evil. It is easier to mistreat and subjugate women if they can be persuaded that they are responsible for the evil and thus deserving of punishment. Even when the actual alienation myths are dismissed by their religious adherents as stories written long ago and therefore not to be taken too seriously, they are often promoted to the sacredness of scripture, and the effects of the stories may be encoded into law. Even though modern religious readers of these alienation myths are able to recognize the implausibility of their events, the negative aspects of the blaming of women for evil may persist for centuries. Women find themselves mistreated for many reasons that have nothing to do with the actual myths, but the treatment is justified by appealing to the sacred scriptures.

This chapter examines religious alienation myths in several cultures that cite women as the cause of the suffering, disease, knowledge of good and evil, hard work, and eventual death of the religion's devotees. As implausible as some of these myths may seem to modern eyes, their far-reaching effects have lasted centuries.

Religious and societal laws built on these myths deprive women of their full participation in the hierarchical religious organization and use the myths to control women's sexual behavior. Because so many men feared the women's reproductive power, they passed religious laws to control women's sexuality, such as menstrual taboos. A double standard arose that governed the sexual behavior of men and women, giving men freedom but demanding virginity from young women and celibacy from widows. By blaming women in myth for the introduction of evil, men justified their attempt to control women's reproductive process; they claimed that only men had the knowledge and rationality to make the correct decisions regarding women's sexual powers. The Hindu and Chinese traditions do not have alienation myths, but their philosophical and religious beliefs supported the establishment of law codes and customs that subjugate women.

However, as unjust as the alienation myths appear toward women, most religions hold hope of salvation open to both sexes. Although in mythical crisis humans lost their harmonious relations with their god and their initial paradisiacal state of unending bliss, they were not left without hope. A future time or event would save these hapless humans from their dismal present state and restore them to their original happiness and unmitigated union with their deity. Women as well as men could avail themselves of this opportunity, so even though a woman might suffer discrimination in the present, she could look forward to the same liberation as men in the future. Since salvation was accessible to women in the same way as to men, women would often continue in religious traditions and practices that appeared unjust and discriminatory, such as cleansing rituals directed at their life-giving capabilities.

Writings That Implicate Women for the Introduction of Evil

Traditional African Religions

Some traditional African myths blame men and animals for their separation from their god. Other tribes describe a god who gave a rule to be observed, such as not eating an animal or the fruit of a certain tree. When humans broke the rule, they suffered separation and tragic consequences. But two African tribes, the Ashantis and the Banyarwanda, blame women for the hard work, disease, and death of their people. John S. Mbiti, an African mythologist, describes an alienation myth told by the Ashantis.

> God originally lived in the sky but close to men. The mother of these men constantly went on knocking against Him with her pestle while pounding the traditional food, fufu. To get away from this knocking, God moved up higher.

The woman instructed her sons to gather all the mortars, pile them and follow God. This they did, but before they could reach to Him, they ran short of construction material. As there was a gap of only one mortar, she advised her children to take the bottom-most mortar in order to fill up the gap. Obediently they did this, only to cause the whole tower to tumble down and kill many of them. The survivors gave up the idea of following God "up there."

Mbiti, 97

In this myth the separation between God and humans was accomplished by an aggressive woman. For her action, she and her whole tribe became alienated from the God who cared for them.

The Banyarwanda tribe also have a myth that blames death on a woman. God provided for the main needs of humankind: food, domestic animals, light, fire, tools, children, medicine, and immortality. God gave the tribe certain rules to observe, and as long as humans kept these rules, their relationship with God remained wholesome and harmonious. One of the gifts that God gave to the people was the capability of death. God regretted this move and decided to take it back. When God came to reclaim death, he could not find it because a Banyarwanda woman had hidden it, even though God had told the people to leave death alone so they could be immortal. When he could not find death, he decided to leave it among the people. As a result, none of the tribespeople would ever be immortal: All would suffer death. A woman was responsible for this sad state of affairs as well as the grief that accompanied death.

By looking at the problems in the world, especially the sorrow caused by the loss in death, religious writers often ascribe the present condition to causes that had their origin many years ago. When these causes can be anchored in the beginning of a culture's history, they can solidify the present practices. Puberty rituals remind young men and women of the hardships they must face in adult life. The East African tribe of the Kipsigis circumcise their boys at the age of puberty to ready them for the difficulties they must face as adults. The initiation rites of the women of the Gikuyu and Nandi tribes of East Africa culminate in the practice of clitoridectomy, or excision of all or a section of the clitoris. Usually the young women are confined until healing occurs. Then the initiate is ready to assume the difficulties of marriage, childbearing, hard physical work, and sorrow caused by death. These tribes believe that young people need physical pain to prepare them for the suffering that results from the evils portrayed in the alienation myths. Christian missionaries have discouraged this practice of genital mutilation, but it is still practiced in many areas where tribes practice traditional African religions.

Hinduism

The Code of Manu

Although Hinduism does not teach an alienation myth that denigrates women, the basic beliefs of the patriarchal Hindu culture support the subordination of women. Knowledge of the Vedas, the sacred texts of Hinduism, was a prerequisite for humans to escape the endless cycle of rebirth and enter the liberated state of salvation, or *mosha*. Because only men were allowed to read the sacred texts, women were doomed to rebirth until they could return as men. Only the men from the three upper classes could receive the thread of the twice born (full initiation into Hinduism), which made them eligible for mosha through the enlightenment that resulted from study. Women were not allowed an education other than domestic, so they were deprived from sharing in the ritual of initiation and thus from full participation in the Hindu religion.

The goddesses of India possessed a power or energy that could destroy as well as create. This power was believed to be passionate, changeable, and emotional; it could whirl out of control. The feminine energy of the goddess, called shakti, needed the control of the masculine energy, which is described as passionless, constant, and reasoned. The *Brahmanas*, or sacred writings, specified the need for the male consort of the goddess to control her so that her boundless energy did not result in chaos and destruction. Denise Carmody and David Kinsley correlate the social conditions of women to the belief that the violent tendencies of the goddesses must not go unchecked. "Many of the social constraints that Hindu culture imposed on women found their final sanction in this fundamental conception of female nature. As the main goddesses show, women have been considered dangerously passionate, possessed of a vital nature that could destroy as well as bring forth new life" (Carmody, 42). The Hindu Puranic (sacred) text, *Devi Mahatmya*, portrays the goddess as the personified shakti, or creative power, of male gods. Since the goddess could produce her own shakti, she was as powerful as the male gods and needed no consort. Kathleen Erndl, a religious scholar, describes shakti as the "primordial power underlying the universe, personified as a female deity who is the Supreme Being, the totality of all existence" (22). This awesome power that a goddess held could be accessible to her female devotee. Fear of this power motivated the influential men in society to legislate control over it.

Law codes are usually developed over a duration of time with periodic additions called commentaries. By the second century CE, the Code of Manu reflected the restrictions placed on the creative power of women. The influence of the law of Manu was perpetuated over centuries through these commentaries, which have strong repercussions for women.

> By a girl, by a young woman, or even by an aged one, nothing must be done independently, even in her own house. In childhood a female must be subject to her father, in youth to her husband, when her lord (husband) is dead to her sons; a woman must never be independent. She must not seek to separate herself from her father, husband, or sons; by leaving them she would make both her own and her husband's families contemptible.
>
> *Code of Manu 5:147–49*

Encouraging life-long dominance of women by men was one of the ways to control this powerful force of the shakti. If a woman could never act independently, she would never be a threat to the patriarchal society. The Code of Manu directed a woman's personal life as well, because it gave explicit directions for her relationship to her husband.

> She must always be cheerful, clever in household affairs, careful in cleaning her utensils, and economical in expenditure. Him to whom her father may give her, or her brother with the father's permission, she shall obey as long as he lives, and when he is dead, she must not insult his memory. For the sake of procuring good fortune to brides, the recitation of benedictory texts and the sacrifice to the Lord of creatures are used at weddings; but the betrothal by the father or guardian is the cause of the husband's dominion over his wife. The husband who wedded her with sacred texts, always gives happiness to his wife, both in season and out of season, in this world and in the next. Though he be destitute of virtue, or seeking pleasure elsewhere, or devoid of good qualities, yet a husband must be constantly worshipped as a god by a faithful wife. No sacrifice, no vow, no fast must be performed by women apart from their husbands; if a wife obeys her husband, she will for that reason alone be exalted in heaven.
>
> *Code of Manu 5:150–155*

The command "to worship him as a god" has provoked many comments from Western women who object to the subordinate position of Hindu wives.

The position of the widow in Hindu society was unenviable because the Code of Manu did not allow her to remarry. She had to live a chaste, virtuous life and remain subordinate to her nearest male relative, usually a son, brother or brother-in-law, or father. Customarily she was forced to sleep on the floor at the house of her in-laws, to whom she became a financial liability. She could attend no social gatherings and had to dress in dark clothes, devoid of ornaments at all times.

> A faithful wife, who desires to dwell after death with her husband, must never do anything that might displease him who took her hand, whether he be alive or dead. At her pleasure let her emaciate her body by living on pure flowers, roots, and fruit; but she must never even mention the name of another man after her husband has died. Until death let her be patient in hardships, self-controlled, and chaste, and strive to fulfil that most excellent duty which is prescribed for wives who have one husband only.
>
> *Code of Manu 9:155–159*

In traditional India today, women's behavior is carefully guarded and ordered by men. Marriage usually takes place at an early age, soon after puberty, according to the arrangements made by the girl's father, who also chooses her husband. In many areas of India girls are betrothed of five to ten years of age, or even at birth. In previous centuries the early age for marriage deprived young girls of the educational opportunities that were open to men. If a girl or woman became a widow—even before the marriage was consummated or as a child bride—she could not remarry, but must live out her life dependent on some willing or unwilling male relative.

Bearing a son allowed a woman to gain acceptance and prestige in the society because a son could carry out the funeral rites of the parents, a ritual action denied to women. Daughters presented an economic liability to parents because they had to raise funds for the dowries required for marriage. The birth of a girl child was not well received by the parents, who often announced the event in the sorry words, "Nothing was born."

Institutionalization of the ill treatment of women is perpetuated by reference to the scriptures and law books that justify and encourage this treatment. When official documents state that women are inferior, legal practices will continue to discriminate against them.

Confucius and the Classics

The philosophy of Confucius, which prevailed in China after the sixth century BCE until the Communist revolution of this century, was centered on a harmonious notion of the cosmos. Each area of the cosmos—the sky, earth, the heavens—functioned in relationship to one another. When the relations stayed harmonious, the forces in the cosmos ran efficiently and well. This cosmic order was maintained in a hierarchical fashion, with the heavens as the most important active force and the earth as the less significant passive force. As long as these forces kept their dominant and subordinate position, the universe would progress in the most desirable and efficient manner. Human relations reflected the cosmic relations. In society, the most important persons held sway over the least important. Therefore, the political leaders expected respect, deference, and obedience from their followers. Families followed this pattern, with the grandfather, father, and sons holding dominion over their wives, daughters, and sisters. If each person on the lower level showed the correct obedience and respect to those above them, the familial relations would be cordial and happy. If the mutual obligations toward each member of the family were not properly carried out, not only would family members suffer, but the elements of the cosmos would fail to function correctly. As a result, there was much pressure placed on all members of society and households to comply with the Confucian ideals.

Unfortunately, the writings of Confucius did not present women in a favorable light. Richard Guisso, summarizing the attitudes toward women in the *Five Classics* of Confucius, describes the view of woman: "The female was inferior by nature, she was dark as the moon and changeable as water, jealous, narrow-minded, and insinuating. She was indiscreet, unintelligent, and dominated by emotion" (59).

The woman, who represented the earth, was considered inferior to the man, who represented the heavens. The man was the dominant person in the political sphere of life, which surpassed the domestic scene in importance. The woman was related to the house, where she obeyed the directions of her father, husband, or son. Relationships in the family were kept harmonious when each person knew his or her place in the hierarchy that placed men at the top and women and children at the bottom.

Most moral teachings of Confucius were directed at people in the lower position, showing them how to give proper respect toward their superiors. However, he directed those in the superior position not to use their power to exploit their subjects, but to treat them with care and concern.

Women had so internalized their inferior position that in the second century CE, a woman, Pan Chao, author of *Instructions for Women,* wrote a guide to help women better live out their destinies as wives and mothers. She described a practice that should accompany the birth of a girl to help the girl identify and accept her future role in life.

> On the third day after the birth of a girl, the ancients observed three customs: first to place the baby below the bed; second to give her a potsherd (a piece of broken pottery) with which to play; and third to announce her birth to her ancestors by an offering.
>
> *Nu-Chieh 1:26–3a in Swann, 83*

Pan Chao explained that placing the baby under the bed showed the proper place for the female child: humble, lowly, and submissive to all. The pottery indicated that she should be hardworking in her domestic area— her destiny as a future wife. She would refer to the ancestors of her husband as her own ancestors, because she would move into his family at marriage. (A woman could expect no record of her birth in her natal home but would be counted among her husband's relatives, to whom she had to give homage.)

When describing the role of the woman in marriage, Pan Chao referred to the corresponding roles of heaven and earth. The husband, like the heaven, had to be strong, firm, and dominant. He was to manage his wife with authority. The wife, like the earth, had to be weak, pliant, and subservient. She had to serve her husband willingly. If either one failed in their execution of these directives, Pan Chao explained, the marriage would fail because the order of the cosmos would be upset. (*Nu-Chieh* 1:45–5a, in Swann, 84).

If people could be persuaded that they were carrying the burden of the cosmos, they would be more likely to uphold the laws that ensure its continuance. Women had just as much responsibility to uphold the cosmic order as men did, so they accepted their inferior position in society. The women also had to maintain the family order through hierarchical family relationships. Women's position called for a great deal of inner strength, because they leave their own family to find an accepted place in a family of strangers, where the women had to prove themselves through selfless devotion. By compliance with the duties prescribed by Confucian precepts, women would reap the same reward given to men. "Parents-in-law boast of her good deeds, her husband is satisfied with her. Praise of her radiates, making her illustrious in district and neighborhood, and her brightness reaches to her own father and mother" (*Nu-chieh* 1:116, in Swann, 88).

The spirit of Confucius applied to both women and men, who looked to him for guidance with family and society. When such a great teacher and philosopher placed women in a subservient position, that position became not only acceptable but also sanctified by his writings. No one dared to upset the harmonious relationships of family and society when that action would upset the forces that kept the cosmos functioning effectively. If one desired the sun, moon, and stars to stay in their orbits, and rain to help the crops grow, one assiduously kept the directives of Confucius.

Judaism

Biblical Views of Women

Perhaps no story equals the alienation myth in the Jewish Bible in its ability to impress lasting effects on the women of the Western world. Jewish, Christian, and Islamic women have been profoundly influenced by the well-known story of the fall of Adam and Eve, an etiological myth in that it tries to explain why evil exists in the world today. The story illustrates the source of alienation that has occurred between humans and God, men and women, and individuals and the environment. It is referred to as the "fall" because it depicts a fall, or change, from a paradisiacal state in which life was easy and happy. Adam and Eve enjoyed a work-free existence in a garden, where they had a harmonious relationship with their god—Yahweh, or God—and with each other. Because humans in real life did not live in a completely peaceful relationship with one another and their environment, they looked for some explanation for that alienation. The authors of the scriptural version of this myth, who lived between the tenth and eighth centuries BCE, were troubled by the human discomfort surrounding death, by the pain of childbearing, and by the frustration of work, sexual desire, and the need for clothing. By writing a story of primal parents who fell from a paradisiacal state to one of discord, war, jealousy, and all the evils caused by humans, the authors could use the myth to explain the present state of alienation from the good.

The Fall
Now, the snake was the most subtle of all the wild animals that Yahweh God had made. It asked the woman, "Did God really say you were not to eat from any of the trees in the garden?" The woman answered the snake, "We may eat the fruit of the trees in the garden. But of the fruit of the tree in the middle of the garden God said, 'You must not eat it, nor touch it, under pain of death.'"

Then the snake said to the woman, "No! You will not die! God knows in fact that the day you eat it your eyes will be opened and you will be like gods, knowing good from evil." The woman saw that the tree was good to eat and pleasing to the eye, and that it was enticing for the wisdom that it could give. So she took some of its fruit and ate it. She also gave some to her husband who was with her, and he ate it. Then the eyes of both of them were opened and they realized that they were naked. So they sewed fig-leaves together to make themselves loin-cloths.

The man and his wife heard the sound of Yahweh God walking in the garden in the cool of the day, and they hid from Yahweh God among the trees of the garden. But Yahweh God called to the man. "Where are you?" he asked. "I heard the sound of you in the garden," he replied. "I was afraid because I was naked, so I hid." "Who told you that you were naked?" he asked. "Have you been eating from the tree I forbade you to eat?" The man replied, "It was the woman you put with me; she gave me some fruit from the tree, and I ate it." Then Yahweh God said to the woman, "Why did you do that?" The woman replied, "The snake tempted me and I ate."

> Then Yahweh God said to the snake, "Because you have done this,
>> Accursed to you
>> of all animals wild and tame!
>> On your belly you will go
>> and on dust you will feed
>> as long as you live.
>> I shall put enmity
>> between you and the woman,
>> and between your offspring and hers;
>> it will bruise your head
>> and you will strike its heel."

> To the woman he said:
>> "I shall give you intense pain in childbearing,
>> you will give birth to your children in pain.
>> Your yearning will be for your husband,
>> and he will dominate you."

> To the man he said, "Because you listened to the voice of your wife and ate from the tree of which I had forbidden you to eat,
>> Accursed by the soil because of you!
>> Painfully will you get your food from it
>> as long as you live.
>> It will yield you brambles and thistles,
>> as you eat the produce of the land.
>> By the sweat of your face
>> will you earn your food,
>> until you return to the ground,
>> as you were taken from it.
>> For dust you are
>> and to dust you shall return."

The man named his wife "Eve" because she was the mother of all those who live. Yahweh God made tunics of skins for the man and his wife and clothed them. Then Yahweh God said, "Now that the man has become like one of us in knowing good from evil, he must not be allowed to reach out his hand and pick from the tree of life too, and eat and live for ever! So Yahweh God expelled him from the garden of Eden, to till the soil from which he had been taken. He banished the man, and in front of the garden of Eden he posted the great winged creatures and the fiery flashing sword, to guard the way to the tree of life.

From the Jerusalem Bible, Gen. 3:1–24

Although the story stands on its own as a good representation of an etiological myth, various interpretations of the scriptural account have left profound effects on the lives of both men and women in Western history. One of the interpretations concerns the subordinate position of women, who will be dominated by their husbands. Some translations say "he will lord it over you," others that "he shall have authority over you" and "he will rule over you." All the translations clearly point to the subordinate position of Eve because she is responsible for the introduction of sin and evil into the world. She needs to be controlled by a man because she is unable to control her passion for food, sex, and power.

The place of the serpent in the story is significant. Later interpreters, influenced by the writers of the Book of Revelation, Augustine, and Milton, have associated the serpent with Satan. However, one must remember that the Hebrews lived near polytheistic religions that worshipped the goddess, whose symbol was the snake. The Hebrew authorities were worried because some of their children were marrying foreigners and bringing these "false" religions into monotheistic Israel. Remnants of the goddess worship in the form of female figures that date from the time of King David have been found in Israel. What better way to rid oneself of the goddess than to demean her symbol, the snake?

The snake, which has been labeled a deceiver, did not lie to Eve in the story, but rather spoke the truth, because Eve and Adam did learn to distinguish good from evil as a consequence of eating the fruit. The serpent—the prophetic symbol of the goddess, who was usually associated with wisdom in neighboring Canaanite culture—would have previously been expected to give wise counsel. In accepting the counsel of the serpent, Eve accepted at the same time the advice of the mother goddess, who was associated with the tree of life and the tree of the knowledge of good and evil. The serpent is acknowledged by the scripture writers as the most subtle of all the animals, so if it were evil, one wonders how it ever got into this paradisiacal garden in the first place. When Eve listened to the serpent and decided to go to the source of knowledge, the forbidden tree, she chose to return to the older religion of the mother goddess, rather than the new Hebrew religion of the male deity, Yahweh. The punishment meted out to Adam and Eve seemed deserving to anyone who preferred the mother goddess of their neighbors to God. The serpent, her symbol, had to be destroyed by a curse. Riane Eisler describes the punishment given to Eve.

Because she—the first and symbolic woman—clung to the old faith more tenaciously than did Adam, who only followed her lead, her punishment was to be more dreadful. Henceforth, she would have to submit in all things. Not only her sorrow, but her conceptions—the number of children she must bear—would be greatly multiplied. And for all eternity she was now to be ruled by this vengeful God and his earthly representative, man.

Eisler, 89

Yahweh's curse on the serpent actually alienated women from their old source of comfort in childbirth—the goddess, in the form of the serpent. Women, who had looked to the goddess for strength and support, were made responsible for crushing her. The end of the goddess religions was thereby effected by women themselves, ensuring the demise of the female deities.

The myth also speaks of the beginning of the alienation between men and women that made the man superior to the woman. The person who has the ability to name another has power over the latter: Yahweh named Adam, and Adam, who named woman and the animals, had domination over the named. No one was ever able to name God because that would give the individual power over God that was impossible to possess. The ability to rename had similar connotations. God changed Abram's name to Abraham and Sari's name to Sarah; Adam renamed woman as Eve (Gen. 3:20). This action reinforces the idea that men participate in the power of God when they perform actions similar to those of Yahweh.

Humans have for centuries sought to be immortal, but life teaches us that mortality is our lot. Gen. 3 describes the cause for death as the separation from the tree of life: Humans shall return to the dust from which they were created. Although Eve and Adam sought the immortality of God, the knowledge they derived from the tree of knowledge was that they were indeed mortal. This knowledge led to their separation from God, who had to expel them from the garden because if they achieved immortality and knowledge of good and evil, they would truly be gods.

Separation results in dualistic divisions between the two separated parties. God is separated from humans, men from women, spirit from dust or matter, reason from emotions, and heaven from earth. Dualism serves patriarchal societies well because it both emphasizes the separation and prioritizes the elements in the dualistic formulas. The element in the first part of the equation becomes the better one, leaving the less desirable features to the less powerful in society. Masters have power over their slaves, monotheists are considered more advanced culturally than polytheists, father gods are viewed as better than mother goddesses, and the father of the family has more prestige than the mother. This dualistic thought has not served women well. The monistic philosophy of the goddess religions emphasized the unity between the goddess and her people, men and women, body and spirit, and heaven and earth. With the suppression of the goddess in Hebrew thought, the dualism of the Hebrew patriarchs replaced monistic philosophy: Women found themselves in the second category.

Another scripture reference that shows the husband's authority over his wife is the Ten Commandments (Exod. 20:14), in which the Hebrew word for husband is *ba al*, denoting him as master or owner of animals or objects. The Israelite man was forbidden to covet his neighbor's possessions, which included the neighbor's wife, slaves, and cattle. The daughter was also considered the property of her father. He had to be compensated for her by the bride price offered by the future husband. If the daughter was raped and her virginity no longer intact, the rapist had to pay the father the bride price and had to marry the daughter. He was not allowed to divorce her, no matter how unhappy their married life was. Since a woman could not divorce her husband, she was condemned to spend her life with the man who had caused her such unhappiness.

Although virginity was demanded of women, it was not required of men. The book of Deuteronomy describes the procedure that a married man who had paid the bride price could follow if he suspected that his new wife was not a virgin. He would have a good judicial case if he could show that he had received damaged goods from the girl's father. The reference to the "cloth" in the following passage depicts the cloth that the new wife was to lie on at the consummation of the marriage. It was to contain the blood that resulted from a pierced hymen.

> If a man marries a woman, has sexual intercourse with her and then, turning against her, taxes her with misconduct and publicly defames her by saying, "I married this woman and when I had sexual intercourse with her I did not find evidence of her virginity," the girl's father and mother must take the evidence of her virginity and produce it before the elders of the town, at the gate. To the elders, the girl's father will say, "I gave this man my daughter for a wife and he has turned against her, and now he taxes her with misconduct, saying, 'I have found no evidence of virginity in your daughter.' Here is the evidence of my daughter's virginity!" They must then display the cloth to the elders of the town. The elders of the town in question will have the man arrested and flogged, and fine him a hundred silver shekels for publicly defaming a virgin of Israel, and give this money to the girl's father. She will remain his wife; as long as he lives, he may not divorce her.
>
> But if the accusation that the girl cannot show evidence of virginity is substantiated, she must be taken out, and at the door of her father's house her fellow citizens must stone her to death for having committed an infamy in Israel by bringing disgrace on her father's family. You must banish this evil from among you.
>
> *Deuteronomy 22:11–21*

The young woman was not consulted as to whether she wanted to spend her life with the accuser. The discrepancy in the punishment that was meted out to the offenders underscores the secondary position of women.

The patriarchs were concerned with controlling the sexuality of women because the female reproductive capacity was so prized. If the woman could control her own sexual capacities, she might become more autonomous, like the women who worshipped goddesses in neighboring countries such as Canaan. The initial alienation myth of Israel continued to alienate men from women, even in marriage, the most intimate of relationships. But perhaps the worst example of alienation occurred when the woman was separated from her own personhood and treated as an object— the possession of a man—as a bride to be bought.

Greek Writings

The Pandora Myth

Most contemporary children from Western civilization are exposed to the myth of the girl, Pandora, whose curiosity got the best of her. She was so self-indulgent that she lifted the cover of the box that she was instructed to leave alone. With that great act of disobedience, the evils of the world— death, disease, famine, wars, crimes—escaped, blemishing the paradisiacal state forever. Curious, sensual women were again blamed for the introduction of evil into the world.

This story has roots in a story told by Hesiod in the seventh century BCE that described hostility among the gods. Zeus was angry at the god Prometheus, who had made life easier for mortals by giving them fire—a possession of the gods. He had punished Prometheus for betraying the gods, but he had not yet punished humans for receiving the fire. Humans then enjoyed a life of ease, happiness, and freedom from work, disease, and old age, which made them too similar to the gods. Zeus looked for an appropriate punishment that would make humans' lives miserable. What better way to introduce evil into the world than through the efforts of a beautiful and treacherous woman? No matter that she was the ploy of the gods, who jealously guarded their lives of immortality and ease. The gods knew that Pandora would be blamed by the humans for their loss of the paradisiacal state and their fall into suffering and death. In his cunning, Zeus enlisted the help of the goddesses to produce this deceitful creature. Hesiod's story has the goddesses eagerly complying with this destructive deed. Then the gods gave Pandora, the victim, with her vessel of evils, as a gift to a human, Epimetheus, who is taken in by her beauty and willingly accepts her. She in turn removed the cover from her vessel and let loose all its evils on humankind.

> Zeus in the wrath of his heart has hidden the means of
> subsistence—
> Wrathful because he once was deceived by the wily Prometheus.
> Therefore he devised most grievous troubles for mortals.
> Fire he hid: yet that, for men, did the gallant Prometheus
> Steal in a hollow reed, from the dwelling of Zeus the Adviser.
> Nor was he seen by the ruler of gods, who delights in the
> thunder.

Then, in his rage at the deed, cloud-gathering Zeus did
    address him;
Iapetionides, in cunning greater than any,
"You in the theft of fire and deceit of me art exulting,
Source of regret for thyself and for men who shall be hereafter
    guides
I, in the place of fire, will give them a bane, so that all
    men
May in spirit exult and find in their misery comfort!"
Speaking thus, loud laughed he, the father of gods and of
    mortals.
Then he commanded Hephaistos, the cunning artificer,
    straightway
Mixing water and earth, with speech and force to endow it,
Making it like in face to the gods whose life is eternal.
Virginal, winning and fair was the shape: and he ordered
    Athene
Skilful devices to teach her, the beautiful works of the
    weaver.
Then did he bid Aphrodite the golden endow her with beauty,
Eager desire, and passion that wasteth the bodies of mortals.
Hermes, guider of men, the destroyer of Argus, he ordered,
Lastly, a shameless mind to bestow and a treacherous nature.
So did he speak. They obeyed Lord Zeus, who is offspring of
Kronos.
Straightway, out of the earth, the renowned artificer
    fashioned
One like a shame-faced maid, at the will of the ruler of
    Heaven.
Girdle and ornaments added the bright-eyed goddess Athene.
Over her body the Graces divine and noble Persuasion
Hung their golden chains; and the Hours with beautiful tresses
Wove her garlands of flowers that bloom in the season of
    Springtime.
All her adornments Pallas Athene fitted upon her.
Into her bosom, Hermes the guide, the destroyer of Argus,
Falsehood, treacherous thoughts and a thievish nature
    imparted:
Such was the bidding of Zeus who heavily thunders; and lastly
Hermes, herald of gods, endowed her with speech, and the woman
Named Pandora, because all the gods who dwell in Olympos
Gave her presents, to make her a fatal bane unto mortals.
When now Zeus had finished this snare so deadly and certain,
Famous Argus slayer, the herald of gods, he commanded,
Leading her thence, as a gift to bestow her upon Epimetheus.
He, then, failed to remember Prometheus had bidden him never
Gifts to accept from Olympian Zeus, but still to return them
Straightway, lest some evil befall thereby unto morals.
So he received her—and then, when the evil befell, he
    remembered.
Till that time, upon earth were dwelling the races of mortals,

> Free and secure from trouble and free from wearisome labour;
> Safe from painful diseases that bring mankind to destruction
> Since full swiftly in misery age unto morals approacheth.
> Now with her hands, Pandora the great lid raised from the
>   vessel,
> Letting them loose: and grievous the evil for men she
>   provided.
> Hope yet lingered, alone, in the dwelling securely imprisoned.
> Since she under the edge of the lid had tarried and flew not
> Forth: too soon Pandora had fastened the lid of the vessel.
> Such was the will of Zeus, cloud-gatherer, lord of the aegis,
> Numberless evils beside to the haunts of men had departed,
> Full is the earth of ills, and full no less are the waters.
> Freely diseases among mankind, by day and in darkness
> Hither and thither may pass and bring much woe upon mortals:
> Voiceless, since of speech high-counselling Zeus has bereft
>   them.
>
> *Hesiod, Works and Days, Chapters 5 and 6*

Although modern writers emphasize the deed of Pandora, Hesiod stressed her creation. He implicated the human man Epimetheus in the introduction of evil as well. It is strange that he classifies hope, a human virtue, as one of the evils that did not escape, although it served as a means of coping with the harm let loose by Pandora.

Hesiod, however, was not the first to tell a myth about Pandora. Long before the Dorian, Achean, and Ionian invaders arrived in Greece with their storm god Zeus around 2500 BCE, the local myths revolved around various goddesses. These powerful, wise, autonomous goddesses contrasted significantly with the petty, jealous, victimized goddesses of the classical era of Homer and Hesiod. One of these pre-Hellenic mother goddesses was Pandora, whose name meant "giver of gifts." Pandora was considered the maiden form of the earth goddess, from whom all material gifts of plants, animals, and food arose. She was pictured as benignly bestowing her gifts and graces upon humans, who did not even have to ask for them. Rather than a cunning creation of the gods, who used Pandora to deceive, as representative of the mother goddess she was the creatrix of humans, the earth, and its fruits. In 1927 Professor Jane Ellen Harrison wrote of the transformation of Pandora by a patriarchal society.

> Zeus the Father will have no great Earth-goddess, Mother and maid all in one
> . . . so he remakes her: woman, who was the inspirer, becomes the temptress;
> she who made all things, gods and mortals alike, is to become their plaything.
> To Zeus, the arch-patriarchal bourgeois, the birth of the first woman is a huge
> Olympian jest.
>
> *Harrison, 285*

By rewriting the myths, patriarchal authors could blame women for introducing evil into the world. When appealing to religious truths for justification, men could almost sanctify maltreatment of women—"this is the way it should be."

Christianity

The Letters of Paul

Because Christians claim the Hebrew Bible as their own, the effects of the Adam and Eve alienation story have penetrated throughout the Western world. In the New Testament, Paul underscores the ramifications of the fall story on the early Christians and affirms the hierarchical order of God over man, and man over women. He incorporates Jesus Christ into his schema, making God, Jesus, and men superior to women. In the letter to the Corinthians, Paul refers to the custom of veiling. Orthodox Jewish women wore the veil to show that they were subject to their fathers and husbands. He encourages Christian women to follow this custom.

> I congratulate you for remembering me so consistently and for maintaining traditions exactly as I passed them on to you. But I should like you to understand that the head of every man is Christ, the head of woman is man, and the head of Christ is God. For any man to pray or to prophesy with his head covered shows disrespect for his head. And for a woman to pray or prophesy with her head uncovered shows disrespect for her head; it is exactly the same as if she had her hair shaved off. Indeed, if a woman does go without a veil, she should have her hair cut off too; but if it is a shameful thing for a woman to have her hair cut or shaved off, then she should wear a veil.
>
> But for a man it is not right to have his head covered, since he is the image of God and reflects God's glory; but woman is the reflection of man's glory. For man did not come from woman: no, woman came from man; nor was man created for the sake of woman, but woman for the sake of man: and this is why it is right for a woman to wear on her head a sign of the authority over her.
>
> *1 Corinthians 11:1–10*

The letter to the Ephesians has been attributed to Paul, although there is some serious doubt that he wrote it. But the very fact that his name is attached to it lends credibility to its contents as a guide for husbands and wives in their moral duties toward each other. The effects of this passage were felt through the 1960s in the United States, when the Catholic Family Movement referred to the husband as the head and the wife as the heart of the family. The author of Ephesians quotes Genesis in the Hebrew Bible when giving the reasons for husbands and wives to live with each other.

> Be subject to one another out of reverence for Christ. Wives should be subject to their husbands as to the Lord, since, as Christ is head of the Church and saves the whole body, so is a husband the head of his wife, and as the Church is subject to Christ, so should wives be to their husbands, in everything. Husbands should love their wives, just as Christ loved the Church and sacrificed himself for her to make her holy by washing her in cleansing water with a form of words, so that when he took the Church to himself she would be glorious, with no speck or wrinkle or anything like that, but holy and faultless.

> In the same way, husbands must love their wives as they love their own bod-
> ies; for a man to love his wife is for him to love himself. A man never hates his
> own body, but he feeds it and looks after it; and that is the way Christ treats
> the Church, because we are parts of his Body. This is why a man leaves his
> father and mother and becomes attached to his wife; and the two become one
> flesh.
>
> *Ephesians 5:21–31*

The most direct reference to Adam and Eve in the writings of the New
Testament is in the letter of an unknown author to Timothy at the turn of
the first century CE. Again the piece has been attributed to Paul to give it
more prestige in the early Christian community.

> Similarly, women are to wear suitable clothes and to be dressed quietly and
> modestly, without braided hair or gold and jewellery or expensive clothes;
> their adornment is to do the good works that are proper for women who
> claim to be religious. During instruction, a woman should be quiet and
> respectful. I give no permission for a woman to teach or to have authority
> over a man. A woman ought to be quiet, because Adam was formed first and
> Eve afterwards, and it was not Adam who was led astray but the woman who
> was led astray and fell into sin. Nevertheless, she will be saved by child-bear-
> ing, provided she lives a sensible life and is constant in faith and love and holi-
> ness.
>
> *1 Timothy 2:9–15*

Here the author tries to justify his position by citing the second story in
Genesis, which depicts the creation of Adam before Eve. He supports his
thesis that women should be subordinate to men with the argument that
Eve sinned first. This passage has been used for centuries to prevent
women from positions of leadership in Christian churches.

Like the Greek writers who justified the subjugation of women through
the Pandora myth, the author of this diatribe against women must have considered it necessary to stop women from participating in church leadership.
If women were not already exercising positions of teaching, preaching, and
authority in the church, would the author have considered it necessary to
discourage the practice? Feminine theologians point out that most practices
are in vogue for a number of years before laws are passed to regulate them.

Christian theologians put more emphasis on the Adam and Eve story as
the beginning of evil than do Jewish theologians. Christian theology, which
takes the scripture as the Divine Revelation of God, places great blame on
Eve for clouding Adam's ability to choose good. Because all men and
women suffer death and disease, even the god-man, Jesus, had to undergo
this evil so humans could regain their paradisiacal state. In the second century BCE, one of the church leaders, Tertullian, let women know how culpa-
ble they were.

> You are the Devil's gateway. You are the unsealer of the forbidden tree. You
> are the first deserter of the divine law. You are she who persuaded him whom

the Devil was not valiant enough to attack. You destroyed so easily, God's image, man. On account of your desert, that is death, even the Son of God had to die.

de Cult Fem 1.1

This misogynist attitude toward women stood in stark contrast to some of the practices of the early church. Women were serving as administrators of churches, were counted among the apostles, and presided over the church services held in their houses. Paul had written to the Romans on behalf of Phoebe, the deaconess, who administered the church at Cenchrae. He sent greetings in Rom. 16 to his fellow workers in Christ Jesus, whose names included 16 women and 18 men. He singled out Prisca and Aquilla as a husband and wife team and referred to Tryphaena, Tryphosa, Julia, and Olympas (women) as active church workers. He designates Junia by the term *apostle*. In his letter to the Galatians (3.28), Paul writes, "There can be neither Jew nor Greek, there can be neither slave nor freeman, there can be neither male nor female—for you are all one in Christ Jesus." Paul's attitude toward women seemed ambiguous, because at one instance he demeaned them when referring to the fall story, but in practice he seemed to uphold their full participation in the early church.

Paul had the example of Jesus upon which to base his acceptance of women. The early Christians were well aware that Jesus chose women as disciples (Luke 8:1–3), befriended them (Luke 10:38–42), and appreciated their presence (Mark 14:3–9). The writers of the second century turned about the example of Jesus and Paul, the first formers of the Christian tradition. The egalitarian church of the first century, in which the spirit was bestowed on women and men together (Acts 2), had allowed women to act as prophetesses. It was overturned by the patriarchal, hierarchical church that emerged by the second century and was recorded in 1 Timothy, in which men were assigning women's roles.

One of the ways that women could escape the role of wife and mother assigned to them by the powerful men in church and society was to declare themselves virgins in love with Christ. During the Roman persecutions of Christians, many young women chose martyrdom over marriage, thus defying their arranged engagements. The legend of Thecla, a courageous woman who emerged victorious from many tortures to carry the message of Christ, is an example of the many stories of women who found in Christianity an alternative to patriarchy. Because the martyr was considered another Christ, women could represent Christ, both in his teaching and his example.

In the popular *Acts of Paul and Thecla*, Thecla is described as adopting this life of chastity as a result of her conversion by Paul. She is then represented as persecuted by the representatives of patriarchal authority of family and state. Thrown to the lions twice, she miraculously escapes, baptizing herself on the second occasion. The female perspective of the narrative is revealed by the fact that all the male authorities, other than Paul, are seen as Thecla's enemies while the females, including the queen and even the female animals in the arena, espouse her cause. Her mother, who identifies with patriarchal claims of the family against Thecla's chosen freedom, is the one exception. But at the end of the narrative Thecla is sent back to Iconium to convert her mother. As a final imprimatur on her authority, Paul is shown commissioning her as an apostle, with the words "go and teach the Word of God."

Roberts and Donaldson, 487 ff.

Islam

The Quran Surah on Women

Although there is much variety in the practice of Islam in Muslim countries, the family law as written in the Quran still prevails in most areas. Muslims, the adherents of Islam, take very seriously their holy book, the Quran, because they believe it to be the direct word of God, dictated by the Angel Gabriel to their founder Mohammed. Although Muslims are found in diverse of cultures worldwide, they share a strict adherence to the Quranic truths, which they believe are divinely revealed. Islam's strongly patriarchal tradition is reflected in the surah on women in the Quran.

> Men have authority over women because God has made the one superior to the other, and because they spend their wealth to maintain them. Good women are obedient. They guard their unseen parts because God has guarded them. As for those from whom you fear disobedience, admonish them and send them to beds apart and beat them. Then if they obey you, take no further action against them. God is high, supreme.
>
> *Surah 2:221–222*

The Quran seems to justify the superior position of men in Arab society, telling women to obey the men who provide for them. Modesty is prized for women who are encouraged to cover their bodies.

Consistent with most patriarchal religions, Islamic societies attempt to control the sexuality of women. By considering women fields to be plowed whenever men please, the Quran appears to give men license for sexual intercourse:

> They ask you about menstruation. Say: "It is an indisposition. Keep aloof from women during their menstrual periods and do not touch them until they are clean again. Then have intercourse with them in the way God enjoined you. God loves those that turn to Him in repentance and strive to keep themselves clean."
>
> Women are your fields: go, then, into your fields whence you please. Do good works and fear God. Bear in mind that you shall meet Him. Give good tidings to the believers.
>
> *Surah 4:35*

The Quran encourages men to have intercourse, but only with their legal wives and concubines. It does not condone sex outside of marriage for either sex.

The Quran gives directives for family life as the basis of prevailing family law in most Muslim countries. A man may marry up to four wives at once, provided he can care for each one equally. A woman can marry only one man at a time. Polygamy established harems, which led to the enforced seclusion of women in their apartments together. Although the stifling conditions and limited opportunities for growth led to rivalries, jealousies, and cultural deprivation among the women, some of its proponents argued that it gave more women a chance to marry and to be provided for by men of means. Harems provided economic benefits to some men because women could work in the fields in the rural areas or perform domestic crafts such as textile spinning and cloth weaving. Women in turn received the protection of a man.

The Quran does allow a woman to keep her dowry and take it with her in case of divorce. She can inherit money, but only half as much as a man can, because he needs more money to provide for his family (Surah 4:11). A Muslim woman is usually married at a very young age, around puberty, to a man secured through an arrangement by her father. Because education is not considered necessary for girls in most Muslim countries, they learn domestic duties from their mothers at home.

Islamic law, called the sharia, is based primarily on the Quran and the sayings and actions of Mohammed. The Quran stresses the inferiority of women and makes the "superior" sex responsible for the care of these dependents. More detailed laws to protect women evolved along with customs to regulate their behavior.

The custom allowing men to divorce women with the triple statement "I divorce you" has caused much pain for women. Some Muslim countries have made the triple repudiation illegal and have added divorce stipulations more favorable to women. "It remains true, however, that men can divorce for less cause than women, and often divorces hung up in the courts with male judges can prove enormously difficult for women to gain" (Young, 239). In the past Islamic divorce law awarded custody of the children to the father after they reached seven years of age. In some Muslim countries the practice is changing, allowing the mother to keep her son until puberty and her daughter until marriage age.

Although the Quran claims that men and women are equal before God and should perform their religious duties faithfully, women have found themselves increasingly excluded from the premises of the mosque. In the home or place of work, religious teachings and prayers occur daily, but all men are expected to attend the mosque, the house of prayer, on Fridays. Because of their impurities during menstruation and childbearing, women were excluded from participation in the communal religious ceremonies and prayers. Even the ritually pure women found themselves moved to the balcony, the side, and finally outside the mosque, where they often could not hear the teachings of the leader, called the mullah. In many countries women were excused or exempted from attending Friday prayers and encouraged to stay home to attend to domestic duties.

In some Muslim countries, such as Iran and Saudi Arabia, Muslim women are turning this discrimination into something very creative and satisfying. They create their own rituals involving music, dance, poetry, and food. Neighboring women visit one another's homes and participate fully in glorifying God through the rituals they themselves construct. Some women make vows to God in which they promise something in return for physical or psychological healing, a good marriage, or the renewed love of their husbands. Other women support them in the fulfillment of these vows. So although women have been deprived of access to God through the male-controlled mosque, they have found their own way to religious consolation outside the paths open only to men.

Women's Adaptation to the Effects of Alienation Myths and Discriminatory Religious Practices

Hinduism

Suttee

The poor treatment of widows in earlier centuries led to a practice called suttee, or sati, in which a widow was expected to immolate herself by climbing on the burning bier and lying down next to her dead husband (Figure 4.1). Because the widow was the shakti, or energy force, of her husband, she was expected to die when he did. Funerals conducted in India usually involved the cremation of the corpse, which was placed on a wooden bier and then set on fire. With such a dismal future to look forward to, completely deprived of all human satisfaction and independence, it is likely that some widows willingly sacrificed themselves in this religious act of burning themselves to death.

According to the commentaries on the Hindu laws, to be a sati (virtuous woman) was considered a great honor. The husband would be happier in the next life if his possessions went with him. Because his wife was his chief possession, she would give him greater happiness by sacrificing herself for him. Her own death was viewed positively because it brought about the reunion of husband and wife. Stories of heroic women who immolated themselves with their husbands were passed down through generations from mothers to daughters, and the widows often were worshipped as goddesses.

FIGURE 4.1   Hindu Ritual of Suttee. (Courtesy of the Los Angeles County Museum.)

There is some question regarding the willingness of the sacrificial victim. Some European travelers through India wrote about widows who were drugged, tied down, or pushed back on the pyre with poles if they tried to get off. Often the widow was blamed for the death of her husband: Her behavior as wife was so poor that it gave him bad karma. Relatives of the husband, and sometimes the wife herself, agreed with this interpretation. It was easier for in-laws to coerce the widow into the ritual of suttee with her cooperation if she accepted the blame for her husband's death. Although the British outlawed suttee in 1829, newspapers give accounts of the practice continuing in contemporary society, especially in rural areas.

Bride Burning

The recent phenomena called bride burning—burning of women for lack of sufficient dowry—gains neither support nor strong protest from orthodox Hindu priests. They cite the ancient laws of Manu, which declare that "it is only a minor crime to kill a dog, a Shudra (lower caste) or a woman." With the intrusion of capitalism into India, some Hindus use the method of bride burning to obtain more material goods. The following story appeared in newspapers in the United States in 1990.

Practice of Burning Wives Still Persists in India

New Delhi, India—When Neelam Gupta accepted a fruit vendor's proposal to marry in 1985, her father borrowed more than $2,600 for her wedding and dowry. It was the equivalent of five years worth of wages.

The teen-age bride moved into her in-laws home with a dowry of a gold ring, wrist watch, dressing table, steel cabinet ceiling fan, and cooking utensils.

It was not enough.

Ms. Gupta said her husband, Rakesh Kumar, and his mother also wanted a refrigerator and tried to kill her by burning her with kerosene last November because her father failed to provide one.

"I screamed loudly," she recalled in a recent interview. "Some neighbors collected, and then my brother-in-law threw some water on me, pretending the fire was an accident."

The woman, who is now 19, cannot sit or sleep on her back because of burns over 20 percent of her body.

She was a victim of "bride burning," where husbands and in-laws set wives ablaze if their families fail to meet demands for more dowry.

Payment of dowry has been illegal in India since 1961, but is still widespread. Women's groups, as well as some doctors and judges, say the bride-burning phenomenon is growing. Police say it isn't, but their critics accuse them of failing to pursue and sometimes ignoring the evidence.

About 300 married women, ages 18 to 30, died of burns in New Delhi during the first six months of 1987, compared to 478 for all of 1986, according to figures issued by Parliament.

Almost every day, New Delhi newspapers carry reports of one or more women "who died of burns under suspicious circumstances."

Often the fire happens in the kitchen, near a kerosene stove. The in-laws call it a cooking accident; usually they are the only witnesses.

Ms. Gupta, who now lives with her parents in a shantytown on the outskirts of New Delhi, said her in-laws waited three days before taking her to a hospital—and that happened only after a neighbor called the police.

"I was too scared to call the police," she said. "My husband had threatened to kill my parents if I did."

In Ms. Gupta's case, police detained her husband and mother-in-law but they were released on bail, even though dowry is a non-bailable offense under the Dowry Prohibition Act. The judge said police did not furnish enough evidence to hold them, according to Ms. Gupta's father, Shanti Swaroop Gupta, a cloth peddler.

Ms. Gupta said her mother-in-law always taunted her for not providing enough dowry.

A visit to New Delhi's major hospitals found several young women patients who had been burned in alleged "cooking accidents." Most were surrounded by in-laws and not willing to say how they were burned.

"It is a problem to get them to tell the truth. Even on their death beds, they don't want to implicate their husbands," said a doctor in the burn ward at Safdarjang Hospital.

Coupled with this is the traditionally low status of women in India, where female infanticide and suttee—where a woman burns herself to death on her husband's funeral pyre—still occur from time to time.

Seema Sirohi, Associated Press

Although these numbers of dowry deaths seem high, the figures are not really accurate, because most people do not report any cases of domestic violence. Elizabeth Bumiller, a correspondent for the *Washington Post*, reports that registered dowry deaths nationwide numbered 1,986 in the year 1987 (48). She has found that although dowry was outlawed in 1961, the law "failed miserably in trying to eradicate the practice" (49). Rather than diminishing, the dowry practice has spread throughout all of India, especially to the middle and lower classes.

Female Infanticide

Perhaps the most astounding misogynist practice against women that is justified by religious beliefs is the practice of female infanticide. A blessing given to women at marriage uses the words, "May you be the mother of a hundred sons." A woman needs sons to be accepted by her in-laws, with whom she goes to live at marriage. She may be forced to act as a servant to her new family until the first male child is born. Should her husband die, she will remain under her son's care until her death. Only he can perform the correct funeral rites that will ensure salvation or a better rebirth in the next life. The mother of a son can demand a dowry at his marriage that will give her the necessary sustenance in her old age.

In past years, the birth of a daughter became an economic liability, because the parents would spend much time and energy to raise the money for an adequate dowry for a desirable marriage. As a result, some girl infants were allowed to die and were sometimes fed poisoned milk to hasten the process. Bumiller found through many interviews with Hindu women that today upper-class women may undergo an immediate abortion once amniocentesis and ultrasound identify the fetus as female. The lower-class expectant mothers cannot pay for the tests that reveal the sex, nor can they pay for the abortion, so they have to wait for the birth of the child to determine their actions. Even the female babies that are allowed to live are often deprived of the necessary nourishment, because they, like their mothers, have to wait until all the men in the family have eaten their fill before they can eat the leftovers.

One wonders how Indian women, even the educated, could endure such sex discrimination for so many centuries. A visitor to both rural villages and large cities will see a new mother singing to and caressing her girl baby in the same way that she treats her son. Although educational opportunities are not as available to girls as boys, more girls and young women are obtaining an education. Whether the increase in the reporting of bride burnings and suttee is really an increase in the number of incidents or a result of greater awareness of the situation remains a question. One would suspect that the feminist groups try to publicize the barbarity in order to expose the evil.

Although the Indian constitution created in the latter half of this century guarantees women complete equality with men, the reality does not mirror the written word. "Over 80 percent of the Indian women [have] never heard of the constitution," because they are too involved in the most "basic concerns—access to clean water, animal fodder, and cooking fuel" (Bumiller, 128). The feminist movement, which is composed mostly of the educated elite from the upper classes, is most frustrated in its attempts to reach poor rural women. The long history of a rigid caste system in the Indian religious hierarchy forms severe barriers between the women seeking reform. However, the urban groups are attempting to expose the issues of dowry deaths, suttee, and the use of prenatal sex-determination tests to determine whether a woman will have an abortion. They are working to raise the consciousness of women concerning the injustice in their own lives.

By forming cooperatives, working women have improved their economic status. Some women have attempted to change the governmental laws and erect new structures that favor women. At times it has seemed easier to get the laws passed than enforced. Nevertheless, women's organizations in India are making concerted efforts that effect results to improve their lives. In rural areas of India, where 80% of the population lives, mobile medical units are reaching pregnant women and sick children. Midwives are receiving modern medical training to replace the unsanitary and dangerous practices that helped give India one of the highest infant mortality rates in the world.

Women's Devotions

Although some Hindu women seek the route to social salvation by changing the structures that cause social injustice, others seek a path of personal salvation through devotion to God. Devotion to God, called *bhakti*, is the method that some Hindu women employ to achieve mosha, or salvation, without having to return to this world as a man. By sincere devotion to and ritual observance of a favored god or goddess, some women find the power to transform their immediate surroundings to more favorable ones. Devotion to the designated deity can influence cruel in-laws to treat a young bride more kindly. Some women believe in the power of certain rituals to make a stubborn and estranged husband more attentive and considerate. They believe in prayers that influence specific goddesses to bring about the birth of a son or keep the husband alive for an aging wife, so she will not have to face the horrors of widowhood. These acts of worship give a woman the comfort that she has done all in her power to effect a satisfying domestic life and has earned salvation in the future by ceasing permanently the endless round of rebirths.

Mirabai, a Rajasthani princess (1498–1546), found the route of devotion to the god Krishna more satisfying than her life with her in-laws, who treated her harshly. Her husband and in-laws forbade her to participate in a group of Krishna devotees. Legend says that her husband and his family were so unhappy with her that they tried to persuade her to commit suicide. Her devotion to the lord Krishna gave her the courage to leave her in-laws' house and move to the town of Vrindavana, which was considered especially sacred to Krishna. She found happiness and satisfaction in her longing for Krishna, which she expressed in poetry that used as its metaphor married passionate love. An example of her poetry describes her longing for Krishna.

> Without my beloved Master
> I cannot live
> Body, mind and life
> Have I given to the Beloved
> Fascinated by his beauty
> I gaze down the road
> Night and day.
> Says Mirabai: My Lord, accept your servant
> It is all she asks.   *Alston, 63*

Another legend involves a woman named Andal, who lived in the sixth century CE in Tamelvad, in South India. Her father taught her devotion to Krishna, which she developed in her youth in terms of passionate, emotional longing and a desire to marry her beloved. When her father suggested that she should marry, she said she could not bear to marry a mortal man because her only love was for the god Krishna. Her father escorted her to the temple one day and prayed that the god would take Andal as his wife. Legend says that the girl, dressed as a bride, walked up and stood beside the image of Krishna. To all the spectators' amazement, she slowly disappeared. Andal's father later learned in a dream that Krishna had taken her as his bride. Andal, like Mirabai and other female devotees, had found an alternative to marriage through their devotion to the divine.

China

Practices and Rituals Affecting Women

Worship of the ancestors whose spirits live on is an important Chinese ritual. The people must keep their ancestors satisfied with rituals, or the spirits will make life unpleasant for their descendants. The Chinese trace their lineage through the male line, so the happiness of the whole family is determined by the satisfaction given to ancestors through the correct performance of rituals. A woman cannot contribute to her father's lineage and perform the necessary rituals for her ancestors. When she marries, she joins her husband's lineage, and her rituals benefit his ancestors and descendants.

If a family has no sons, the parents may fear that they will become disgruntled or hungry ghosts after death because they have no one to perform the necessary ancestor worship for them. The need for male children is therefore paramount in China in order to ensure happiness for the parents and harmony in the lives of the descendants. The need to perpetuate the male lineage led to preference for male children, female infanticide, ill treatment of women (especially those who do not bear sons), and censure of widow remarriage.

It is said that Confucius discouraged the practice of female infanticide by exposure of the newborn to the elements. The practice, though not as widespread as in earlier times, does continue in some areas of China. One missionary Sister in the 1930s and 1940s combed the city dump of a large city in China each morning to retrieve the newborn girls. She would bring them to the orphanage run by her order of nuns that gave hundreds of young women a chance at life.

Since the communist regime, women have become more accepted by society because of China's rejection of the Confucian doctrine. However, the practice today of allowing only one child per family in order to control the population does not favor the birth of girls.

Young women under Confucian custom were held to strict standards of chastity in their homes. The sexes were usually segregated and the marriages arranged by the parents. Within marriage the wife was expected to be chaste and produce sons for her husband. Although wealthy Chinese husbands could have concubines, wives and daughters were held to a strict code of sexual morality. The wife could never initiate divorce proceedings, but her husband could divorce her on such grounds as being disobedient to her husband's parents, failing to bear a son, being promiscuous or jealous, having an incurable disease, talking too much, or stealing (Kelleher, 143). The husband had some restrictions regarding divorce: He could not divorce his wife if her parents were dead, because he could not then send her home to them, or if he came into riches after the marriage and simply wanted to discard his wife. Similarly, he could not divorce her if she had participated in the ancestral mourning rites of one of his parents: Her participation would mean that she had been inducted into her new lineage and that his ancestors had become her ancestors. If the husband died, the widow was expected not to remarry because it would upset the cosmic order of the ancestral line. It would cause confusion as to whose lineage she belonged and raise questions regarding who should perform the ancestral rites for her.

The education of young girls was directed at preparation for marriage. Whereas young boys went out to schools to prepare them for life in the political sphere, girls stayed at home to learn weaving and sewing. The Chinese character for the word *woman* was a broom, symbolizing the domestic work for which she was destined. A young woman was expected to marry, by age twenty, a young man picked out for her by her parents.

Marriage was important to the Chinese because it continued the line of the family that was started by their ancestors. The birth of male children would continue the performance of religious rites that kept the spirits of the ancestors happy and thus prevented them from disrupting the lives of their descendants.

The Chinese *Book of Rites* emphasizes the connection between the generations as the purpose of marriage. The groom—who is the active agent, like heaven—goes to the home of the bride, who, like earth, is the passive agent. He takes the initiative to fetch the bride and bring her to his familial home. Before she leaves her natal home, her parents instruct her to be reverent and obedient to her new parents-in-law. The *Book of Rites* suggests equality for the bride and groom in that they eat and drink from the same bowl and cups, "showing that they now formed one body, were of equal rank, and pledged to mutual affection" (Legge, 2:430). Although the wife must dedicate herself to the servitude of her parents-in-law, she receives a place in the ancestral line of her husband, a niche that she never had in her own home. She will be assured of the performance of the correct ancestral rites, which her male children and their descendants will perform for her just as she honors her new ancestors. She will be honored by her new family for bearing sons, who will continue the rituals that perpetuate the lineage and keep the cosmos moving in an orderly manner.

The communist revolution in the latter part of the twentieth century improved the quality of life for women by treating both sexes equally and offering education to women as well as men. Communists gave occupational opportunities to women that the previous regimes had barred. Recent years have seen some resurgence of the old traditions, which the Chinese see as offering them order and harmony because everyone then knew his or her place in the cosmic order. Traditional religious rites that had been outlawed by the communists, who labeled ancestral rites superstition, are appearing again all over China. It is difficult to guess what effect this revival will have on the future of women in that country.

Judaism

The Position of Women in the *Mishnah*

The *Mishnah* is a book of legal rules written in the second century CE by the sages living in Palestine. The framers of the *Mishnah* tried to apply the written law of the sacred scriptures to everyday life. They devoted one of the sections to women, although they did not include a corresponding section on men.

The sages were caught in the tension of two opposing views of women, as contained in the scriptures. One view recognized women as individuals with rights, such as the right of a daughter to inherit her father's property if he had no sons. The other view regarded women as property to be controlled by male relatives. Most of the control centered on a woman's biological powers of reproduction, whether she was an unmarried daughter, a wife, or a widow. In the tribe of Levi, for example, a man was expected to marry the widow of his brother in order to keep the children in his family.

In this way, the dead former husband would be remembered, and the living brother would name the first male child of the new union after him. This control of women's sexuality was made easier if women were confined to the private sphere rather than allowed in the public domain. They would not meet other men who might be tempted by them if they remained in the safety of their own enclosure.

Rules regarding ritual purity were one way to keep women in the home. Male warriors were dubious about women's menstrual periods because they had seen so many deaths from loss of blood. Yet women could lose their blood monthly, and this blood became life producing, rather than death dealing. By calling this menstrual period a curse that demanded purification, men could confine women to their homes so that they would avoid contaminating anyone they met. According to the *Mishnah*, men were contaminated by the presence of a menstruating woman and so they were not allowed to perform the religious practices of ablutions and prayer said over food in the home. At the end of her menses, the woman had to undergo a purification ritual so that men would no longer become contaminated by her presence.

One of the methods used by the writers of the *Mishnah* to confine women to their homes was to deny them participation in public prayers. Although they used the word *exempt*, which makes the denial sound like a privilege, in reality this "privilege" implied an unworthiness on the part of women. Even though the scriptures were to be observed by all Israelites, the sages exempted women from duties that were to be performed at specified times. Judith Romney Wegner cites such exemptions.

1. [With respect to] every scriptural duty owed to sons by parents [such as circumcision or redeeming the firstborn], men are obligated but women are exempt. [Such duties devolve on the father but not on the mother.]
2. But [with respect to] every scriptural duty owed to parents by sons [such as the commandment to "honor" and "revere" the father and mother], both men and women are obligated. [A duty owed to the parents devolves on sons and daughters alike.]
3. [With respect to] every precept that accrues at a specified time [such as reciting the Sh'ma', binding t'fillin, hearing the shofar, or dwelling the sukkah], men are obligated but women are exempt. [Though the sages gave no reason, later interpretations (e.g., the fourteenth-century *Sefer Abudarham*) suggest that the rule stemmed from a fear that such observances would interfere with a women's domestic chores.]
4. But [with respect to] every positive precept that does not accrue at a specified time [such as reciting the T'fillah or giving charity] both men and women are equally obligated. [A woman can and must carry out such precepts when her other duties permit.]
5. And [with respect to] every negative precept, whether or not it accrues at a specified time, both men and women are equally obligated [because observance of a prohibition merely requires abstention, which is not time-contingent] (Wegner, 150).

These exemptions made it impossible for Jewish women to enter into communal prayer, denying them the mutual enrichment that men gained from studying and reciting the Torah as a group. Although women could read the scriptures privately as individuals, they lost the opportunity for the intellectual growth and support that resulted from shared insights.

Jewish rabbis and scholars began to apply the laws of the *Mishnah* to new situations as they arose.

> In many academies in Babylonia and Israel, notes and questions were append- ed to individual laws, and in time this material—the *Mishnah* together with explanatory matter, relevant anecdotes, and abstracts of philosophical and theological discussions—coalesced into a work called the *Talmud*, literally the teachings.
>
> *Hauptman, 185*

As a result, the *Mishnah* laws that were incorporated into the *Talmud* continued to influence the lives of women until modern times. Until recent- ly, with the establishment of Reformed and Conservative Judaism, women were encouraged to send their boys to study the Torah in the schools and to enable their husbands to have time to discuss the Torah with the rabbis. The wife arranged to free her husband's time by taking on more work, which sometimes meant that she had to tend to his business when her own domestic duties were done.

The most important duty incumbent on women was to become the mother of sons. According to *The Law of Property Baba, Batra* (16.b) "Happy is he whose children are sons and woe to him whose children are daughters." The sons could be counted in a minyan, the quorum of ten men necessary for a prayer service. The mother could neither take part in the minyan nor preside at the prayer service.

Contemporary Developments

Although other branches have made reforms, Orthodox Judaism still sep- arates the sexes at most religious functions. Orthodox Jews rigorously fol- low the *Talmud*, which severely restricts the role of women. Some reform- ers within the orthodox branch have sought to relieve women from the exemption rule. In order to persuade women that their prayer is as influen- tial as that of men, reformers are mounting pressure to allow women to be eligible for the minyan or quorum and for the reading of the Torah, as is allowed in other branches. Women who do not have a husband to pray for them—such as widows, divorcees, and single women—want to feel more accepted by their religious community. And because Jewish religious and civil laws are so connected, Jewish feminists also feel the need to forgo the protection that the latter provides. Civil laws prohibit a woman from appearing in civil court and from remarriage at the death or desertion of her husband unless she has a baby. She still finds it difficult to obtain a divorce, receive an inheritance equal to that of her brothers, or marry the person of her choice. Feminists say that Orthodox Jewish women must become rabbis and judges so they can change the rules, but they cannot gain the credentials necessary if they cannot study the Torah in a seminary setting.

Reform Judaism has a much broader interpretation of the scriptures and *Talmud*. Women are studying at reformed Jewish seminaries, where they make up nearly one half of the student population. There are presently more than 250 women ordained as rabbis in the less traditional reformed, conservative, and reconstructionist branches of Judaism. One woman was recently ordained in Israel. Although these women clergy must work toward equal pay and opportunities within their institutions, they are accomplishing much toward the incorporation of new rituals. For example, it has been customary for a Jewish woman to remain silent during the wedding ritual, which signified her silence in the future of the couple's life together. Jewish feminists are devising new rituals for marriage along with bas mitzvah rites of passage for young girls. Women cantors are appearing at the synagogues, which contributes to women's move from the private sphere of the home to the public arena, where capable spiritual women can make an impact on the world.

Greece

The Teachings of Aristotle

Most of the Western world has looked to Greece as the origin of its civilization. The dualistic philosophy of the Greeks has influenced the world view of most Europeans and their emigrants. Greek philosophers looked to their patriarchal religion to illustrate and justify their ideas of superiority and inferiority. The male gods were superior to the goddesses, and so were men to women. The philosophers ascribed to men the characteristics of rationality, objectivity, intellectual activity, initiative, and spirit. The philosophers assign the opposite and less desirable traits to women, such as passion, subjectivity, emotion, passivity, inertia, and body.

Aristotle extended his philosophical knowledge to the realm of science. He claimed that men's participation in the act of reproduction was far superior because the man contributed semen, containing the soul, whereas the woman contributed only the matter. Because the soul was so superior to the matter, the power of reproduction must certainly belong to the male. This mystical power of men, Aristotle said, was manifested in the result of birth: The perfect child would be male, and the imperfect, or the mistake, would be female. In fact, he considered the girl child so imperfect that he referred to her as misbegotten and mutilated.

> For just as the young of mutilated parents, are sometimes born mutilated and sometimes not, so also the young born of a female are sometimes male and sometimes female instead. For the female is, as it were, a mutilated male.
> *De Generatione Animalium II, 732a, 8–9*

Once Aristotle had proclaimed the biological inferiority of woman, it was an easy step to establish her inferior ability to reason or make decisions. She was thought to be unable to control her passions because rational abilities resided in men. With no soul to guide her, woman was believed capable of the worst mistakes, leading to Aristotle's description of the need for men to rule over women.

> Again, the male is by nature superior, and the female inferior; and the one rules and the other is ruled; this principle of necessity extends to all mankind.
> *De Generatione Animalium II, 124b, 4–6*

One might dismiss such musings as ridiculous, but the implication of this thinking has affected not only Greeks, but Christians as well. Even democratic Athenians denied the vote to women and slaves in the first millennium BCE. During Greek classical times, upper-class women were restricted to the women's quarters. Women were denied the educational opportunities that men received, which in turn barred them from public life. Polytheistic Greece did allow some freedom to women, who could petition their goddesses for favors. The sculpture of classical Greece portrays women as beautifully as men. Sappho of Lesbos contributed poetry emphasizing the wonder of love over the marvels of war, which seemed to be the focus of so much male Greek poetry.

Women must have provoked some controversy, because a few male Greek authors chose to write about them. Aristophanes, the playwright, poked fun at women who met in groups to discuss issues in the same manner as men. One of the issues the women espoused was a concern for peace. Aristophanes satirized their attempts to withhold their sexual favors from men who insisted upon waging war. Through the medium of plays, which were very popular in classical Greece, male authors would ridicule women by trivializing their interests and achievements. The very fact that these authors felt it necessary to put down women indicates that Grecian women were active in promoting their own causes. Devotion to goddesses continued, as evidenced by one of the seven wonders of the ancient world, the huge and beautiful temple to Aphrodite in Ephesus. The oracle at Delphi continued to be a woman who answered the queries of kings and warriors. The sorriest part of Greek history and literature is the absence of women. Male writers did not think it was necessary to include the activities of women in their literature, depriving the Western world of the insights and contributions of women, who were much more than "misbegotten men."

Christianity

Limitations Placed on Women in Patristic and Medieval Times

The age of the fathers, as the patristic era connotes, spanned the second to the eighth centuries of the Christian church. The influence of St.

Augustine, one of the prominent fathers of the early church (fourth century), resounds even today. In his dualistic thought, Augustine identified women with the body and men with the mind. He said that woman could not image God as well as man because she could image only the body. Because God is spirit, or mind, only men could image him. Woman had to unite herself to man, her head, in order to possess the fullness of God. Man could possess the image of God by himself, without the assistance of woman.

Another theologian, Saint Albert the Great, continued the teaching of Aristotle during the middle ages:

> Woman is less qualified [than man] for moral behavior. For the woman contains more liquid than the man, and it is a property of liquid to take things up easily and to hold onto them poorly. Liquids are easily moved, hence women are inconstant and curious. When a woman has relations with a man, she would like, as much as possible, to be lying with another man at the same time. Woman knows nothing of fidelity. Believe me, if you give her your trust, you will be disappointed. Trust an experienced teacher. For this reason prudent men share their plans and actions least of all with their wives. Woman is a misbegotten man and has a faulty and defective nature in comparison with his. Therefore she is unsure in herself. What she herself cannot get, she seeks to obtain through lying and diabolical deceptions. And so, to put it briefly, one must be on one's guard with every woman, as if she were a poisonous snake and the horned devil.
>
> *Quaestiones Super de Animalibus XV, q. 11*

St. Thomas Aquinas tried in the thirteenth century to apply Aristotle's science to theology. Aquinas may have been recognized as a great theologian, referred to as "the light of the church,' but a biologist he was not. He claimed that women were conceived during the blowing, moist, south winds, which cause the fetus to have a high water content (*Summa Theologica*, Iq 92al). He identifies the weak will of women with the limpid condition of the water. "Because there is a higher water content in women, they are more easily seduced by sexual pleasure" (*Summa Theologica* III, q. 42a 4 and 5).

Aristotle's premise that the man is the active agent in the act of intercourse led Thomas to believe that each sperm contained a perfect little man. When something went wrong, an imperfect creature was born—a woman. This strange attitude extended to the education of children for Thomas. Because the father of the child had such superior mental and spiritual abilities, he would be the natural teacher. Aquinas said that "the woman is in no way adequate" to educate children because the father has "more perfect reason" and "stronger virtue" (*Summa Theologica Contra Gentiles* III, 122). Aquinas believed that woman's inferior position should deprive the mother of her children's love. "The father should be loved more than the mother, because he is the active principle of generation, while she is the passive one" (*Summa Theologica* II/II q. 26a10).

Although this attitude toward women seems difficult to accept in today's world, medieval theologians based their argument on New Testament interpretations that women were inferior because Eve gave in to the temptation of the devil (serpent) and persuaded her husband to do the same. The combination of the Old Testament myth and Aristotle's Greek philosophy served to alienate women from God, men, birth, and their children.

Response of Women in Monasteries

Women in medieval times found an alternative to the oppression heaped on them by celibate male clerics such as Albert and Aquinas. They, too, found their way to monasteries, where they contributed much to the fields of learning and health care. The first hospitals were provided by the monastic nuns, who opened their convents to the infirm and often nursed them back to health. Many of these women left to posterity their beautiful artwork, including many tapestries. Their love of learning provided many balanced contributions to philosophy, theology, science, literature, and even physics. During feudalistic times, the abbess of the female monastery, usually elected by the nuns as leader, could rule over the fief as bishops did. She could exact taxes, appoint administrators, raise armies, coin money, and rule over the towns in her jurisdiction. The abbess was also the spiritual ruler in that she had the right to credential the priests who operated in her territory. Because she had the jurisdictional power of a bishop, she carried his accoutrements—his crosier and miter. Unfortunately, the female monasteries lost much of their power when the centers of learning moved from the monasteries to the great universities. Not only were women forbidden to attend these universities, but the bishops also imposed rules of cloister on the nuns, forbidding them to leave the enclosure of their convents. Perhaps the low point of female spiritual power preceded the Council of Bishops in 900 CE, which finally ended the debate whether women had souls when the Irish bishops broke the deadlock vote in favor of women.

Devotion to Mary

The one model afforded women in the institutional church of the middle ages was that of Mary, the mother of Jesus. She is a controversial figure in that she has been interpreted as both a help and a hindrance to women's position in society. On one hand, she has been linked to the mother goddess figures of old in that she bears many of their characteristics. Charlene Spretnak, a mythologist, describes the connection.

> In the Christian tradition, the Virgin Mary is clearly rooted in the older Goddess religion because she produces her child parthenogenetically. (And Jesus himself is true to the older pattern of the Goddess' son/lover dying at the Spring Equinox and being reborn at the Winter Solstice.)
>
> *Spretnak, 27*

The church fathers were careful not to make Mary a goddess, however, but to retain her human stature. She was not to be worshipped as a deity, but venerated only as the mother of God, whom she conceived by a virgin birth. The gospel authors write of the action of the Holy Spirit in the birth of Jesus and deny any contribution of Joseph (Luke 1:26–38 and Matt. 1:48–25). Spretnak believes that the church used the goddesslike characteristics of Mary to pacify some of its followers.

> The church co-opted Mary in order to make converts. She is not included in the core symbols, i.e., the trinity, but the church fathers discovered they could not attract followers in the heavily Goddess-oriented Mediterranean and Celtic cultures, which then stretched from the Balkans to the British Isles, without a Goddess on their banners: Mary, Mother of God, formerly God herself. Far from "elevating the feminine," the church demoted her, stripped her of her power, and rendered her docile and sexless.
>
> *Spretnak, 27*

The hindrance to women was the fact that the symbol of Mary confused women: Although they were urged to imitate this "new Eve," they could not conceive virginally. They could model themselves on her docility and silence, where "she kept all things in heart" (Luke 2:51) as she suffered her quiet martyrdom through the life and death of her son. On the other hand, she appeared to be the new Eve who would crush the head of the serpent, as promised in Genesis with God's words to the serpent:

> I will put enmity between you and women,
> and between your offspring and hers,
> it (her offspring) will bruise your head
> and you will strike its heel.
>
> *Genesis 3: 15–16*

Mary has also been associated with the woman in the book of Revelation: "Now a great sign appeared in Heaven: a woman robed with the sun, standing on the moon, and on her head a crown of twelve stars" (Rev. 12:1). She escapes the great dragon, or primeval serpent, who is waiting to devour the child she is about to deliver. Here she appears to be a celestial figure with a divine child who has the power to subdue evil.

During the Middle Ages, Mary was considered the mediator between the male authorities in heaven and her beloved people on earth. Just as Jesus was considered the divine redeemer, Mary began to take on the role of redemptrix. It became difficult for the common people to distinguish between the divine redeemer, Jesus, and the human mediator, Mary. Divinity and humanity tended to blur in their eyes as they approached their "mother of mercy" in prayer and supplication.

Medieval art and architecture glorified the position of Mary, and most of the cathedrals of Europe were erected in her name. Orthodox and Roman Catholicism, with their glorious mosaics and icons of Mary, continued the devotion to the mother of God, as she was defined by the Council of Ephesus in the fifth century CE. Before the introduction of the printing press, much of the popular religious literature was portrayed on church walls and windows in picture form of events in the life of Mary and Jesus. Statues of Mary, sometimes holding the child Jesus, were common and popular; religious processions carried them for veneration by the faithful. The rosary to Mary became popular for those who could not read and did not have scripture books available to them. Perhaps the devotion to Mary is best described by Saint Alphonsus Liguori, a noted moral theologian of the eighteenth century:

> This divine mother, with her powerful prayers and assistance, has obtained for us paradise, if we place no obstacle to our entrance there. Wherefore those who are servants of Mary, and for whom Mary intercedes, are as secure of paradise as if they were already there. To serve Mary and to belong to her court, adds Saint John of Damascus, is the greatest honor we can attain; for to serve the queen of heaven is to reign already in heaven, and to live in obedience to her commands is more than to reign.
>
> *Liguori, 279*

Mary has taken on some of the titles, such as "queen of heaven," that were originally attributed to mother goddesses such as Isis and Ishtar. She counted men and women among her devotees but gave especially to women a model of dignity to which they could aspire. Appearances or apparitions of Mary have resulted in the establishment of shrines. The shrine of Our Lady of Lourdes in France has gained international prominence for the well-documented cures that have occurred at the miraculous spring. Shrines at Fatima in Portugal and Guadalupe in Mexico have become pilgrimage sites for Catholics from all over the world where devotees honor the Virgin Mary, whom they treat as their beneficent mother.

Limitations Placed on Women in Modern Times

Liberal Protestantism

The Protestant Reformation of the sixteenth century did not bring much relief to women. Martin Luther perpetuated these myths of inferiority as just punishment for the sin of Eve.

> The rule remains with the husband, and the wife is compelled to obey him by God's command. He rules the home and the state, wages war, defends his possessions, tills the soil, builds, plants, etc. The woman on the other hand is like a nail driven into the wall. She sits at home. . . . Just as the snail carries its house with it, so the wife should stay at home and look after the affairs of the household, as one who has been deprived of the duty of administering those affairs that are outside and that concern the state. She does not go beyond her most personal duties.
>
> *Luther, 203*

John Calvin, the reformer, continued the double standard that was applied to women in that he thought women should remain within the domestic sphere. He resurrected the biblical laws that said adulterous wives should be stoned to death although the unfaithful husband should not be punished.

The Puritans, who set up their household with the husband as the little minister and the wife and children as his obedient congregation, failed to liberate women in the same manner that they attempted to liberate men.

Some Protestant groups did attempt to improve the condition of women. In the seventeenth century the Quakers, thanks to the efforts of Margaret Fell, advocated the equality of men and women with the argument that both were created in the image of God. Fell substantiated her plea for the acceptance of women as preachers with quotes from the New Testament that portrayed women preaching by word and example.

Anne Hutchinson, in her break with the Puritans, likewise stressed that the spirit of God need not be confined to ordained clerics, but could empower all spiritually minded Christians, regardless of their sex. She was persecuted by the dominant Puritan group, which upheld the patriarchal notion that divine revelation could be interpreted only through the divinely ordained ecclesiastics, who were all male.

The Shakers, under the guidance of Mother Ann Lee, taught that God was androgynous, having both female and male characteristics. Therefore the redeemer who would restore the human race to its pristine glory before the fall needed to be both male and female. Christ had already come as the male redeemer, and the Shakers believed Mother Ann Lee to be his female counterpart. She had many followers, who lived as members of a spiritual community, but the group died out because of its policy of enforced celibacy.

The philosophy of the Enlightenment, which was proposed in the seventeenth and eighteenth centuries, stressed the equality of all humans. Philosophers taught that each person was given inalienable rights that were rooted in humanity. The theology of domination gave way to a theology of social justice that advocated such rights as equal opportunity to political, economic, and cultural power.

This liberation theology laid the basis for the liberal feminist theology advocated by American women in the early nineteenth century. Conscious of the injustices toward slaves, these women allied themselves with the abolitionist movements. The Grimké Sisters, Lucretia Mott, Elizabeth Cady Stanton, and Susan B. Anthony extended the concept of slavery reforms to the reform of other social institutions such as churches, government, and the family. They identified the cause of the oppression of women as rooted not in the female nature as their religious leaders proclaimed, but rather in the socialization process that kept women in subordinate roles of domesticity. At Seneca Falls, New York, in 1848, these women called for the overthrow of the male monopoly of the pulpit because they saw the close connection between civil law and church teaching on equality for women.

Protestant congregations began to recognize the gifts of women and ordained women to the ministry in the early 1900s. By the middle of the twentieth century, the mainstream Protestant denominations—including Methodists, Presbyterians, and Lutherans—had voted to ordain women. The Episcopalian church in America and, recently, its parent Anglican church in England have ordained women candidates. Only the conservative fundamentalist Protestant groups and the Roman and Eastern Orthodox Catholic churches have refused to allow women full participation in their congregations through ordination.

Christian women have been creative in directing their energies to the dissemination of the Christian message. Protestant women have worked as Sunday school teachers in their homeland and in many mission countries. Roman Catholic orders of nuns have established and administered schools, colleges, hospitals, and homes for the aged. The nuns' missionary work has carried them all over the globe as they promote the gospel message of Christ. The Catholic sisters have not been entirely free from the harassment of patriarchal Catholic church leaders, who would like to interfere with the nuns' independence, but the hierarchy finds it hard to argue with the gospel message of service.

Islam

Isolation of Women

Although the Quran teaches that both men and women have access to salvation and that both have the duty to submit to God, women have in practice had to submit to men. Men have defined women's roles through separation of the sexes according to the law of the Shariah. Wealthy men were thought more prestigious if they could keep their wives and daughters segregated in the home. If a woman had to go out, she was expected to cover herself from head to foot so that men would not be tempted by her appearance. The sexes were separated on issues of morality also, as Susan Schaefer Davis found in her study of rural Moroccan women:

> Although the attributes of a pleasing character, including kindness, verbal skill, and a good sense of humor, are similar for men and women, what constitutes a moral man is different from what constitutes a moral woman. A respectable or moral man is *nisban*, or honest (literally, "straight" in his interactions), supports his family well, and does not gamble or drink or go to prostitutes *too* often. A respectable woman promotes the welfare of her family as a good wife and mother, is an excellent and thrifty housekeeper (*hadga*), and keeps her family's honor pure by never interacting with strange men, staying inside, and not spreading affairs of the family around the village. One gossips, of course, but about *others*, while keeping family problems out of the public realm.
>
> *Davis, 92*

FIGURE 4.2   Muslim Women Wearing the Chador, Afghan Refugee Camp. (Courtesy of Sonja Iskov/Impact Visuals.)

The idea of veiling—covering one's whole body, including parts of the face, with a garment called a *chador*—had some beneficial effects for women in that it afforded them anonymity and thwarted unwanted advances by men (Figure 4.2).

Modern Developments

The issue of veiling has become prominent in modern times because it is such a strong visual symbol of traditional values. The recent changes allowing education of women and employment outside the home in some Islamic countries such as Turkey and Egypt have created fears that the purity of Muslim practices may be threatened. If women dressed in the styles of their Western counterparts, the traditional beliefs regarding the separation of the sexes might be compromised. In Iran, especially, after the fundamentalists revolution, women returned to the traditional clothing in order to

ward off the intrusion of the culturally imperialistic Western world, epito-
mized by the United States.

Women's role has been strongly identified with procreation in Islam. A
woman is still especially honored if she can be the mother of sons whom
she can control in the household. This control would extend to her daugh-
ter-in-law in the same fashion, giving her some power and prestige. But in
some Muslim countries, the state has intervened to reform the religious
laws regarding polygamy, separation and isolation of women, and the educational and occupational limitations placed on one half of the population.
States such as Egypt and Turkey denounce these practices "because they
created ignorant mothers, shallow and scheming partners, unstable marital
unions, and lazy and unproductive members of society" (Kandiyoti, 10).
Kandiyoti describes the tension that all Arabs are under as they try to balance the needs of emerging industrial societies with the religious traditional
laws. Some women would like to return to the traditional ways when they
did not have to bear the financial responsibility for the family. Others are
willing to bear the responsibilities that come with increased opportunities.
Regardless of their stance toward changing ways, Muslim women are caught
between their desire for reform and their certitude that the Quran and their
Islamic community is God's chosen path for humankind.

Summary

Humans have always needed to cope with the evils they confront in the
world, especially suffering, death, disease, and alienation from one another.
Some religions try to explain the origin of these evils in our world by telling
myths that depict a change from a paradisiacal, blissful state of being to one
of separation from the divine. Evils accompany this state of separation.
These myths often blame women for the introduction of evil, as in some
traditional African, Jewish, Greek, and Christian religions. Although the
Hindu and Chinese religions do not have alienation myths, many of their
discriminatory practices against women have their basis in fundamental religious beliefs.

Women have suffered as a result of prejudice that became justified by
religion. Sometimes oppressive actions toward women were sacralized by
scriptures; other times they were encoded into law, as in the Code of Manu
and the *Mishnah* and Shariah. Religious leaders communicated attitudes
toward women that stressed their inferiority to men, and because religion
and society were so tightly connected in earlier times, women's place in
society also suffered. Religious and state laws based on scriptures served to
restrict the sphere of women to the home.

Women, however, found creative ways to overcome many of the religious
barriers. Some women simply bypassed the patriarchal structures to reach
the divine through devotion, such as in Hinduism.

Changes in state systems—in China, for example—helped to improve the place of women in traditional society.

Jewish women in the conservative and reformed branches of Judaism have successfully overcome the exemption rule and now contribute to their religious groups in leadership roles.

Greek philosophy has influenced the Western world so deeply that Christian women have been challenged to overcome the discriminatory attitudes handed down to them by Greek thinkers and canonized by the early church fathers. Competent women rose above the accusation of inferiority in the Middle Ages and headed monasteries as abbesses, contributing to the education and health care of their communities. Although Christian women of the later Middle Ages were deprived of leadership roles in their institutional churches, they found a role model in Mary, the mother of Jesus. Many Protestant women in America led the movement for abolition of slavery and social reform as an outgrowth of their religious beliefs that respected the dignity of each individual.

Islamic women are caught today in the tension between respect for their traditional religious beliefs and practices and the intrusion of Western values.

Although women have suffered discrimination from their own religious traditions, they have found ways to derive comfort and challenge from their religious beliefs. They admit to the presence of evil in the world, but modern women see no need to carry the blame for its origin.

Questions for Discussion

1. How have patriarchal cultures used religion to justify their negative treatment of women in the following traditions?
    Traditional African religions
    Hinduism
    Confucianism
    Judaism
    Greek religion
    Christianity
    Islam
2. Why do laws that govern the behavior of women develop out of religious scriptures?
3. How are the Adam and Eve myth and the myth of Pandora similar?
4. When alienation myths reach the status of scripture, their effects become most profound. Discuss the ramifications of this statement.
5. Some religions do not have alienation myths per se, but their authoritative writings affect the lives of their adherents. Give examples from some religious traditions.
6. How have women coped with their own religious traditions that appear to oppress them?
7. Why have patriarchal religions sought to control the sexual behavior of women? Give some examples.

8. Why is the Virgin Mary a difficult model for behavior for Christian women?
9. Why do so many religions have rituals of purification for women?

Works Cited

Abudarham, David. *Sefer Abdudarham*. [Seville, 1340]. Ed. A. J. Wertheimer. Jerusalem: Abudarham ha-Shalem, 1950.

Alston, A. J. *The Devotional Poems of Mirabai*. Delhi: Motilal Banarsidass, 1980.

Aquinas, Thomas. *Summa Theologica*, trans. and ed. A. M. Fairweather. Philadelphia: Westminster Press, 1954.

Aristotle. *Politica*, trans. Benjamin Sowell, ed. W. D. Ross. New York: Oxford University Press (Clarendon), 1921.

Brandt, Leopold. *Die Sexualethik des hl*. Albertus Magnus, 1954.

Bumiller, Elizabeth. *May You Be the Mother of a Hundred Sons*. New York: Random House, 1990.

Buffalo News. Buffalo, New York, newspaper. March 16, 1990.

Buhler, Georg, trans. *The Laws of Manu*. Sacred Books of the East, vol. 25. New York: Oxford University Press, 1886.

Burnett, J. *Early Greek Philosophers*. London, 1930.

Carmody, Denise Larder. *Women and World Religions*. Englewood Cliffs, N.J.: Prentice Hall, 1989.

Davis, Susan Schaefer. "The Determinants of Social Position among Rural Moroccan Women." In *Women in Contemporary Muslim Societies*, ed. Jane I. Smith. Lewisburg, Pa.: Bucknell University Press, 1980.

Eisler, Riane. *The Chalice and the Blade*. New York: Harper & Row, 1988.

Erndl, Kathleen. *Victory to the Mother*. New York: Oxford University Press, 1933.

Guisso, Richard. "Thunder Over the Lake: The Five Classics and the Perception of Women in Early China." In *Women in China*, ed. Richard Guisso and Johannesen. New York: Philo Press, 1981.

Harrison, Jane Ellen. *Myths of Greece and Rome*. London: Ernest Benn, 1927.

Hauptman, Judith. "Images of Women in the Talmud." In *Religion and Sexism*, ed. Rosemary Ruether. New York: Simon and Schuster, 1974.

Huhler, G., trans. *The Laws of Manu*. Delhi: Motilal Banarsidass, 1975.

Kandiyoti, Deniz, ed. *Women, Islam and the State*. Philadelphia: Temple University Press, 1991.

Kelleher, Theresa. "Confucianism." In *Women in World Religion*, ed. Arvind Sharma. Albany: State University of New York Press, 1987.

Kinsley, David. *Hindu Goddess Visions of the Divine Feminine in the Hindu Religious Tradition*. Berkeley: University of California Press, 1986.

———. *Hinduism: A Cultural Perspective*. Englewood Cliffs, N.J.: Prentice Hall, 1993.

Legge, James. *Book of Rites*. 2 vols.; ed. C. C. Chai and W. Chai. New York: University Books, 1967.

Liguori, Alfonso. *The Glories of Mary*. New York: Kennedy, 1952.

Lipman, Eugene, ed. *The Mishnah*. New York: W. W. Norton, 1970.

Luther, Martin. "Lectures on Genesis." In *Luther's Works*, vol. 1, ed. Jaroslav Pelikan. St. Louis: Concordia Press, 1958.

Mbiti, John. *African Religions and Philosophy*. New York: Praeger, 1969.

Meyers, Carol. *Discovering Eve*. New York: Oxford University Press, 1988.

The New Jerusalem Bible. New York: Doubleday, 1985.

Pan Chao, D. U. "Na-Chieh." In *Nu ssu-shu*, ed. Wang Hsiang. Naikaku: Bunko, 1844.

Ranke-Heinemann, Uta. *Eunuchs for the Kingdom*. English trans. New York: Doubleday, 1990.

Roberts, Alexander, and James Donaldson, eds. "Acts of Paul and Thecla." *Ante-Nicene Fathers*, vol. 8. New York: Scribners, 1885, 1897.

Ruether, Rosemary Radford. *Womanguides*. Boston: Beacon Press, 1985.

Smith, J. A., and W. D. Ross. "De Generatione Animalium." In *The Works of Aristotle*. New York: Oxford University Press, 1912.

Spretnak, Charlene. *Lost Goddesses of Early Greece*. Boston: Beacon Press, 1992.

Swann, Nancy Lee. *Pan Chao: Foremost Woman Scholar of China*. New York: Century, 1932.

Wegner, Judith Romney. *Chattel or Person: The Status of Women in the Mishnah*. New York: Oxford University Press, 1988.

Young, Katherine K. "Hinduism." In *Women in World Religion*, ed. Arvind Sharma. Albany: State University of New York Press, 1987.

Suggested Readings

Alastruey, Gregory. *The Blessed Virgin Mary*, 2 vols.; trans. Sr. M. Janet La Giglia. St. Louis: B. Herder, 1964.

Altekar, A. S. *The Position of Women in Hindu Civilization*. Delhi: Motilal Banarsidass, 1959.

Andors, Phyllis. *The Unfinished Liberation of Chinese Women 1949–1980*. Bloomington: Indiana University Press, 1983.

Arthur, Marylin. "Origins of the Western Attitude Toward Women." In *Women in the Ancient World: The Arethusa Papers*, ed. John Peradatto and J. P. Sullivan. Albany: State University of New York, 1984.

Avalon, Arthur (Sir John Woodroffe). *Shakti and Shakta*. New York: Dover, 1978.

Bachofen, J. J. *Myth, Religion and Mother Right*, reprint. Princeton, N.J.: Princeton University Press, 1967.

Beck, Lois, and Nikki Keddie, eds. *Women in the Muslim World*. Cambridge: Harvard University Press, 1978.

Bennett, Lynn. *Dangerous Wives and Sacred Sisters: Social and Symbolic Roles of High-Caste Women in Nepal*. New York: Columbia University Press, 1983.

Bird, Phyllis. "Male and Female, He Created Them: Gen. l:27b in the Context of the Priestly Account of Creation," *Harvard Theological Review* 74, no. 2 (1981).

Brown, Peter. "The Notion of Virginity in the Early Church." In *Christian Spirituality, Origins to the Twelfth Century*, ed. Bernard McGinn, John Meyendorff, and Jean Leclerq. New York: Crossroads, 1985.

Carmichael, Calum M. *Women, Law and the Genesis Traditions*. Edinburgh: University Press, 1979.

Chen, Ellen. *Tao As The Great Mother and the Influence of Motherly Love in the Shaping of Chinese Philosophy*. Chicago: University of Chicago Press (Religious Heritage Series), 1972.

Eberhard, Wolfram. *Folktales of China*. London: Routledge & Kegan Paul, 1965.

Foley, Helen, ed. *Reflections of Women in Antiquity*. New York: Gordon & Breach Science Publications, 1981.

Gatwood, Lynn E. *Devi and the Spouse Goddess: Women, Sexuality, and Marriages in India*. Riverdale, Md.: Riverdale, 1985.

Glennon, Lynda. *Women and Dualism: A Sociology of Knowledge Analysis*. New York: Longman, 1979.

Harris, Kevin. *Sex, Ideology and Religion: The Representation of Women in the Bible*. Totowa, N.J.: Barnes and Noble, 1984.

Jacobson, Doranne. "The Women of North and Central India: Goddesses and Wives." In *Many Sisters: Women in Cross-Cultural Perspective*, ed. Carolyn Matthiason. New York: Free Press, 1974.

Jacobson, Doranne, and Susan Wadley. *Women in India: Two Perspectives*. New Delhi: Manohar, 1977.

Jain, Devaki. "India: A Condition across Caste and Class." In *Sisterhood is Global: The International Women's Movement Anthology*, ed. Robin Morgan. Garden City, N.J.: Anchor Books, 1984.

McClure, K. *The Evidence for Visions of the Virgin Mary*. Wellingborough: Aquarian, 1983.

MacDonald, D. R. *The Legend and the Apostle*. Philadelphia: Westminster, 1983.

Monaghan, Patricia. *Women in Myth and Legend*. London: Junction Books, 1981.

Musurillo, Herbert. *The Acts of the Christian Martyrs*. New York: Oxford University Press (Clarendon), 1972.

Naidoff, B. D. "A Man to Work the Soil: A New Interpretation of Genesis 2–3," *Journal for the Study of the Old Testament* 5 (1978): 2–14.

Otwell, John. *And Sarah Laughed: The Status of Women in the Old Testament*. Philadelphia: Westminster, 1977.

Russell, L. M., ed. *Feminist Interpretation of the Bible*. Philadelphia: Westminster, 1985.

Schafer, Edward H. "Ritual Exposure in Ancient China," *Harvard Journal of Asiatic Studies* 14 (1951): 130–84.

Shulman, David Dean. *Tamil Temple Myths: Sacrifice and Divine Marriage in the South Indian Saiva Tradition*. Princeton, N.J.: Princeton University Press, 1980.

Smith, Jan I. "Women in Islam: Equity, Equality, and the Search for the Natural Order," *Journal of the American Academy of Religion* 47 (December 1979): 517–37.

Tabari, Azar. "The Women's Movement in Iran: A Hopeful Prognosis," *Feminist Studies* 12 (Summer 1986): 343–60.

Thompson, Laurence G. *The Chinese Way in Religion*. Belmont, Calif.: Dickenson, 1973.

Trenchard, W. D. *Ben Sira's View of Women*. Chico, Calif.: Scholars Press, 1981.

Trible, P. "Depatriarchalizing in Biblical Interpretation," *Journal of American Academy of Religion* 41 (1973): 30–48.

———. "Eve and Adam, Genesis 2–3 Reread," *Andover Newton Quarterly* 13 (1973): 251–58.

Umansky, Ellen. "Women in Judaism: From the Reform Movement to Contemporary Jewish Religious Feminism." In *Women of Spirit*, ed. Rosemary Ruether and Eleanor McLaughlin. New York: Simon and Schuster, 1979.

Vawter, B. *On Genesis: A New Reading*. New York: Doubleday, 1977.

Wadley, Susan. "Hindu Women's Family and Household Rites in a North Indian Village." In *Unspoken Worlds: Women' Religious Lives in Non-Western*

Cultures, ed. Nancy Auer Falk and Rita Gross. New York: Harper & Row, 1980.

Walsh, J. T. "Genesis 2:4 and 3:24—A Synchronic Approach," *Journal of Biblical Literature* 96 (1977): 161–77.

Williams, John A. "A Return to the Veil in Europe," *Middle East Review* 11, no. 3 (1979): 49–59.

CHAPTER 5

Competent Women Who Helped Shape Their Religious Traditions

With all the oppression that women suffer at the hands of institutional religion, one wonders why so many women stay active in their institutional religious communities. Surprisingly enough, women make up more than one half of the membership of organized religion. There must be some reason for the power of religion to attract the very members that it seems to oppress.

The sacred scriptures of most religions either marginalize women or ignore them altogether, yet women find consolation, challenge, and encouragement from these very writings. However, it is difficult for women to identify with the sacred scriptures of most religions because the authors write little about the feminine religious experience. Because most of the known scripture writers were men, they wrote about activities, ideas, and experiences to which men can relate. Even so, women are able to find in most scriptures some role models whose ideals and actions are worth imitation. Often these role models appear as the exception to the usual female experience or take on the roles usually assigned to men. In other instances, some women are considered heroines because they keep their place in the patriarchal society and adhere to the roles assigned them by men.

Women have helped change their religious traditions to become more inclusive and affirmative of their experience. Most often these women reformers accomplish their feats by calling men back to the original tenets of their religion. Feminist theologians have tried to investigate their religious scriptures and traditions in the light of the human experience, both men's and women's.

The field of reclaiming women's experience is not limited to theology or scripture studies: Extensive efforts also have been made by feminists in the fields of history, psychology, education, and literature. This new focus has caused women to reexamine and reformulate their religious commitments in new terms and on new evidence. Rather than forming their allegiance to a religion on the basis of blind obedience to male religious superiors, women have made their own religious commitments based on credible evidence utilizing their own experience. Women from all religious traditions have used their own creativity, intelligence, and effort to derive satisfaction from the very religion that seems to oppress them.

As we study the various traditions from which competent women have emerged, we notice that these women often did not and do not follow the established behavior for women. As a result they have challenged the status quo and caused some rethinking about "holy" traditions. In some cases this critical examination has led to constructive changes that have improved the lives of both men and women. In other cases, however, religious hierarchies have dismissed these outstanding women as exceptions to the rules of their religious traditions. Whatever the result, these extraordinary women have given evidence by their lives that all women have access to the supernatural and are free to interpret their religious truths in light of their own experience rather than the limited experience of the men who wrote the scriptures and codified the laws.

Women who have challenged religious traditions often were and are treated poorly by the powerful in their religious communities. All prophets are persecuted by their own people; likewise, strong women who challenge a social system of patriarchal control of the female sex cannot expect support and acclaim. These women must be driven by some other force that sees religion as a power for the betterment of all humankind rather than for the benefit of a few. Whether motivated by their love for God or by a desire to embody the nurturing and beneficent characteristics of the mother goddess, many generous women spend their lives in the selfless service of others.

North American Indians

Egalitarian Practices Among the Iroquois

Each tribe of the North American Indians assigns different traditions, rituals, and roles to women. The Iroquois tribe—composed of the League of the Five Nations: the Cayuga, Mohawk, Oneida, Onondaga, and Seneca—has one of the most accessible histories to trace. Although few of the North American Indians have written scriptures or traditions, the French Jesuit priests, who set about to convert them to Christianity, have left many written records describing their native religious practices. France sent missionaries to upper New York state and southern Ontario to spread the faith to its territory in the New World.

The Iroquois seemed to be egalitarian before their conversion to Christianity. Both men and women lived together in the longhouse, which was divided into male and female areas; abided by the same rules; and participated in most of the same rituals, although women dominated the agricultural rituals. The members of the clan traced their heritage through the mother, in matrilinear fashion, and families named children after deceased relatives from the mother's clan group.

Although a woman could not serve as chief of the clan, women could elect or depose the chief. In some cases, the responsibility for choosing the successor to the chief fell to the dead chief's matron, the woman who held his wampum beads (beads used as money, ceremonial pledges, and ornaments). A council of chiefs had to approve her choice; if they failed to do so, she had to choose another candidate. The matron was not necessarily the chief's widow: Usually she was chosen for that position because of her knowledge of the Iroquois traditions and rituals and her leadership ability in maintaining them within the tribe. Members of the tribe sought the matron's advice for names for newborn children, for medicinal or healing rituals, for the enactment of commemorative feasts, and for counsel for family problems.

The matron was esteemed because she participated in the power of the Great Creator, who was believed to inspire her choices. The Iroquois paid great respect to their matron and to fortune-tellers, the majority of whom were women. They believed that the Great Creator, or Spirit, inspired the fortune-tellers with wisdom to dispense good medicinal cures, to conduct rituals using healing herbs, and to dispense good advice to the seekers. Women conducted many of the longhouse religious ceremonies.

Today most Iroquois ceremonies are conducted in the longhouse, which is no longer a home but a place of worship. The most important contemporary ceremonies are connected with the agricultural cycle of seed planting and harvesting. Women sing and devise special dances, such as the squash dance, corn dance, and women's shuffle dance, to celebrate the rituals. Men are included in the ceremonies and often contribute their own songs, but the ritual cannot be conducted without the participation of women. With the shift from the male rituals of hunting and war to the agricultural domain of women, women leaders called deaconesses, or faithkeepers, have assumed more leadership rules in the ceremonies. Although men still retain the preaching role at contemporary religious ceremonies, the deaconess performs most of the organizational services. Working with the male deacons, she sets the date for the ceremonies—a very prestigious job. The deaconess then organizes the rituals, assigning the intentions, or purposes, and roles to the preacher, singers, and dancers.

There are certain women's ceremonies as well as men's ceremonies. The male and female faithkeepers cooperate in the planning of the male ceremonies, but women have the last say regarding their own rituals.

In recent years, the chief and the matron roles are now receding. Many of their past political duties have fallen to the deaconesses, who now accept or reject new members, keep the names, and settle quarrels. A deaconess can be elected by the female members of the longhouse or inherit the office from her mother's line. Longhouse religious ceremonies are held seasonally on the Iroquois reservation in New York state and southern Ontario.

Although men control their own ceremonies and retain the role of preacher for all rituals, women have complete power in the ceremonies of their own domain. Following the example of Iroquois women, many feminists from different religions are planning and executing their own rituals. The Iroquois provide a model of egalitarian participation in religious ceremonies in which all the members are recognized for their talents and contributions.

Hindu Tradition

Although most models for Hindu women center on the traditional roles for women in society, some extraordinary women are making inroads into the roles that men have kept for themselves. In the past men have presented women with such models as Sita, who underwent the fire ordeal to preserve her husband's honor, and Sati, whose self-sacrifice for her husband was held up as heroic virtue. They offered the example of Savitri, whose devotion to her husband could even bring the dead back to life and who embodied the virtues of chastity, long suffering, and faithfulness.

Hindu tradition generally discourages women from using ascetic practices such as fasting, exposure to the elements, or wandering and begging for food because they believe these practices bring with them some kind of power. Women are encouraged to engage in *tapas*, or ascetic practices, if they use the power produced from them for the betterment of their husbands, but not for themselves. These ascetic practices prepare one for the higher forms of devotion, which produce trancelike states of deep meditation called *samadi*. Samadi paves the way for mosha, or liberation from the endless rounds of rebirth, and women have been traditionally discouraged from using this rigorous method of asceticism. Hindus commonly believe that a person must be born male in order to achieve mosha and that women must await this male rebirth.

Gargi

Gargi, a woman philosopher, lived in India during the seventh century BCE, around the beginning of the period of Upanishad philosophical writing. The Brhadaranyaka Upanishad tells the story of a philosophy tournament at King Janaka's court in which the prize of 1,000 silver coins and 10,000 gold coins would be awarded to the winner. The contestants were to demonstrate their knowledge of ultimate reality, or Brahman, which is both a transcendent reality and a force permeating everything. The impersonal nature of Brahman made it very difficult to use concepts and language that made it intelligible to humans.

The Upanishad tries to provide insights into Brahman by using a philosophic method of inquiry: One question leads to another and finally to a conclusion. In the story of the philosophy tournament, the male philosophers interrogate the teacher Yajnavalkya regarding his ideas, and during the questioning it is the only female philosopher, Gargi, who demonstrates her outstanding knowledge. She ties her questions to the Vedas (Hindu sacred writings) using the familiar images of weaving but at the same time shows an understanding of the newer philosophy of the Upanishads. Gargi, using a regressive questioning method to get Yajnavalkya to expose his views on the first principle, or absolute reality, challenges him so clearly that he tells her to stop questioning him. Gargi accepts the rebuff diplomatically and falls into silence. She picks up the questioning again, the only one to have that opportunity. She gets Yajnavalkya to begin to disclose his theory of negation, because when Yajnavalkya cannot explain absolute reality, he tries to say what it is not. He says it is not a thread, not a stone, not short, not long, and so on. Gargi gets him to say that absolute reality, or Supreme Brahman, is not limited by any attributes. It is beyond all description that can be understood by the human mind.

A. S. Altekar, a Hindu writer, extols the knowledge and skill of Gargi, the only female philosopher at the tournament:

> The subtlest philosophical questions were initiated for discussion by the lady philosopher, Gargi, who had the honour to be the spokesman of the distinguished philosophers at court .... The searching cross-examination of Yajnavalkya by Gargi shows that she was a dialectician and philosopher of high order.
>
> *Altekar, 207*

Gargi was not content to use the usual method to gain intellectual knowledge by meditating on the Vedas or asking the guru for his teachings on the subject. Instead she had the intellectual skill and courage to pursue knowledge through questioning based on her own experience. Her own philosophical competence won the acclaim and admiration of the men philosophers who engaged in the religious discussion and reflection on supreme reality.

Sri Sarada Devi

One of the routes Hindu women have for advancement is a revered or powerful husband. Women of most cultures have found that marriage to a socially high-ranking spouse increases their own opportunities for growth and material happiness. Sarada Devi found the path to spiritual advancement through the instruction and example of her husband, Ramakrishna, but after his death, she independently continued his role as guru and extended her help to her many disciples.

Sri Sarada Devi, whose life spanned the nineteenth and early twentieth centuries, seemed from early childhood to be a child of promise. She was betrothed at the age of six to Sri Ramakrishna, who had a marked religious influence on her. As a young woman, Sarada was gifted with a vision of a woman, who brought her an instant cure to a fever.

Ramakrishna, known for his holiness and ascetic practices of tapas, would fall into religious trances easily. One day after he addressed the divine mother present in Sarada Devi, the husband and wife fell into deep samadi. They both could see Sarada Devi's complete identification with the mother goddess. She had experienced the union of the worshipper with the worshipped, which is usually a temporary phenomena. But Sarada retained the consciousness of the divine presence within her for the remainder of her life. After Ramakrishna's death, Sarada continued his work as leader of a group of devotees. She performed miracles of healing and reported them to the authorities.

Sarada took on the role of guru after having a vision of her dead husband in which he gave her the secret mantra necessary for the disciple's initiation. In her role of guru, Sarada refused to wear the dull, drab attire of the widow and refused to shave her head. The other widows denigrated her for this behavior, but Sarada continued to lead her group of disciples, detached from their criticism. She had no children to care for her as she aged; rather, she found herself caring for her younger siblings and their children. The position of guru is taken very seriously, as is noted by Swami Ghanananda.

> The power of the guru is transmitted through the mantra to the disciple. That is why the guru at time of initiation takes on himself the sins of the disciple and suffers so much from physical maladies. It is extremely difficult to be a guru, for he has to take responsibility for his disciples' sins.
>
> *Ghanananda, 112*

Sarada Devi seemed to suffer physically for the disciple when the disciple touched her feet in a reverent gesture. She felt a burning sensation in her feet that could be diminished only slightly when she bathed them in Ganges River water. This suffering never deterred her from dispensing motherly advice or offering gentle hospitality to the throngs of men and women who came to her. Her divine motherhood extended to everyone; she was able to transcend natural motherhood and include the whole world in her concerns. Her teachings include the following.

> If you want peace of mind, do not find fault with others. Rather see your own faults. Learn to make the whole world your own. No one is a stranger.
>
> One should not hurt others even by words. One's sensibility is lost if one has not control over one's speech.
>
> As clouds are blown away by the wind,
> the thirst for material pleasures will be driven away
> by the utterance of Lord's name.
>
> *Sri Sarada Devi*

These teachings of Sarada Devi stress the underlying unity of all humankind. Rather than emphasizing the differences that separate us, Sarada Devi suggests that there are no such things as strangers versus family, men versus women, old versus young, yours versus mine, or any of the other dichotomies that divide humanity. Everyone is an image of God, whether that god is conceived of as the divine mother or father. Her teachings offer a recipe for practical living that implement the principles of unity and harmony for all peoples. Her disciples, both men and women, are still trying to spread these principles to all who will listen.

Sarada Devi used the path that many women take for salvation. Through prayer and meditation, she experienced the ultimate being in a most satisfying manner. She went directly to God, rather than using the mediating experiences of the brahmin priests. It did not seem to bother her that she did not receive the thread ceremony of the upper-class men, which entitled them to prepare for mosha. She had an internal awareness that she could achieve salvation even though she had been taught that only men could attain it. Sarada Devi is an example of a self-confident woman who would not be cowed by patriarchal religious practices, but emerged as a strong, wise woman of faith.

Ma Jnanananda

Many have witnessed the absorption of Ma Jnanananda into trancelike states during the latter half of this century. Born in 1931, Jnanananda—whose official name is Her Holiness Satguru Swami Shri Jnanananda Saraswati—presently lives in Madras, India. She was born into wealth because her father had a prominent position with Southern Railway. After marriage and five children, Ma Jnanananda renounced her wealth and practiced such austerities that in 1975 she secured the power to reach samadi. She was initiated into the role of female *sannyasi*, or holy woman, by a renowned religious teacher and began her role of guru.

It was most unusual for a woman to be a disciple of a male guru because she could not wash his feet or enter into the personal relationship demanded for spiritual growth. She could not spend time in private or talk with him about intimate details of her life because of severe social restraints about relations between men and women who are not married. Ma Jnanananda offered the opportunity for spiritual growth to members of her sex, who treated her as their guru. Realizing her great holiness, many people have sought her advice, and she has even reluctantly taken on some of these people as disciples in her distinguished role of guru. The guru assumes a special relationship with the disciple, which is usually begun by giving the initiate a secret mantra. The mantra comes to the guru in prayer and is to be shared with no one but the disciple. The relationship between Ma Jnanananda and her disciples is so intense that she can communicate with them even if they are miles apart. Educated women seek her out for advice and meet with her individually or in groups, usually in homes. People besiege her with requests, such as help obtaining suitable jobs, mental and physical health, favors for relatives and friends, and instructions in prayer. Her message, as observed by Charles White in 1979, centers on the need to surrender oneself to God:

> God realization should be one's entire goal in life, and everything else should be secondary. All else in the world pales alongside God realization. As you come closer to it, the valuable things of the world will draw you less because they will be less attractive. You should become aware of the passage of life from childhood to old age. Nothing lasts—the joys or the sorrows. So much is fated, the result of past karma. We cannot avoid anything. But the attitude toward events, the type of attention we give to them, these are within our control. That is where we exercise freedom.
>
> *White, 23*

David Kinsley, a professor of Hindu religion, says many of those who come to her are women, and she acknowledges that women may find her less intimidating than a male guru and that she is better than men at understanding many women's problems (148). Surprisingly, however, men as well as women number among her numerous disciples. Professor White explains.

> Over the weeks, months, and years that I have been meeting Ma, I have felt increasingly attracted to her. What part of my attraction has to do with her being a woman? I think most people would like to have a mother like her— without apparent inner conflicts, dignified, wisely admonitory, and, at the same time, completely accepting. But beyond that, as far as I can tell, her spiritual knowledge stems from a profound inner life that seems to illuminate general human experience, a man's as well as a woman's. True, she has a powerful personality, and this is especially meaningful at a time when women are seeking leading roles in all areas of human endeavor. But Shri Jnanananda Saraswati, the guru-goddess, will be most attractive to anyone, female or male, who wants to know about the depth of the spiritual reality from one who is amazingly articulate in stating her perception of it.
>
> *White, 24*

Although Ma Jnanananda is difficult for Hindu women to imitate, they can use the path she took to holiness. They may never become gurus, but they can practice the tapas that will help them gain the self-control necessary for deep and satisfying meditation. Ma Jnanananda allows women the opportunity to achieve an intimate personal relationship with a guru who will help them to grow spiritually, a relationship that is usually prohibited to women with a male guru.

Ma Jnanananda has been severely criticized by traditional men and women because she refuses to wear the widow's garb, shave her head, or stay in the role assigned to widows. Her inner faith in God has engendered a faith in herself that gives her the courage to transcend the criticism of others.

Buddhist Tradition

Nuns

Nuns have been a part of Buddhism, the religion to which much of the Asian world belongs, from its early history. Following the advice of his aunt, Buddha had permitted the nuns to form their own religious community. Although they were dominated by the monks, who acted as the teachers, disciplinarians, preachers, and conductors of their rituals, the order of nuns did offer women in India an alternative to marriage. When other women were coping with arranged marriages, dowry prices, and misuse by the in-laws, women who chose to be nuns could leave their homes and commit their lives to following Buddha. They lived a celibate life with other women and dedicated themselves to meditation and prayer, which they believed would lead them to enlightenment and finally to an end to the countless rounds of rebirth.

As Buddhism spread to include more of the laity in the Mahayana branch, both men and women were taught the principles of the religion. The Buddhist communities began to recognize and revere certain leaders, called *bodhisattvas*, who had achieved enlightenment through meditation and then spread the teachings of Buddha and techniques of prayer to others. A bodhisattva could be of either sex, and many women achieved this ideal.

One of the teachings of Buddhism was the merit of giving material goods and food to the monasteries. Prosperous laywomen had contributed to the Buddha himself and had been responsible for the building of shrines and housing for the monks and nuns. Many women from nobility and royalty were generous in this endeavor and enlisted the help of their husbands in support of Buddhism.

Sanghamitra

One of the reasons that Buddhism spread so quickly throughout Asia was its followers' missionary work. The son and daughter of King Asoka, a Buddhist king of great renown, were responsible for the conversion of Ceylon (Sri Lanka). King Asoka had given special attention to the education of his daughter, Sanghamitra, and her brother, Makendra, in the Buddhist teachings. They both renounced their inheritance to the throne and joined Buddhist orders. Makendra went to Ceylon, where he gained fame as a teacher and practitioner of Buddhist doctrines. He formed an order of Buddhist monks in Ceylon in the third century BCE. Queen Anula of Ceylon was so impressed with his teachings that she asked to be admitted into the order. Knowing the ambivalent teaching of Buddha toward nuns, Makendra sent for Sanghamitra to come to Ceylon with the required number of nuns (10) to initiate the queen and her retinue of 500 maidens into the order.

Sanghamitra arrived with 11 nuns and a branch from the sacred Bo tree, under which Buddha had achieved enlightenment. She granted ordination to the queen and her maidens, thereby establishing the first order of Buddhist nuns in Ceylon. "This was the first time in history that the daughter of a great emperor, well trained and educated, set out to give the message of peace and love to the women of a foreign land, and the enthusiasm with which this news was greeted by the Indian people can hardly be imagined by us today" (Handoo, 155).

The order of nuns founded by Sanghamitra prospered until the eleventh century CE. The nuns taught the fundamentals of Buddhism, nursed the sick, and fed the hungry. King Mahinda IV built them a monastery in the tenth century CE along with kitchens and medical halls (Geiger, 154). With the support of the king, the nuns received official recognition for their work, which was so integral to the inhabitants. Buddhist women were not only able to learn and practice the religious doctrines but entrusted to pass them on to other women. One can imagine that this opportunity for bonding among women carried with it many benefits. Rather than competing with each other within in-law families or harems, women could work together in a cooperative manner to achieve their salvation. Missionary work called for many sacrifices on the part of the women, who left their familiar abodes to preach the Buddhist message. But the satisfaction the missionaries derived from witnessing the happiness and bliss that their message brought more than compensated for their inconveniences. The selfless women who followed the model of Sanghamitra achieved personal growth and fulfillment and were able to imbue other women with enthusiasm for such an experience.

Kuan-yin Bodhisattva

When the male bodhisattva Avolokitesvara was transported from India to China, he underwent a sex change. He became a beautiful woman called Kuan-yin, who carried the feminine, or yin, symbol of the Chinese polarity. Although a bodhisattva, she appears in some legends to take on some characteristics of the goddesses. Kuan-yin usually wore a white dress and carried flowers. Chinese women pursued Kuan-yin as an object of devotion, and she helped them overcome the restrictions of the patriarchal Confucian-defined society. Devotion to Kuan-yin helped to free some Chinese women from some of the culturally defined roles that had existed in society and family since the tenth century CE. She was especially effective in granting requests for healthy children and salvation from physical or natural disasters.

Buddhist nuns and mothers spread the devotion to Kuan-yin Bodhisattva by educating their young children regarding her legends and appearances. Her stories and paintings depicted her wondrous healing power, which was believed to arise from her strong compassion. She showed intense compassion toward the natural sufferings of women. Blood of menstruation and childbirth were considered especially polluting in popular Chinese religion, but Kuan-yin could intervene and save women even if they died in this miserable state by leading them to the Pure Land, where they could achieve enlightenment.

The legends about Kuan-yin gave women an example of an alternative to arranged marriages, which could be unhappy in the Chinese culture. Kuan-yin has the ability to transform herself into a different person in different legends in order to help people in distress. In one of her legends Kuan-yin appears as a Chinese princess, Miao-shan, who revolts against her father's command to marry. She runs away to join a Buddhist convent to become a nun, similar to the renunciation of Buddha. When her father tries to burn the convent and the nuns in retaliation for her lack of filial piety, princess Miao-shan holds no enmity toward her father. In typical Buddhist compassion, she heals his blindness by cutting off her own arm and then heals both her parents spiritually by preaching the message of the Buddha to them after she becomes a bodhisattva. In her form as Miao-shan, Kuan-yin provided an alternative to marriage for Chinese women, that of Buddhist nun. Because she resisted marriage in the traditional Chinese society, she also provided a model for young women who desired to do likewise.

Marjorie Topley reports that a group of laywomen in the nineteenth and twentieth centuries did not wish to marry, but neither did they care for the restrictive lives of Buddhist nuns. They were members of the silk industry and financially independent, so they banded together to form sisterhoods in order to avoid marriage. Women interviewed by Topley said that they wanted to avoid the oppression of loneliness of marriage, the lack of financial independence, and the pain and punishment (pollution) of childbirth (79). These women looked to Kuan-yin as their model in the form of Miao-shan and as their patroness and goddess in her own right.

Kuan-yin has gained popularity in Taiwan in recent years, and her representations appear in many temples. She is usually portrayed as a white-robed Chinese woman holding a willow branch and vase. Her image is a source of devotion in home altars, is sometimes visible in protective charms, and is even the subject of recent novels, films, and television shows. Sometimes treated as a goddess, other times as a bodhisattva, Kuan-yin provides inspiration and consolation in suffering for her female devotees.

Jewish Tradition

Women in Biblical and Contemporary Times

Miriam

Although the social position of women in ancient Israel left them dependent on the men in their family and marginal in their scriptures, a few women rose to prominence in the Hebrew Bible. Exodus tells us of Miriam, the sister of Moses and Aaron, who is favored by Yahweh to receive the gift of prophecy. She exercises her office of prophet together with her brothers. After the Israelites had been delivered from Egypt and had crossed the Red Sea, they watch in relief as the Pharaoh's army drowns. Miriam, as a prophetess, leads the women in the song and dance of rejoicing to glorify the power of Yahweh, who had performed such a great deed for his people.

> For when Pharaoh's cavalry, with his chariots and horsemen, had gone into the sea, Yahweh brought the waters of the sea back over them, though the Israelites went on dry ground right through the sea.
>
> The prophetess Miriam, Aaron's sister, took up a tambourine and all the women followed her with tambourines, dancing, while Miriam took up from them the refrain:
>
> "Sing to Yahweh, for he has covered himself in glory,
> horse and rider he has thrown into the sea."
>
> *Exodus 15:19–22*

Later Miriam and Aaron criticize Moses for marrying a foreign woman: They call themselves God's people and believe that foreigners may contaminate their worship of the one God by introducing some of their polytheistic gods and goddesses. God comes to the defense of Moses and punishes Miriam with what appears to be leprosy. Aaron and Moses beg God to heal her, which he does after seven days.

> Miriam, and Aaron too, criticized Moses over the Cushite woman he had married. He had indeed married a Cushite woman. They said, "Is Moses the only one through whom Yahweh has spoken? Has he not spoken through us too?" Yahweh heard this. Now Moses was extremely humble, the humblest man on earth.
>
> God's answer.
>
> Suddenly Yahweh said to Moses, Aaron and Miriam, "Come out, all three of you to the Tent of Meeting." They went, all three of them, and Yahweh descended in a pillar of cloud and stood at the entrance of the Tent. He called Aaron and Miriam and they both came forward. Yahweh said:
>
> "Listen to my words!
> if there is a prophet among you,
> I reveal myself to him in a vision,
> I speak to him in a dream.
> Not so with my servant Moses;
> to him my whole household is entrusted;
> to him I speak face to face,
> plainly and not in riddles,
> and he sees Yahweh's form.
> How, then, could you dare
> to criticize my servant Moses?"
>
> Yahweh's anger was aroused by them. He went away, and as soon as the cloud left the Tent, there was Miriam covered with a virulent skin-disease, white as snow! Aaron turned to look at her and saw that she had contracted a virulent skin disease.

The prayer of Aaron and Moses
Aaron said to Moses:

"Oh, my Lord, please do not punish us for the sin we have been foolish enough to commit. Do not let her be like some monster with its flesh half eaten away when it leaves its mother's womb!"

Moses pleaded with Yahweh. "O God," he said. "I beg you, please heal her!"

Yahweh then said to Moses, "If her father had done no more than spit in her face, would she not be unclean for seven days? Have her shut up out of the camp for seven days, and then have her brought in again."

Miriam was shut out of the camp for seven days. The people did not set out until she returned. Then the people moved on from Hazeroth and pitched camp in the desert of Paran.

Exodus 12:1–16

Although the Israelites were traveling through the desert, they waited the seven days for her to join them before breaking camp. Miriam must have been held in high esteem among her kinsmen for her gift of prophecy. Miriam was not forgotten, because the prophet Micah writes about her again a number of centuries after the first episode supposedly took place. Micah names Miriam with Moses and Aaron as God's appointed leaders.

My people, what have I done to you,
how have I made you tired of me? Answer me!
For I brought you up from Egypt.
I ransomed you from the place of slave-labour
and sent Moses, Aaron, and Miriam
to lead you.

Micah 6:3–5

Deborah

Deborah is named as a judge, which was one of the most important leadership roles in Israel in the twelfth century BCE. The kingship had not yet been established, so the judge performed services similar to those of the king, such as deciding cases, arbitrating disputes, and dispensing wise counsel. According to Judges Deborah takes on the role of prophetess also in that she tells the leader of the Israelite army, Barak, that the enemy general, Sisera, will be killed by a woman. She sends him to the battle, but the faint-hearted Barak is afraid to go without her.

Deborah, a prophetess, wife of Lappidoth, was judging Israel at the time. She used to sit under Deborah's Palm between Ramah and Bethel in the highlands of Ephraim, and the Israelites would come to her for justice. She sent for Barak son of Abinoam from Kedesh in Naphtali, and said to him, "Has not Yahweh, God of Israel, commanded, 'Go! March to Mount Tabor and with you take ten thousand of the sons of Naphtali and the sons of Zebulun. I shall entice Sisera, the commander of Jabin's army, to encounter you at the Torrent of Kishon with his chariots and troops; and I shall put him into your power?' " Barak replied, "If you come with me, I shall go; if you will not come, I shall not go, for I do not know how to choose the day when the angel of Yahweh will grant me success." "I shall go with you then," she said, "but, the way you are going about it, the glory will not be yours; for Yahweh will deliver Sisera into the hands of a woman." Deborah then stood up and went with Barak to Kedesh. Barak summoned Zebulun and Naphtali. Ten thousand men marched behind him, and Deborah went with him.

Judges 4:4–10

They destroy Sisera's army, but the enemy general escapes, only to fulfill Deborah's prophecy that he will fall at the hands of a woman. The woman is Jael, who invites him into her tent and then drives a tent peg through his temple and kills him as he sleeps.

The Israeli people composed a hymn to Deborah and Jael in which they hail Deborah as "mother in Israel" and praise Jael as the "most blessed of women" for her bravery and action.

> The villages in Israel were no more,
> they were no more
> until you arose, O Deborah
> until you arose, mother of Israel!
>
> *Judges 5:7,8*

> Most blessed of women be Jael
> (the wife of Heber the Kenite);
> of tent-dwelling women, may she be most blessed!
>
> He asked for water; she gave him milk;
> She offered him curds in a lordly dish.
> She reached her hand out to seize the peg,
> her right hand to seize the workman's mallet.
>
> She hammered Sisera, she crushed his head,
> she pierced his temple and shattered it.
> Between her feet, he crumpled, he fell, he lay;
> at her feet, he crumpled, he fell.
> Where he crumpled, there he fell, destroyed.
>
> *Judges 5:24–27*

Both women were considered heroines who had led their people to victory even though they had stepped out of the traditional roles assigned to women at the request of Yahweh. Neither one of them asked the priests or male religious leaders for permission to follow the revealed word of God. They could interpret the urgings of the spirit without checking with the officials of Israel. Deborah and Jael exemplify the ability of women who act as prophetesses to interpret the spiritual powers directly, rather than appealing to the patriarchal structures of their religion for interpretation.

Ruth

Ruth is another biblical woman who, although a Moabite, became a revered heroine in Israel. The book of Ruth tells us that she lives in her own land of Moab with her Jewish husband; her mother-in-law, Naomi; and her

husband's brother and his wife, Orpha. When all three women are wid-
owed, Naomi decides to return to Judah and tells her daughters-in-law,
Ruth and Orpha, to return to their Moabite relatives. Orpha leaves, but
Ruth insists upon accompanying Naomi back to her native land. Ruth
speaks the well-known words illustrating friendship between women:

> Wherever you go, I shall go,
> wherever you live, I shall live.
> Your people will be my people,
> and your God will be my God.
>
> Where you die, I shall die
> and there I shall be buried.
> Let Yahweh bring unnameable ills on me
> and worse ills, too,
> if anything but death
> should part me from you!
>
> *Ruth 1:16–17*

Ruth and Naomi are examples of mature women who pledge their loyalty
to each other in a form of religious bonding that is based on their friendship with God. They lack the protection of a man and therefore have no
place in Jewish society, yet they support each other in grief, poverty, and
insecurity. Their bonding and mutual support seems to be pleasing to God,
who provides for them by supplying a wealthy husband, Boaz, for Ruth.
Their child becomes the grandfather of the future King David, thus bringing
the happiness and fulfillment warranted by the loyalty of Ruth and Naomi.

Contemporary Jewish Women

The bonding of Ruth and Naomi provides a model for female bonding in
groups. Women have found the strength that derives from the combined
effort of a group. The results of their efforts, directed through various organizations, have contributed a great deal to the betterment of the members
of Judaism and the larger community of citizens.

Jewish women, who have traditionally been deprived of active roles in
synagogue worship, have directed their energies toward service to other
members of their community. They find fulfillment and satisfaction through
the organizational work of their sisterhoods. Creative women find ways to
serve the congregation other than the routes of the rabbis, readers, or cantors. These sisterhood groups often fund adult education programs and
study groups for like-minded women. Sometimes they direct the programs
of religious education for children and provide materials for some of the
synagogue celebrations. They raise funds for equipment and books for their
libraries.

In the United States, the sisterhoods have extended their activities
beyond their congregations. The National Council of Jewish Women, found-

ed at the turn of the century, has involved itself in many areas of social legislation, such as adequate housing for low-income groups, pensions for
women, slum clearance, food and drug regulations, and wage and hour
laws for women. Their efforts draw from most branches of Judaism as they
bond together to cope with the problems that face their own congregations
and the larger community of their country. The Hadassah group has been
active in helping the country of Israel to found a medical program by establishing a medical university hospital in Mt. Scopus. Hadassah doctors help
many third world countries establish their own medical services. In the
United States, one of the better known women's organizations is B'nai
B'rith, which funds the college student group of Hillel, the Anti-Defamation
League, Roosevelt Four Freedoms Library in Washington, D.C, and other
worthy projects. They work to improve the status of women by urging the
passing of the Equal Rights Amendment, enlarging opportunities for
women in politics and business, and improving family conditions.

These women's groups that call for equality in society are often unable
to demand the same equality within their own religious congregations.
They have worked hard to improve social conditions, but many of their
own religious congregations reject some of the benefits of their talents and
energy. With the ordination of some women rabbis, perhaps more women
can contribute to the decision-making process within the synagogue system. Many women believe that the religious congregations should derive
some benefit from the talents of gifted, generous Jewish women by allowing them fuller participation in the synagogues, rather than marginalizing
them and letting them direct their valuable energy toward social services for
others.

Berta Pappenheim

Berta Pappenheim lived in Frankfort, Germany, at the end of the nineteenth century. Her upper-middle-class background did not prepare her for
the sights she saw in a welfare center, where Jewish refugees fled from the
pogroms of eastern Europe. Berta volunteered at the center, which was run
by Jewish women to feed homeless and hungry Jews, the elderly, and the
children of Jewish heritage.

> She could have lived, if she wished, like her mother, in quiet leisure, with
> money enough for endless entertainment and travel. But something within
> her cried out for a life that held deeper meaning.
>
> She did not know how to seek this kind of life however until the day she
> stood in the soup kitchen, surrounded by the persecuted men, women, and
> children. She felt she must help these stricken souls.
>
> *Freeman, 64*

Realizing that the refugees needed more than food, Berta began to vol-
unteer at the girls' orphanage with other Jewish women. Some of the children were illegitimate or unwanted; others had parents who were unable

to support them. Her contact with these children led her to crusade against the white slave market. The poverty that existed in eastern Europe had caused some parents to sell their daughters into prostitution. Other unscrupulous opportunists persuaded young women to leave their homes to find work in factories or stores, only to drag them into slavery. Berta founded the League of Jewish Women in 1904, which enrolled about 20 percent of all Jewish women as members. "Among its concerns were equal participation of women with men in the Jewish community, providing career training for Jewish women, and combatting all forms of immorality, especially white slavery (prostitution)" (Kaplan, 213).

Berta recognized the need for education for the girls at the orphanage and tried to prepare them for life outside of marriage. Besides giving them the usual education for domestic chores, Berta wanted to teach them to read, think, and make reasonable decisions. Having been deprived herself of the opportunity for higher education, she wanted to prepare the girls at the orphanage to take advantage of all occasions that would better their lives. She put her own organizational and administration abilities to work in an organization she founded called "Care by Women," in which various groups took responsibility for founding nursery schools, foster homes, and family counseling and career preparation.

When Berta died, Margarethe Susman gave the following tribute to the woman who never forgot her Jewish roots but extended her efforts to improve the quality of life for all women.

> We all know that with the death of Berta Pappenheim a great woman, a real fighter, a true Jewish person, has left us, that a life is gone which will not reappear in Judaism for generations, because of the drastically changed living conditions. We know her life was interwoven with a wide and fateful web of Jewish and German influences, that she lived through the developments of our times with an alert and passionate mind, never yielding her original position, no matter how intensely the changes of the era affected her. Her personality, her life, were from the beginning to the end a single flaming protest against the religious and moral dissolution of the time in which lived.
>
> *Freeman, 266*

Christian Tradition

Women Saints of the Early Church

The early church recognized two paths to authority among its members: the cultic, or authority of office, and the charismatic, or authority given directly to a person through the gifts of the Holy Spirit. In the beginning of Christianity, women exercised leadership in both areas. By the second century, however, they had been excluded from the official office of leadership because men had established the church's hierarchical structure and kept for themselves the cultic authority. Because at Pentecost the Holy Spirit had descended upon everyone, both men and women, it had brought everyone the gifts of teaching, preaching, and administering (Acts 2:1–4). Peter said that the gift of prophecy had been bestowed on women, who used this gift for the benefit of the whole church (Acts 2: 17, 18). Rosemary Ruether says that these prophetic gifts gave women the power to preside over the Eucharistic meals. "Prophetic gifts were seen as giving power to preach and to bestow the blessing over the Lord's Supper" (20).

The early Christian community reflected the egalitarian attitudes of its founder, who had called both men and women to discipleship. Early church members lived the equality formula of Paul (Gal. 3:27), which said there was no difference between men and women, Jews and Gentiles, slaves and free people, but that all are united in Christ. Luke describes this egalitarian society: "Each day, with one heart, they regularly went to the temple, but met in their houses for the breaking of the bread, they shared their food gladly, and generously. They praised God and were looked up to by everyone" (Acts 2:46). The new Christians still used the Temple for the recitation of the psalms and prayers but chose to celebrate the Eucharist in each others' homes, which they called house churches. The leadership of this house community rested on the owner of the house. For example, Acts 12:12 refers to a Christian community that met at the house of Mary, the mother of John Mark. In his letters Paul refers to the house churches that met in the homes of Lydia, Nympha, and Prisca, or Priscilla. The house of Priscilla still stands outside of Rome, over the catacombs that hold the graves of the early Christian martyrs. A chapel that dates back to the first century has frescoes on the wall that depict women presiding at the eucharistic supper held in the home.

Paul stresses the egalitarian structure of the early church by referring in his letters to both women and men by name as coworkers. He does not attribute higher or lower authority to them, but considers them equals. The Christian message has been entrusted to both men and women, he says, who spread it by their teaching and example. Paul even calls the woman Junia an apostle in his letter to the Romans (Rom. 15:16), because she had converted to Christianity before he did.

The office of leadership held by Phoebe in Paul's letter to the Romans has received a variety of interpretations. She is called the deacon of the church of Cenchrae, which means that she could have served the church in charitable work or as leader of the congregation. The office of deacon was recognized for its teaching and preaching capacity in the official church. Phoebe, in some translations, is also referred to as the leading officer or administrator, demonstrating her recognized authority in the community. Unfortunately, the patriarchal church of the second century downplayed the role of deacon and deaconess in favor of the office of bishop. Writings that referred to the service of women have not been as extant as writings that describe the position of men in the early church. Was the leadership of these women left unrecorded because it was taken for granted in an egalitarian church? Or were the women excised from authority by patriarchal fathers? These questions necessitate the effort of more women's research in the field of ecclesiology to discover the reasons for the absence of women's contributions.

The office of prophecy, which was believed to be given directly by the Holy Spirit, was bestowed on the martyrs. Those who were willing to give their lives as a testimony to their faith in Christ were highly regarded by the early Christians. The Roman persecutions that began with Nero in 65 CE and ended with Constantine in 313 CE offered many faithful Christians the opportunity to test their faith. For those who would not give up their faith under torture and threat of death, the kingdom of heaven offered a hero's welcome. In the early church, both men and women were encouraged to offer their lives in faith and were revered as prophets through whom the Holy Spirit spoke. The opportunity for martyrdom offered many young Christian women an alternative from marriage. By choosing Christ as their bridegroom, they were free to reject suitors and their parent's arranged marriages. These young women, such as Agnes, Thecla, Perpetua, and Felicitas, were filled with the gifts of the Holy Spirit, which gave them the strength and courage to undergo tortures. They gained much esteem and stature in the eyes of the early Christians, who admired the courage of those who would willingly die for their faith.

There has been some debate as to whether women were ever ordained priests. In fact, the place of the priesthood in the early church has been seriously challenged by many theologians. Dorothy Irvin, an archaeologist and theologian, describes the frescoes that she discovered in Rome. "A fourth century catacomb fresco found in Rome shows a woman ordained a Bishop. I do not know of any scenes of the ordination of a man, although all agree the men were ordained at that time" (8). Irvin describes some frescoes of women and men dressed in liturgical vestments and standing in attitudes of leaders of the ceremonies. Janice Nunnally-Cox, an Episcopal priest, says, "Women most certainly functioned as leaders in the early Christian community, doing charitable acts, opening their homes for meetings, and functioning liturgically as well" (129). As more women researchers uncover some of the evidence that documents women's contributions to the early church, the work of more outstanding Christian women of that era will emerge. The efforts of many women researchers have uncovered a tradition of full participation by women who served as liturgical leaders in the early church. This evidence is valuable because it supports the argument that women should gain full participation in their Christian churches today. If women of the past had access to both routes of authority—charismatic gifts of the spirit and the cultic as well as decision-making office of the institutional church—it is difficult to build a credible argument forbidding this same action in the present.

Women Saints of the Medieval Period

Just as the martyrs of the early church were perceived as bearers of the Holy Spirit, the medieval saints are recognized for having power that they derived from their holiness. Women saints contributed to an understanding of human spirituality that included the mind, the body, and the affections. They incorporated into their holiness a balanced personality composed of all facets of human development—minds, emotions, and bodies. They were not afraid to mention love of God, self, others, and nature as the most important ingredients of spirituality. Their vision of God as lover served as an impetus on their road to holiness. Because they blended their affections with substantial learning, they were esteemed as teachers, counselors, and models of the spiritual life. By integrating love and learning, the medieval saints were recognized as able administrators who governed well those entrusted to their care.

Two examples of these medieval saints are Saint Brigit of Kildare, Ireland, and Saint Catherine of Siena, Italy. Both were recognized by the official church after their deaths as saints because of their holiness, intelligence, competence, teaching, and administrative ability in their spread of the Christian message.

Saint Brigit of Ireland

Saint Brigit was born in Ireland in the fifth century CE to a Christian slave-woman and a minor Celtic prince, Dubthack. When her mother was sold to a druid, Brigit went with her. From the druid she learned many secrets of nature from traditional Irish lore—the healing herbs and the uses of water and fire—that would help her in her care of others. Images of Saint Brigit connect her with the goddess Brigit because, according to Felime O'Briain, her biographer, "we find flames coming from her head, just as they had from the Goddess" (18).

Brigit devoted herself to monasticism as the monks did. But she did not enter a life of retreat and isolation; instead, she dedicated herself to a life of service to her community. She attracted many young women to join her at a time when most women did not participate in societal activities. When receiving Brigit's vows to live as a nun in the service of God, Bishop Mel, the representative of the Pope, used the words for ordination of a bishop rather than the words for the dedication of a nun. An acknowledged scholarly text, *Lives of the Saints from the Book of Linsmore*, describes the scene:

> The bishop being intoxicated with the grace of God, there did not recognize what he was reciting from his book, for he consecrated Brigit with the orders of Bishop. "This virgin alone in Ireland," said Mel, "will hold the episcopal ordination."
>
> *Lives of the Saints, 323*

Brigit exercised her power as abbess of her monastery and passed on this gift to her future abbesses. She was able to establish peace between warring factions, mediate disputes, and offer herbal cures for humans and livestock. She is noted not for wondrous miracles, but for a practical wisdom that expressed itself in loving care of others.

Saint Brigit founded many monasteries, traveling all around Ireland in a chariot. These foundations, which became centers of great learning, were extensive, self-supporting settlements that included monks, nuns, and lay-people. In the monasteries people received instructions in carpentry, farming, harvesting, weaving, herbal and food nutrition, and care for the sick. No one who wanted to learn was turned away from the monasteries.

Brigit was not a dour ascetic, but encouraged laughter and gaiety and incorporated music into her community celebrations. Her love for God overflowed to love for all members of her community, to whom she rendered kindly service. Brigit is associated most often with the foundation at Kildare, where she spent most of her life. The *Annals of Ireland* declares that she died in 525 CE and was buried in the same tomb as Saint Patrick. Her namesakes have continued over the centuries, with families today naming their daughters Brigit, Bridie, Bride, or Brigid in her memory.

Saint Catherine of Siena

Saint Catherine was born in Siena, Italy, in the fourteenth century CE. From early childhood she showed a propensity for devotion and love of God. After a religious experience in which she sensed the presence of God, she told her parents that she would dedicate her life to Christ. Although they were disappointed that she refused to marry, they gave her a room in their house. She seldom left this room at first, living her life as a hermit in constant communion with God. In one of her mystical experiences, however, she discerned that Christ wished her to leave her solitude and contemplation for active service in caring for the poor and sick of the city. She performed her service so lovingly that she attracted a group of followers who participated in her prayer and ministry. Her prayer was so intense and her service so generous that she gained a reputation for vigorous sanctity.

Her spiritual vigor showed itself in her concern for the papacy, which was undergoing division at the time. She insisted that the Pope, who was living in Avignon, France, return to his rightful place in Rome as successor to Peter. Catherine was also a prudent diplomat in that she successfully mediated a dispute between two cities that no one else could bring to a peaceful conclusion. Glimpses of Catherine's competence, wit, sarcasm, humility, and intelligence were faithfully preserved through her numerous letters. Her powerful personality, vitalized by the Holy Spirit, gave her an energy that propelled her to offer peace proposals to warring factions, reform the church hierarchy, and work for the salvation of all people.

Catherine's one desire was to do God's will. Rather than living in slavish obedience to her male religious superiors, she wished to obey the will of

God, with whom she held such a loving relationship. At God's urgings she set about to reform the patriarchal church by returning the Pope to his rightful place in Rome. In this endeavor she tried to conform to Christ by taking on herself the sins of the world. She willingly suffered for others so that they would become acceptable to God and achieve salvation. Catherine presented an ideal of Christian spirituality that integrated prayer, action, intelligence, and piety. Her dedication to church reform gained her the respect of the patriarchal church fathers as well as of the men and women who enthusiastically followed her leadership.

Saint Brigit and Saint Catherine both showed evidence of their spiritual authority, which they derived from their personal holiness. They developed the gifts that were bestowed upon them directly through the Holy Spirit. Instead of traveling the route of the institutional office of ordination, they effected great spiritual influence through the prophetic office of the Holy Spirit. Their union with God empowered Brigit and Catherine to preach by example the true Christian message of the gospel. The official church recognized their gifts and held them up as worthy examples for imitation by canonizing them as saints.

Contemporary Times

Dorothy Day

Born in 1897, Dorothy Day lived during her childhood for a short time in a very poor section of Chicago. After witnessing the poverty, hunger, and homelessness in the city, Dorothy saw a need to dedicate her life to issues of social justice. Her journalistic background provided her with the necessary skills to influence the thinking of others through the press. After her conversion to Catholicism, she cofounded a penny paper called the *Catholic Worker* with her friend Peter Maurin. It was dedicated to principles of social justice and called for proper compensation, reasonable hours, and better conditions for workers. Her writings, which encouraged others to adopt these ideals, raised the consciousness of early twentieth century Americans to the inequalities in our capitalist system. The paper's dedication to the ideal of peace caused some controversy during World War II, the Korean war, and the war in Vietnam. Dorothy Day remained true to her rejection of war, violence, and bloodshed in spite of the criticism leveled at her by her more military-minded contemporaries. She even spent time in jail as a witness to her beliefs of pacifism and nonviolence.

The concepts of the *Catholic Worker* grew into the Catholic Worker movement, and as Dorothy wrote about the social inequalities, she put her ideas of social justice into action. Although she was a traditional Catholic, she did not ask permission from the Catholic hierarchy to establish her homes of hospitality for the needy and homeless. The homes were autonomous units, some situated in cities or on farms, that always offered the warm atmosphere of a family. Dorothy knew the value of a community that recognized each person's gifts, and she did her best to encourage the talents of each individual. The Catholic Worker homes were not luxurious, but they provided for the basic needs of its inhabitants. Their spirit of community and zeal for social justice attracted young college graduates to the movement. Debra Campbell, a professor of religion, describes the attraction of these young people to the Dorothy Day's movement. "The Catholic Workers represented a way to be involved in the struggle for social justice and still avoid the more radical movements condemned by the church" (30).

The Catholic church opposed communism, anarchism, and some forms of socialism in the 1950s because of their close ties to atheism. Dorothy Day and the Catholic Workers movement were at times suspected of socialist leanings because of their demand for consideration of the poor and oppressed. Day was not content just to house the poor, clothe the naked, and feed the hungry; she also aimed at changing the structures that caused their oppression. She raised the consciousness of the injustice of war and poverty through the newspapers and encouraged her followers to protest and demonstrate against the violence and inequality. Debra Campbell gives us a good insight into the relevance of Dorothy Day for women today.

> What can Dorothy Day's life teach us about women's power in the Roman Catholic Church? It shows that it is at least possible for a woman to form and lead a decentralized movement for peace and justice and still remain a faithful, even a devout Roman Catholic. It indicates that the hierarchical model of authority does not exhaust the possibilities open to the church; the extended family model might, in fact, be more compatible with a strong stand on peace and social justice. Implicitly, Day's experience illustrates the wisdom and practicality of confronting the issues rather than the authorities whenever possible. Granted, Dorothy Day had no trouble making this clear-cut distinction because for her, the authority structure was not one of the issues.
>
> *Campbell, 32*

Catholic Women Religious

Catholic women religious are women who live in community, bound together by vows of poverty, chastity, and obedience. Even though Roman Catholic nuns, or sisters, as they are called, have to submit their communities' constitutions to male church authorities, they have enjoyed many of the freedoms and opportunities for which feminists have longed. They have become economically independent, received advanced education opportunities, and held the executive positions in their own institutions. Sisters have founded and conducted schools, hospitals, orphanages, nursing homes, colleges, and religious education centers in Europe and North America and in mission countries all over the world. Their vows of celibacy free them from the responsibilities of marriage and motherhood, yet do not deny them the satisfaction of deep and lasting friendships with members of both sexes. They find great support in living in community with like-minded individuals who share their goals and aspirations. When their ministries are no longer needed, they adapt their services to the changing times. For example, since issues of social justice have become apparent, the sisters have operated soup kitchens, food pantries, and homes for battered women and have engaged in lobbying efforts to change the structures that cause injustice. The sisters have engaged in campus ministries, prison ministries, and peace and justice activities, and with the shortage of priests they have become administrators of parishes and diocesan offices.

The sisters enjoy the personal fulfillment that derives from the opportunity for meaningful and satisfying work and constantly examine their motives for that activity. As women dedicated to the Christian message, they see their service to others as an outgrowth of their service to God. Although they work for the Roman Catholic church, the sisters perceive their mission as coming directly from God. Like the women of early Christianity, they participate in the prophetic or gifted mode of authority from the Holy Spirit rather than the cultic or official authority of the hierarchy. The sisters cooperate with the hierarchy in order to spread the Christian message but do retain their independence from some clerical regulations.

Protestant Women

The social gospel has a special appeal for Protestants, who traditionally have seemed dedicated to helping people they consider less fortunate than themselves. The U.S. movement to abolish slavery arose in Protestant churches in the north, and the civil rights movement had its origins in Protestant churches in the south. Such Protestant institutions as the Young Women's and Young Men's Christian Associations (YWCA and YMCA) began with concern for housing for the unmarried young people away from their familial homes. Social action concerns extended to hospitals, nursing homes, and orphanages. Florence Nightingale was a member of the Anglican church in England when she heard God's call to revolutionize the field of nursing. The Grimké sisters belonged to a Quaker group whose thoughts on nonviolence led them to work for the abolition of slavery. Women from various Protestant denominations left their homes to spread the word of God in mission fields abroad. Dedicated women continue today to work for human rights and the betterment of the human condition, motivated by religious faith that originated in their Protestant churches.

The Grimké Sisters

Fundamentalist religion is usually considered allied with political conservatism. In Iran the fundamentalist Muslim Shiites hold to traditional religious and social values. American evangelical fundamentalists associate themselves with conservative anti-abortion and anti–gay-rights movements and usually do not support government social programs. The Grimké sisters, however, proved that they could combine a deeply pious evangelical religion with zealous, social action. Sarah (1792–1873) and Angelina (1805–1879) Grimké were born to wealth on a South Carolina plantation before the Civil War. Leaving their mainline Protestant religious denomination for the Quakers, they developed a deep personal relationship with Jesus, whom they considered their lord. They viewed themselves as disciples of Christ and felt the moral responsibility that accompanied that discipleship.

Angelina was so convinced that her moral principles came from her belief in Christ that she said, "True believers had but one Leader, who would if they followed Him, guide them in all truth" (Du Pre Lumpkin, 24). A part of the truth that Angelina embraced was the teaching of Jesus regarding treating others as one would wish to be treated. She found this teaching especially inconsistent with the practice of slavery. She asked slave owners pointed questions, such as "Wouldn't thou be willing to be a slave?" (Lumpkin, 48). She based her argument against slavery on the moral obligation for everyone to reach moral and spiritual perfection. Slave owners failed in their moral responsibility toward the slaves in denying them full opportunity to pursue their perfection through freedom and moral education. Angelina saw no distinction between moral rights for men, women, or slaves as she wrote in a letter:

> My idea is that whatever is morally right for a man to do is morally right for a woman to do. I recognize no rights but human rights . . . . For in Christ Jesus there is neither male nor female.
>
> *Du Pre Lumpkin, 120*

Sarah, in her goal to free the slaves, wrote her wishes to Angelina's husband, Theodore Weld:

> To spend and be spent in the cause of the enslaved . . . . One of the best means of serving this cause is by the holiness of our lives that the mouths of the gainsayers may be stopt, and that by near communion with the Lord Jesus we may be thoro'ly instructed in his will in all things.
>
> *Barnes and Dumond, Letters, vol. 1*

The sisters believed they could discern the will of God through the Bible and gave lectures on the passages in the Old and New Testaments that they thought opposed slavery. Sarah preached that God was the god of the poor and needy, the despised and the oppressed. She linked her biblical studies that decried slavery to a concern for woman's rights. She stressed the need for correct interpretation of scriptures because they tended to favor the experience of men and cited the need for female biblical scholars to find a more complete and accurate rendition of the word of God.

Against some of the false translations of some passages by men. . .and against the perverted interpretations by men who undertook to write commentaries thereon. I am inclined to think, when we (women) are admitted to the honor of studying Greek and Hebrew, we shall produce some various readings of the Bible, a little different than we have now.

Sarah Grimké

Both sisters joined the abolitionist movement for the emancipation of the slaves but demanded that it follow the nonviolent principles of the gospel. They were willing to suffer persecution, even death, for their cause. They lectured and wrote against the violation of human rights that such a deplorable system engendered. In refusing to call anyone lord and master except Christ, they saw no reason for slave owners to assume that title. The Grimkes saw the relationship between sexism and racism and appealed to all women to oppose slavery because slave women "are our sisters; and to us as women, they have a right to look for sympathy with their sorrows, and effort and prayer for their rescue" (Lerner, 161).

The social action of the Grimké sisters, radical in those times, was motivated by their love of Jesus and their commitment to the lordship of Christ, to whose moral principles they adhered. What they grasped personally, the Grimké sisters tried to implement socially, trying to apply these principles to the abolition of slavery and the improvement of the position of women.

The Protestant Reformation enabled many spirit-motivated women to rise to prominence in their denominations. In the more democratic settings of some Protestant churches, women's rights were recognized and their participation encouraged. Although some denominations maintained the hierarchical structures of the Catholic church, many of them respected the musings of the spirit, which could be given directly to their members. With the development of the printing press, lay people could read and interpret the scriptures as well as the educated clergy. Many intelligent and courageous women, empowered by the Holy Spirit, made invaluable contributions to their churches and society.

Florence Nightingale

One outstanding English Protestant was Florence Nightingale, who completely revolutionized the profession of nursing. After a religious experience in her youth, Florence decided to accept the call of God. Her wealthy Anglican family had expected her to conform to the social roles for women of the nineteenth century, but she, pondering her God-given mission, refused to marry the wealthy suitor they had encouraged. She believed that the restrictions that would be placed upon her as a wife would severely limit the activities that she came to realize were part of her call.

Instead of devoting her energies to the polite conversations of English society, Florence decided to follow the gospel message of caring for the sick by working in the dirty hospitals of England, which were filled with disease and death. In order to prepare herself for her vocation, she left Anglican England to attend a new medical training school established by a Lutheran pastor in Germany. From there she went to Paris and Rome to learn the techniques of Catholic sisters who administered hospitals. Although a member of the Anglican religion herself, she had no qualms about accepting the ideas of other religions that would enhance her mission.

Florence is best known for her dedicated and competent service to the soldiers during the Crimean War. One of the English nurses who went with her, Sarah Anne, wrote about the conditions of the British military hospital in Turkey. Her words are recorded by Robert Richardson:

> These wards were at this time very unfit for use. The roof let in water; the windows were rickety, and were sometimes blown in on dying men; the broken windows were stuffed with rags—everything looked deplorable and depressing . . . . One poor dying fellow, called Nicols, seemed to be neglected by the orderlies because he was dying. He was very dirty, covered with wounds, and devoured by lice. I pointed this out to the orderlies, whose only excuse was—"It's not worth while to clean him; he's not long for this world." I washed his face and hands, cut away his hair, and tried to make him a little less uncomfortable . . . . His flannel shirt was dark, and seemed moving with lice, it stuck into his bed-sores . . . . Daily we saw men carried in whose state of filth no words can describe, and with death written on their discoloured faces.
>
> *Richardson, 87*

Florence and her nurses transformed this hospital from a death-dealing trap to a life-giving oasis. Under her capable administration, the death rate decreased from 36 percent to 5.2 percent in one year (Richardson, 48). Jealous doctors and bureaucrats made life difficult for her as she increased her efforts to reform the medical profession. Her love for God overflowed to her love for the soldiers, whom she considered worthy of nursing back to health. This idea conflicted with the attitudes of the military men, who found the wounded soldiers no longer useful parts of their war machine. When her humanitarian efforts were blocked by the military as well as the medical profession, Florence appealed directly to the queen of England, and the queen supported her efforts.

After the war, Nightingale established a school for nurses in England. The graduates were expected to train others in the medical practices that would alleviate suffering and restore life. Her vision continued through these dedicated women, whose efforts transformed the nursing profession.

Florence was acquainted with many of the medieval female mystics and was attracted to the female English mystic Julian of Norwich. Her own experience of God seemed to fill her with the energy to spread that loving experience to others by helping them to attain the unity and harmony that she had known. She performed her service so inspiringly that the beneficiaries were stimulated to do likewise.

Missionaries

Protestant missionaries traveled all over the world, sponsored by the women's missionary groups in each of their churches. Single women found in foreign missions activity an alternative to teaching or nursing at home. Helen Montgomery reports about the activities of a Methodist missionary to India, Isabella Thoburn:

> We have found sickness and poverty to relieve, widows to protect, advice to be given in every possible difficulty or emergency, teachers and Bible women to be trained, houses to be built, cattle and horses to be bought, gardens to be planted and accounts to be rendered.
>
> *Montgomery, 175*

Many Protestant missionaries accepted the challenge to do missionary service, which enabled them to develop their talents in worthwhile activities and improve the position of other women all over the world. In the early twentieth century, rules forbidding the ordination of women in the mainline Protestant churches barred the full participation of women. Creative and talented women prepared themselves for other church roles and served, for example, as trained religious educators, social workers, and youth directors. Because these women were educated, they could demand a salary commensurate with their background.

World War II blurred gender roles in both Europe and the United States. Harvard and Yale Interdenominational Divinity Schools began to accept women as seminarians in the 1950s with the intention of ordination. Many Protestant denominations have ordained women ministers since the 1950s to serve their churches in full and assistant leadership capacities. Recently the Anglican and Episcopal churches have ordained women to the priesthood, and the latter group has allowed women to become bishops.

The efforts and talents of generous, dedicated women are being recognized as they arrive at full participation in their churches. Some women wonder if the female ministers, priests, and bishops will adapt pliantly to their patriarchal churches or use their power to transform these institutions to more egalitarian organizations that serve the interests of all their members.

Islam Tradition

Medieval Islam

The outstanding Islamic women described here were either examples of the ideal Muslim woman as promoted by the fundamentals of Islam or women who skirted the official structures to arrive at union with Allah through mystical techniques. Fatima, a daughter of Mohammed, is held up as a model of ideal behavior for women. Rabiah is called a saint because of her extraordinary powers, which arose out of her mystical experience.

Fatima

Fatima was the daughter of Mohammed who survived her brothers. In the early seventh century she married the heroic Ali, from whom the Shiite Muslims trace their heritage. Her two sons, Hasan and Husain, were martyred for their faith. She should have derived her fame from her role as their mother, but the contemporary Iranian writer, Roma Chaudhuri, says that Fatima had an identity in herself rather than deriving it from her sons.

> The value of Mary lies with Jesus Christ whom she delivered and nourished. The value of Assiyeh, the wife of Pharaoh lies with Moses, whom she nourished and befriended. The value of Khadyih lies with Mohammed whom she befriended and with Fatima whom she gave birth to and nourished.
> And the value of Fatima? What can I say? To whom does her value belong? To Khadyh? To Mohammed? To Ali? To Hosein? To herself!
>
> *Chaudhuri, 165*

Fatima has been revered for her loyalty to Mohammed's teaching and her patient suffering after the deaths of her husband and sons. She can serve as an intercessor for the faithful even today among the Shiites. Saadia Chishti, who writes on female spirituality in Islam, depicts Fatima as a heroine who is remembered fourteen centuries after her death (according to the Muslim calendar). "The Muslims unanimously recognize her as the fountainhead of female spirituality in Islam, because she occupied herself with the purity of the Oneness and Unity of God, and was confirmed in her absolute sincerity in the beliefs and tenets of Islam" (Chishti, 207).

Rabia

Rabia (Rabe'a) lived in the eighth century CE and gained prominence by embracing the mystical life. She is an extraordinary example of Sufi mysticism, in which the aspirant seeks God in a disinterested way that avoids all selfish desires. She rid herself of the motives of hope for heaven in her love for God and cast away her fear of punishment for sin. Instead she sought a pure love that needed no rewards. Her disinterested love led her to practice voluntary poverty, which deprived her of her physical comforts but cleansed her heart of all selfish desires, turning it toward God alone. Rabia embraced the Sufi teaching of gratitude, in which one thanks God not only for prosperity but for adversity as well. Her love for God was an all-absorbing love, for which she prepared with deep asceticism and self-control.

Left an orphan at an early age, Rabia learned self-control after being sold into slavery. Her master noted her mystical tendencies: When he watched her at prayer one night, he saw a lighted lamp appear over her head that illumined the whole room. Immediately he set her free, and she went to the desert to live in quiet solitude and meditation. Her reputation for holiness spread because she combined her mystical prayer with actions of unselfishness and sacrifice for others. Numerous influential suitors offered proposals for marriage along with imposing dowries, but she refused them all, choosing to live a celibate life of union with God.

One of the stories told about Rabia illustrates her love for God, which was so strong that she had no interest in human love. Hasan was a friend who often spoke with her.

> "Do you desire for us to get married?" Hasan asked Rabe'a.
> "The tie of marriage applies to those who have being," Rabe'a
> replied. "Here being has disappeared, for I have become naughted to self and exist only through Him. I belong wholly to Him. I live in the shadow of His control. You must ask my hand of Him, not of me."
> "How did you find this secret, Rabe'a?" Hasan asked.
> "I lost all 'found' things in Him," Rabe'a answered.
> "How do you know Him?" Hasan enquired.
> "You know the 'how'; I know the 'howless,'" Rabe'a said.
>
> *Attar, 46*

A woman mystic was not always respected by the men of Islam. She had to defend her position to skeptics, who questioned her abilities because of her sex.

> A party of men once visited her to put her to the test, desiring to catch her out in an unguarded utterance.
> "All the virtues have been scattered upon the heads of men," they said. "The crown of prophethood has been placed on men's heads. The belt of nobility has been fastened around men's waists. No woman has ever been a prophet."
> "All that is true," Rabe'a replied. "But egoism and selfworship and 'I am your Lord, the Most High' have never sprung from a woman's breast. No woman has ever been a hermaphrodite. All these things have been the specialty of men."
>
> *Attar, 48*

Rabia's prayers are well known for a mystical quality that stressed her detachment from all worldly goods and heavenly rewards.

> O God, whatsoever Thou hast apportioned to me of worldly things, do Thou give that to Thy enemies; and whatsoever Thou hast apportioned to me in the world to come, give that to Thy friends; for Thou sufficest me.
>
> O God, if I worship Thee for fear of hell, burn me in Hell, and if I worship Thee in hope of Paradise, exclude me from Paradise; but if I worship Thee for Thy own sake, grudge me not Thy everlasting beauty.
>
> O God, my whole occupation and all my desire in this world, of all worldly things, is to remember Thee, and in the world to come, of all things of the world to come, is to meet Thee. This is on my side, as I have stated; now do Thou whatsoever Thou wilt.
>
> *Attar, 51*

Roma Chaudhuri, a professor from India, describes Rabia's fame.

> Rabia died in 801 CE and was buried in Basra. Her last hours were worthy of her long, dedicated life of constant prayer and union with God. Calm and unafraid, she surrendered herself completely to her Beloved, and was welcomed by Him to Life Eternal.
>
> *Chaudhuri, 262*

Rabia is an example of a woman who bypassed the traditional religious structures to achieve union with God through the mystical states. She was loyal to the Sufi tradition of mysticism and holiness of life, but she was unable to exempt herself from the numerous restrictions placed on women by patriarchal Islam. She is an example to Muslim women who wish to seek an alternative to the traditional lifestyle designated for them by Muslim law.

Contemporary Islam

Benazir Bhutto

One of the ways that women can rise to power and contribute to their religious traditions is to be associated with a powerful man. In some cases widows carry on the work of their dead husbands, arrive at their own identity, and gain respect for their own contributions to their religious communities. Another method that women use to gain prominence is the legacy of a powerful father. If violence and chaos have robbed the family of vigorous male representation, sometimes a daughter can replace her father's influence.

In 1988 Benazir Bhutto became the first prime minister of a Muslim county when at age 35 she was elected to that office in Pakistan. Born in 1953 in Karachi, Pakistan, she was the daughter of Pakistan's late ruler Zulfikor Ali-Bhutto.

Her wealthy father sent her to America for schooling at Harvard (Radcliffe College), where she graduated cum laude with a degree in government. Before leaving home for America, her father had spoken of her debt to the people of Pakistan, "of a debt you can use to repay God's blessing by using your education to better their lives" (Bhutto, 1988, 12). She went on to Oxford University, her father's alma mater, with plans to join his regime in the foreign service upon her return to Pakistan. Her plans were thwarted by the execution of her father at the hands of the new military dictator. Before he died, Bhutto visited him in his cell and heard his parting words, "My daughter, should anything happen to me, promise me you will continue my mission" (Bhutto, 1988, 22). She took his mission very seriously and, with her mother, replaced him as head of his Pakistan People's Party. She and her mother were jailed, where she suffered physically from an ear infection that was denied treatment. She was finally sent into exile for medical treatment.

Bhutto writes of her father using the term *shakeed*, which means a martyr for Islam. In the Muslim state of Pakistan, religion and politics are so closely tied that a dead political hero or leader may be considered a martyr for the faith. Bhutto campaigned for office with the image of her martyred father in the background of all of her campaign pictures. As she said in *The Way Out*,

> The same dedicated workers whose courage is higher than the mountains and whose dedication is deeper than the oceans are even now ready to come forward and to sacrifice, inspired by Shaheed Bhutto and in the manner of sacrifice known only to the political descendants of Muslim Martyrs.
>
> *Bhutto, 1988, 34*

Bhutto's campaign was successful in spite of the opposition from Muslim religious scholars, who argued that a woman, especially a Western-educated woman, should never rule over men or lead an Islamic state. *Time* claimed, "Bhutto's installation which ended years of military domination was the most peaceful transition to democracy in Pakistan's politically troubled history" ("Now the Hard Part," 40). Even with clerical opposition of the mullahs, Benazir Bhutto, who headed her father's Pakistan's People's Party, captured voters' imagination by promises of freedom, prosperity, education, and improved conditions for women.

After her election Bhutto tried to conform to Muslim customs of wearing the veil and consenting to an arranged marriage. She cited family, religious, and political considerations as the basis for her decision, saying that Western-style dating would be inappropriate for a Muslim woman, especially in her position as leader of a Muslim party. Her supporters agreed that marriage would give her respectability and freedom of movement that single women cannot enjoy in Pakistan.

Her term of office was plagued by rumors of corruption, and her husband was jailed for backing a plot to extort $800,000 from a businessman based in Britain. Her real opponents appeared to be the fundamentalist Muslims who thought that women should stay enclosed in their homes. The religious affairs minister, a mullah, Mr. Niazi, called her an infidel "who is liable for the death penalty" because she opposed him on his plan to replace some of Pakistan's national laws with the Islamic religious law ("Nearer, My God, to Theocracy," 38). She also opposed his proposal to make the Quran and the sayings of Mohammed, the *sunna*, into the supreme law of the land. Replying to Mr. Niazi, Bhutto said

> "I believe in the Koran and *sunna* but the law of God should not be subordinated to that framed by hand-picked individuals from the *sharia* court. The government has ganged up with the mullahs to kill me." The next day Mr. Niazi backtracked. "I never said she should be killed," he said.
>
> *Economist (September 5, 1992): 38*

Twenty months after her installation, Benazir Bhutto was removed from office, but she made history as an educated and competent woman who could wisely lead an Islamic state. She constantly had to validate her father's legacy, adapt to Islamic laws that hampered her work, and confront religious leaders. In spite of all the obstacles, she left the example that a peaceful transition of government was a possibility that was worth the cost.

Summary

Although most religious traditions have kept women in subservient or marginal positions, some women have made significant contributions to their religions and to society. Some have served as role models for other women, as in the appearances of Kuan-yin in China. The Iroquois Indians from New York state and southern Ontario are role models for an egalitarian society that uses the gifts of women to create religious rituals. By searching their sacred writings, Hindu women find the respect given to Gargi, a model of female intelligence. Jewish women do the same to find the respect given to Miriam for her prophetic abilities and to Deborah for her wisdom. Christians see in their scriptures exemplary women from the early church who appeared to act in cultural and prophetic manners equal to men.

One of the benefits that women can derive from their religious tradition is the example of groups of women working together. Ruth's bonding to Naomi provides a striking example of the good that many Jewish women have sought to emulate through their religious organizations. Buddhist and Roman Catholic nuns, together in religious communities, exemplify the good that can be obtained through the group effort of dedicated women. The establishment of orders of nuns has also given women an alternative to marriage that releases them from the single option of life as wife and mother.

One of the characteristics of these outstanding women was their courage to challenge the status quo of their religious traditions. Ma Jnanananda stepped out of her role as passive observer in Hinduism to take on the esteemed role of guru. Catherine of Siena had the nerve to confront a pope and convinced him to return to his rightful position. Brigit of Ireland was the abbess of male and female monasteries. Protestant missionaries left the comfort of their homes and protection of their families to pass on the Christian message in foreign countries. Rabia dared to assume the role of a mystic in Islam.

Social work provided an outlet for the creative energies of many religious women. Berta Pappenheim nurtured Jewish children in Europe. Dorothy Day provided for the homeless in the United States. The sick soldiers of the Crimean war as well as the whole nursing profession benefitted from the unselfish service of Florence Nightingale. Motivated by personal piety, the Grimké sisters worked for the abolition of slavery before the Civil War in America.

Some women found help in their endeavors from husbands and fathers. Sarada Devi followed in the footsteps of her husband to act as guru and spiritual advisor to his followers. Benazir Bhutto claimed the legacy of her father to help her ascend to high political office in Islamic Pakistan. These women had to overcome the obstacles placed before them by their patriarchal religious traditions in order to excel in whatever mission they determined themselves called by God. As gurus, founders, mystics, saints, teachers, or social workers, the ideals of their religious traditions were reflected in their lives. The inner power of holiness that manifested itself in the direct experience of the ultimate overshadowed the patriarchal power inherent in institutional structures and practices.

Women researchers are adding to the body of knowledge of past and contemporary women, who integrated their own experience with the ideals of their religious beliefs in order to provide more satisfying lives for themselves and others.

Questions for Discussion

1. Why do women in patriarchal religions find it difficult to adopt the cooperative aspects of the Iroquois Indian longhouse rituals?
2. How do Hindu women cope with the patriarchal concepts that say they must return in the next life as a man before they can achieve mosha?
3. Why must women use their own experience when relating to religious scriptures and rituals?
4. Why did the lives of Buddhist nuns seem so attractive to Asian women?
5. Why do we know so little about Miriam and so much more about her brothers, Moses and Aaron?
6. How do Deborah and Jael exemplify the gift of prophecy rather than the cultic office of the official Hebrew religion?
7. What is the relation of Ruth to contemporary Jewish women?
8. What happened to change the position of women from full participation in the early Christian church to their secondary positions of today?
9. Why were medieval women saints extolled for their virginity?
10. How do contemporary Christian women cope with discrimination in their churches?
11. How can the newly empowered women in ministry change the structures of their patriarchal churches?
12. How do the women of Islam skirt some traditional rules but at the same time become models for emulation?

Works Cited

Altekar, A. S. *The Position of Women in Hindu Civilization*. Delhi: Motilal Banarsidass, 1956.

[Annals of Ireland.] Annala Rioghachta Eireann, trans. John O'Donovan. Dublin: Hodges, Smith, 1854.

Attar, Farid al-Din, *Muslim Saints and Mystics*. Trans. A. S. Arberry. London: Routledge & Kegan Paul, 1973.

Barnes, Gilbert, and Dwight Dumond, eds. *Letters of Theodore Dwight Weld, Angelina Grimké Weld and Sarah Grimké 1822–1844*, 2 vols. New York: Appleton–Century, 1904.

Bhutto, Benazir. *The Way Out: Interviews, Impressions, Statements and Messages*. Mahmood Publications, 1988.

———. *Daughter of the East*. New York: Simon & Schuster, 1990.

Campbell, Debra. "The Catholic Earth Mother." In *Unspoken Worlds*, ed. Nancy Auer Falk and Rita M. Gross. Belmont, Calif.: Wadsworth, 1989.

Carroll, Theodora Foster. *Women, Religion and Development in the Third World*. New York: Praeger, 1983.

Chaudhuri, Mrs. Roma "Rabia" Ghanananda, Swami, and Sir John Stewart-Wallace, eds. *Women Saints, East and West*. Hollywood, Calif.: Vedanta Press, 1955.

Chishti, Saadia, and Khawar Khan. "Female Spirituality in Islam." In *Islamic Spirituality Foundation*, ed. S. H. Nasr. New York: Crossroads, 1987.

Du Pre Lumpkin, Katherine. *The Emancipation of Angelina Grimké*. Chapel Hill, N.C.: University of North Carolina Press, 1974.

Freeman, Lucy. *The Story of Anna O*. New York: Walker, 1972.

Geiger, Wilhelm, ed. *The Culavamsa*. London: Luzac, 1980.

Ghanananda, Suami. "Sri Sarada Devi the Holy Mother." In *Women Saints East and West*, ed. Swami Ghanananda and Sir John Stewart-Wallace. Hollywood, Calif.: Vedanta Press, 1955.

Grimké, Sarah. "Province of Women: The Pastoral Letter," *The Liberator* (October 6, 1837).

Handoo, Chandra. "Women Saints of Buddhism in India." In *Women Saints East and West*, ed. Swami Ghanananda and Sir John Stewart-Wallace. Hollywood, Calif.: Vedanta Press, 1955.

Irvin, Dorothy. "Archeology Supports Women's Ordination," *The Witness* 63, no. 2 (February 1980).

Kaplan, Marion. "Jewish Women in Imperial Germany." In *Jewish Women in Historical Perspective*, ed. Judith Baskin. Detroit: Wayne State University Press, 1991.

Kinsley, David. *Hinduism: A Cultural Perspective*. Englewood Cliffs, N.J.: Prentice Hall, 1992.

Lerner, Gerta. *The Grimké Sisters from South Carolina*. New York: Schocken, 1971.

Lives of the Saints from the Book of Lismore. Anecdota Oconiensia Medieval and Modern Series 5. Oxford: Oxford University Press (Clarendon), 1890.

Montgomery, Helen Barrett. *Western Women in Eastern Lands*. New York: Macmillan, 1911.

"Nearer, My God, to Theocracy," *Economist* (September 5, 1992).

The New Jerusalem Bible. Garden City, N.Y.: Doubleday, 1985.

"Now the Hard Part: Governing (Prime Minister Bhutto)," *Time* 132 (December 112, 1988): 47.

Nunnally-Cox, Janice. *Foremothers*. New York: Seabury Press, 1980.

O'Briain, Felime. "Brigide." In *Dictionnaire de Histoire et des Geographie Ecclesiastique*, ed. Alfred Bowdrillart. Paris: Letouzey, 1935.

Radhakrishna, Sri, ed. and trans. *The Principal Upanishads*. London: George–Allen, 1953.

Richardson, Robert, ed. *Nurse Sarah Anne with Florence Nightingale at Scutari*. London: John Murray, 1977.

Ruether, Rosemary, and Eleanor McLaughlin. *Women of Spirit*. New York: Simon and Schuster, 1979.

Shariati, Ali. *Fatima Is Fatima*. Trans. Laleh Bakhtiyar. Tehran: Shariati Foundation, 1980.

Sri Sarada Devi, The Holy Mother. Madras: Ramakrishna Math.

Topley, Marjorie. "Marriage Resistance in Rural Kwangtung." In *Women in Chinese Society*. Stanford, Calif.: Stanford University Press, 1975.

White, Charles. "Mother Guru: Jnanananda of Madras, India." In *Unspoken Worlds*, ed. Nancy Auer Falk and Rita M. Gross. Belmont, Calif.: Wadsworth, 1989.

Suggested Readings

Albers, Patricia, and Beatrice Medicine (Lakota). *The Hidden Half: Studies of Plains Indian Women*. Lanham, Md.: University Press of America, 1983.

Andrews, Lynn V. *Medicine Woman*. New York: Harper & Row, 1981.

Banner Lois W. *American Beauty*. New York: Knopf, 1983.

———. *Women in Modern America: A Brief History*. New York: Harcourt Brace Jovanovich, 1974.

Barker-Benfield, G. J. *The Horrors of the Half-known Life: Male Attitudes Toward Women and Sexuality in Nineteenth Century America*. New York: Harper & Row, 1976.

Beane, Wendell Charles. *Myth, Cult and Symbol in Sakta Hinduism: A Study of the Indian Mother Goddess*. Leiden: Brill, 1977.

Bennett, Lynn. *Dangerous Wives and Sacred Sisters: Social and Symbolic Roles of High-Caste Women in Nepal*. New York: Columbia University Press, 1983.

Berkin, Carol Ruth, and Mary Beth Norton. *Women of America: A History*. Boston: Houghton Mifflin, 1979.

Bernard, Jessie. *The Female World*. New York: The Free Press, 1981.

Bernikow, Louise. *Among Women*. New York: Crown Publishers, 1980.

Bordin, Ruth. *Woman and Temperance: The Quest for Power and Liberty 1873–1900*. Philadelphia: Temple University Press, 1981.

Cameron, Anne. *Daughters of Copper Woman*. Vancouver, B.C.: Press Gang, 1981.

Chafe, William H. *The American Woman: Her Changing Social, Economic and Political Roles 1920–1970*. New York: Oxford University Press, 1972.

Christ, Carol P., and Judith Plaskow, eds. *Womanspirit Rising: A Feminist Reader in Religion*. New York: Harper & Row, 1979.

Conrad, Susan Phinney. *Perish the Thought: Intellectual Women in Romantic America 1830–1860*. New York: Oxford University Press, 1976.

Deloria, Vine Jr. (Lakota). *God Is Red*. New York: Grosset and Dunlap, 1973.

Douglas, Ann. *The Feminization of American Culture*. New York: Knopf, 1977.

Dubois, Ellen Carol. *Feminism and Suffrage: The Emergence of an Independent Women's Movement in America 1848–1869*. Ithaca, N.Y.: Cornell University Press, 1978.

Epstein, Barbara Leslie. *The Politics of Domesticity: Women, Evangelism and Temperance in Nineteenth-Century America*. Middletown, Conn.: Wesleyan University Press, 1981.

Evans, Sarah. *Personal Politics: The Roots of Women's Liberation in the Civil Rights Movement and the New Left*. New York: Knopf, 1979.

Foreman, Carolyn Thomas. *Indian Women Chiefs*. Washington, D.C.: Zenger, 1976.

Green, Rayna. *Native American Women: A Bibliography*. Bloomington, Ind.: Indiana University Press, 1983.

Hori, Ichiro. *Folk Religion in Japan*. Chicago: University of Chicago Press, 1968.

Kingston, Maxine Hong. *The Woman Warrior: Memories of a Girlhood Among Ghosts*. New York: Vintage Books, 1977.

Morgan, Robin, ed. *Sisterhood Is Powerful: An Anthology of Writings from the Women's Liberation Movement*. New York: Random House, 1970.

Mullet, G. M. *Spider Woman Stories: Legends of the Hopi Indians*. Tucson: University of Arizona Press. 1979.

Nash, S. H., ed. *Islamic Spirituality: Foundations*. New York: Crossroads, l987.

Niehammer, Carolyn. *Daughters of the Earth: The Lives and Legends of American Indian Women*. New York: Collier, 1977.

Porterfield, Amanda. *Feminine Spirituality in America: From Sarah Edwards to Martha Graham*. Philadelphia: Temple University Press, 1980.

Ruether, Rosemary Radford, and Rosemary Skinner Keller, eds. *Women and Religion in America*. 3 vols. New York: Harper & Row, 1981.

Smith, Jane, ed. *Women in Contemporary Muslim Societies*. Lewisburg, Pa.: Bucknell University Press, 1980.

Spretnak, Charlene, ed. *The Politics of Women's Spirituality*. Garden City, N.Y.: Doubleday, 1982.

Swidler, Leonard. *Women in Judaism*. Metuchen, N.J.: Scarecrow Press, 1976.

Tavard, George. *Women in the Christian Tradition*. Notre Dame, Ind.: University of Notre Dame Press, 1985.

Upadhyaya, Bhagwat Saran. *Women in Rgveda*. New Delhi: S. Chand, 1974.

Vicinus, Martha. *Suffer and Be Still: Women in the Victorian Age*. Bloomington, Ind.: Indiana University Press, 1972.

Witherington, Ben. *Women in the Ministry of Jesus*. Cambridge: Cambridge University Press, 1984.

Yang, C. K. *Religion in Chinese Society*. Berkeley: University of California Press, 1970.

CHAPTER 6

Language As a Representation of Reality

Reality is communicated to individuals through language, the instrument necessary for humans to communicate and to record the ideas and events in their lives. Without language humans' relationship with the sacred being and one another could not be conveniently ensured. People's sense of self is enhanced or diminished by the words and images communicated to them by others through language. If people receive encouragement and support through the comments of others, their self-esteem will be enhanced. Derogatory remarks will induce debilitating effects on the personality.

When speaking of the sacred, humans are especially challenged to find appropriate language to describe a reality that is composed of opposite concepts, such as transcendence and immanence. The contrasting attributes of personal and impersonal become problematic in our attempts to name the sacred. Because the inclusion of women's experience has been neglected in contemporary descriptions of the sacred, this chapter examines recent attempts at gender-inclusive language by monotheistic faith communities.

Language is central to our construction of reality. Not only do we view reality through language, but we need the symbol system of words to interpret the meaning of our existence. The words often describe images that contribute to our understanding of the categories and concepts that make our reality comprehensible. The meaning of the words, categories, and concepts are influenced by the society that produces them.

If the society is patriarchal, the words reflect the dualistic thinking that assigns lesser and greater designations for each category. Thomas Groome says "the historical evidence is that gender exclusive language originated and was intended to maintain the connection that men are superior to women and are the natural norms of humanity" (8). Thomas Wilson, an English grammarian, indicated in 1503 that male superiority should be demonstrated by always naming men before women, as in *man and wife*. A

century later Joshua Poole, another English grammarian, said the male terminology has "pride of place" in language because the male gender is the
worthier one. The English Parliament recognized the use of language to
reinforce male power by passing a law in 1850 decreeing that *he* legally
stands for *he and she*.

In patriarchal societies religious writers use language to justify the superior position of men by also designating the deity as male. Because the male
person reflects the male deity, male superiority is justified. Mary Daly, a feminist theologian, explains this concept by declaring that in the Judeo-
Christian tradition, "God is male and male is God" (1). She says that this
means men are viewed as taking on the characteristics of God, whereas
women possess the lesser characteristics of humans.

One of the most critical elements of language is the terminology used in
a society's religious myths. Myths explain reality to the members of its culture, so the words used for metaphors and images have lasting effects on
the religious community and the whole society. Mythological stories help
humans explain events that they normally cannot understand. Creation stories are told to help humans understand their origins or to give them identity as individuals or a group. For example, the Hopi Indians tell a myth that
describes the formation of tribal identity. They relate the process that divided humans into the many tribes in the southwest United States.

> After Spider Woman had bent her wise, all seeing eyes upon the thronging
> creatures about her, she wound her way among them, separating them into
> groups. "Thus and thus shall you be and thus shall you remain, each one in
> her own tribe forever. You are Zunis, you are Kohoninos, you are Pah-
> Utes. . . .
>
> *Lemming, 38*

One feels secure in an identity that is dispensed by a deity, especially if
the designation is given a specific name. The name acquires a special significance to the group or individual bearing it. Sometimes the myths are short-
ened to become extended metaphors. The myth that some college professors and students remain aloof from the problems of the real world is realized in such metaphors as "ivory tower" or "egghead." The very identity of a
school whose myths depict it as athletically inclined takes on the title of a
"jock school." If the students are considered to spend more time partying
than studying, the title "party school" is applied. When the myth surrounding the school emphasizes scholars and study, the school is often called a
"brain school" by the creators of metaphors.

Psychology as well as religion has made use of myths to identify humans
and their relationships. Psychologists such as Sigmund Freud have used the
Greek myths to name aspects of personality, as in Freud's so-called Oedipus
and Elektra complexes. The names *Oedipus* and *Elektra* became extended
metaphors to name parent fixations in the field of psychology. Carl Jung is
recognized for his use of myths to arrive at his theory of the collective

unconscious and archetypes. By studying the patterns of myths from various cultures, Jung found common themes that he believed help humans adjust to their society.

Myths and extended metaphors have the power to elevate or degrade persons, institutions, and societies. Whoever has the power to create the metaphor or the myth possesses great authority in a society. The persons of influence usually name buildings, streets, parks, and ceremonies, for example, that are used by the larger population. Religious authorities name the deities and construct the myths and metaphors that make these deities relevant to the populace. If the myths constantly extol the male members of the society as so many hero and quest myths do, it is likely that the male members of that society will gain prominence. If women are ignored or become marginal in the religious myths, their position in their religious communities will often reflect that situation. If the metaphor used for the deity is always masculine, women may feel excluded from full participation in that religion. Because myths and metaphors help to form one's identity, it is difficult for a woman to integrate herself favorably when she cannot identify with a male god. If the maleness of God is constantly reinforced by personal pronouns that refer to God as *he* or *him*, the difference between the woman and God is widened.

Language metaphors are usually resistant to change. Persons in religious authority who have charge of the myths and metaphors are rarely eager to change the instruments that give them their power. To change the religious myths may be unacceptable to the followers of the tradition, but to change some of the metaphors for the deity may enhance the self-awareness and identity of the members who perceive themselves as excluded from their religious organization. The deity may sometimes be referred to in feminine terms or neuter forms in the English language. Religious ceremonies, books, and rituals could contain language that would be more inclusive of all its members.

Some of our myths have adjusted to the changing times. Science has added many insights to our knowledge of natural forces, so we no longer talk about a god of thunder to explain the sounds made by storms. Science has also given us a new myth for the creation of the universe. The big bang theory is now gaining prominence over previous scientific myths that depicted the origin of the earth, such as earth flying off the tail of a comet. In a recent myth advocated by scientist Thomas Berry, earth is considered a part of the universe that exploded from a primeval fireball. Not only do the myths change, but metaphors evolve that are contained in the myth.

Adherents of religious myths who are reluctant to change the story are sometimes willing to change the metaphor. If the metaphor for the deity is always masculine, they may accept making the metaphors more gender inclusive. The myth of the macho man so prevalent in some Caribbean cultures, for example, is giving way as society sees a more egalitarian relationship evolve between the sexes. The myth of the husband as sole breadwinner in many cultures is being replaced as the participation of both partners becomes necessary to the economic well-being of the family. The metaphors of macho man and male breadwinner are no longer considered the ideals in changing societies. Likewise, metaphors for the deity no longer have to be exclusively male in religious institutions that see a need to adapt to changing times.

Language develops in a social situation that contributes to our sense of self and our relation to the community. If the community is strongly patriarchal, the words enforce the domination of men over women. Feminine theologians point out that women internalize the values of the patriarchal society when they repeatedly mouth the words that exclude them. If their prayers and rituals constantly emphasize a male god, women will come to feel devalued because they are forced to use language that represents a reality that does not relate to their experience.

Naming the Sacred— Transcendence Versus Immanence

Theologians recognize that the sacred transcends all human categories, so all references to it must be metaphorical and all definitions provisional. "The dilemma of religious language is that categories for speaking of the sensible world of material bodies and persons are inadequate for speaking of the ultimate that transcends all categories" (Gilkey, 290–91). The sacred remains a mystery that words and definitions can neither encompass nor exhaust.

In its totally other, different-from-us aspect, the sacred is often referred to as transcendent. This mysterious other can be revealed to humans as it manifests itself in the experience of the religious community. Some tribal religions meet the awesome power of the sacred transcendent in volcanoes, thunder, fire, and tidal waves. The Israelites saw the transcendent power of God in the cloud that led them through the desert by day and in the pillar of fire by night. The early Christians felt the power of the Holy Spirit manifested as fire and wind at Pentecost. Although the power of the Tao is more passive, it is experienced as the cause of all that is. Buddhists experience the sudden insight of nirvana, although they do not try to explain or interpret this contact with the ultimate. Since the sacred in the form of the transcendent is so different from us, no human words, concepts, or categories can adequately describe it.

Writers of religious literature usually have been men, who have often referred to transcendence as power. Power is evident in the philosophical categories devised by men to describe the transcendent God in the Judeo-Christian and Islamic faith communities. Such titles as *all powerful*, *all knowing*, *almighty*, *eternal*, and *omnipresent* ascribe strength and authority to the transcendent one. The sacred writers of the Hindu Vedas described Brahman as the dynamic power that gives energy and strength to all things.

The Quran depicts God as so transcendent that nothing in human experience is commensurable.

> Allah, in One, the Ultimate Source
> He does not give birth, nor was he born (of anyone)
> And there is nothing comparable to Him.
>
> *Quran, Surah 112*

The pronoun *he* is used to depict this indescribable power, although it is beyond all human categories and concepts. The Almighty Allah is so powerful that he commands complete submission from his Muslim followers.

This transcendent power that is so totally other to human experience has the ability to be close to humans and reveal itself to the followers. Peter Berger describes God as "totally other, yet accessible in human experience" (112). Many traditional religions say that the high creator God, who is distant and all powerful, is also present in other spirit beings who reside in sacred places that are accessible to the believer. Jews feel that the totally other God has been present in the ark of the covenant and in Hebrew scriptures. And just as Christians believe the divine power of God became embodied in Christ, the Hindus believe that the creator of all became incarnated in Krishna and Rama. In most religious traditions, the almighty transcendent power can become immanent by permeating the cosmos and dwelling with the devotees. Sometimes the presence penetrates nature or dwells within persons. When trying to illustrate the immanent presence of God, Dag Hammarskjold wrote, "We must learn to pierce the veil of things and comprehend God within" (123). In order to show how close God is to the believer, Saint Teresa of Avila taught that God dwelled in the "deeper center of the soul" (213).

Trying to find words to describe the sacred that will combine the characteristics of immanence and transcendence presents an exciting challenge to theologians. It is difficult to harmonize two opposite concepts in words that lend themselves to human experience. The monotheistic religions have used the words *Allah*, *God* or *G-d.* to name the sacred. Eastern religions combine the transcendent-immanent categories by naming the abstract reality *Brahman*, which manifests itself in the immanent form of gods and goddesses. It is difficult to find a metaphor for the feminine that encompasses the transcendent and immanent characteristics of the divine.

The Sacred As Personal and Impersonal Powers

The multifaceted divine power, which can be transcendent and immanent at the same time, can also assume impersonal or personal dimensions. The impersonal power of Brahman or the Tao is venerated by the Hindus and Taoists, but the devotees often find it necessary to relate to personal powers such as gods and goddesses. Humans communicate best to other humans in images, metaphors, and words that relate to the human condition. But men and women perceive the human condition in different terms and thus relate to it differently.

Nancy Chodorow, a psychologist, notes that men and women differ from each other in personality attributes and the roles they undertake in society. She says there is "a reproduction within each generation of certain general and nearly universal differences that characterize masculine and feminine personality and roles" (43). She does not ascribe these differences to physiology but rather to the involvement of women almost exclusively with early child care. The relationship of the mother to her child is intense and central to most women. A mother sees herself connected to the child and the child to her. These connections extend to other children, the spouse, the parents, the siblings, and everyone that is part of her immediate environment. Soon women perceive themselves as the hub of a web of relationships. Chodorow concludes that "in any given society, feminine personality comes to define itself in relation and connection to other people more than masculine personality does" (44). Chodorow argues that women desire more intimacy or closeness in their relationship with God. They want a God who can be close to them, whose immanent presence they can feel.

Andrew Greeley, a priest sociologist, has similar beliefs about women's view of God. He surveyed practicing Catholic women to determine the reasons they had stayed in their church through the years. He found that most of the women who remained faithful related to God in a personal and intimate manner—as a lover. Women, whose chief concerns (according to Carol Gilligan) revolve around fulfilling their multiple responsibilities toward others, prefer a personal God who emphasizes the nurturing, attentive, protective characteristics consistent with their present needs.

The opposite categories of personal and impersonal also present a challenge when we try to describe the sacred. To portray an entity that is transcendent, impersonal, immanent, and personal at the same time requires a combination of words that do not fit our human language. Therefore we must use figures of speech such as analogies, images, and metaphors to describe a reality that our language cannot encompass.

Metaphoric Images That Enhance Women's Relation to the Sacred

Religious writers define the sacred as "that which is ultimate (nothing greater) and nonordinary (a mysterious, incomparable power)" (Schmidt, 490). Because the sacred is beyond all categories of thought, metaphors illumine our concepts or understandings of one experience in light of another. Metaphors generate new insights, make associations, and appeal to our emotions, all of which make learning more appealing, but they must be critically examined because they are created by the powerful in a society or institution. Just as the dualistic categories of God over humans, spirit over matter, reason over emotions, men over women, and good over evil serve to alienate women, metaphors for the sacred that are exclusively male can reinforce patriarchy.

Philip Wheelwright demonstrates the use of the *up–down* metaphor to show desirability (112). Because up is a more difficult direction to go than down, it is associated with achievement. Images of ascent connote loftiness, excellence, regality, and spirituality. Fires burn upward to give light, just as the heavenly sun gives us illumination and wisdom. The opposite metaphor illustrates falling down into emptiness, ignorance, and loss. In the up–down tension, the sky god of light surpasses in excellence the dark womb of Mother Earth. The male sky god metaphor seems superior to the Mother Earth metaphor, and women are subsequently perceived as the inferior part of the dyad.

Chinese philosophers developed the concept of yin and yang to explain the complementary forces that hold the universe together. The cosmos operates harmoniously as a result of the balance of these two forces. The yin is the negative force that manifests itself in darkness, coolness, moistness, femaleness, the earth, and the moon. The positive force, yang, is seen in lightness, brightness, warmth, dryness, maleness, and the sun. Although no value judgments designate yin as evil and yang as good, in the *Tao Te Ching* the categories themselves reveal a dualism that can suggest inferiority and superiority in a patriarchal society.

The danger of metaphors is that they can be taken literally and inflict their negative connotations on innocent victims. Particularly in dichotomous metaphors that try to inform by contrasting opposites, women are usually shortchanged; the male authors ascribe to them the less desirable characterizations. Aristotle's dualistic schema portrays men admirably as rational and spiritual but calls women emotional and material. Using the metaphor of perfection, Thomas Aquinas tells us that the perfect child is male and the imperfect is female.

One of the metaphors used to describe God is the image of God as parent. The parent image includes mother as well as father, but unless the deity is referred to as mother-father god, as suggested by Elizabeth Cady Stanton a century ago in the *Woman's Bible*, this abstract term does not resonate with the personal presence of God. Rosemary Ruether underscores the negative aspect of the parent metaphor. "It suggests a kind of permanent parent-child relationship to God. God becomes a neurotic parent who does not want us to grow up" (160). Ruether emphasizes the danger in patriarchal societies of modeling one's image of God on the nuclear family because of stereotypical roles assigned to mothers and fathers. Patriarchy extols the role of the father, so the powerful God will mirror him and downplay the importance of the mother. The teachings of Jesus on prayer have influenced the Christian attitude toward God. He addressed God as "Abba," a term that describes the relationship between Jesus and God as an intimate one. Jesus deviated from the style of the Old Testament, or Hebrew Bible, which does not address God directly as father or imply closeness in the passages that do refer to god as a father. The twelve citations that speak of a father in the Hebrew Bible describe the responsibilities between God and the king and the relationship between God and Israel; the speaker does not call God *Father* in the close manner of Jesus' speech.

> Five of the references to God as father concern the special relation of God to the king (2 Sam. 7:14; 1 Chron. 17:13; Ps. 89:26; 1 Chron. 22:10; [and 1 Chron] 28:9) and thus do not apply to the ordinary person. The other seven references (Ps. 103:13; Deut. 32:6; 18 Jer. 3:4–5 [and] 31:9; Isa. 63:16; Mal. 1:6), all refer to God in the context of Israel's sin, repentance and restoration, and God's endless forgiveness.
>
> *Tennis 82–83*

The father metaphor in the New Testament does not represent a patriarchal figure that serves as a model for a patriarchal family. Rather, the father metaphor resembles more closely the father figure in Jesus' parable of the prodigal son. He is a forgiving father who shows patience and compassion toward the erring child, receiving his son back into the family with joyous celebration. Similarly, Jesus chooses imagery of closeness with God, not of God as a powerful patriarch who ruled his family in a formidable fashion.

The prodigal son or forgiving father is the third in a sequence of Jesus' parables that depict images of God in human form. All of these parables stress the loving compassion and forgiveness of God, who seeks out sinners and welcomes them back into the community. The first image, of God as shepherd, refers to either sex. The second image, of the woman who seeks the lost coin, portrays God as a woman. The woman does the same thing as the father of the prodigal son: She seeks out and restores what was lost. There is no reference to patriarchal power or dominating force in these metaphors used by Jesus to image God.

The Old Testament metaphors for God also include the characteristics of motherhood. Deuteronomy 32:18 depicts a "God who gave you birth." God tells Israel that God cherishes people with a mother's love (Isa. 49:15) "As one whom his mother comforts so will I comfort you." (Isa. 66:13). God is compared with a woman in labor, "panting and gasping for air" (Isa. 42:14). However, this metaphor is paired with the image of the warrior God who helps Israel defeat the enemies who worship idols. This mixing of metaphors makes one hesitant to construct idols out of images by taking them literally. It is difficult to justify a patriarchal society that reflects a patriarchal God when the metaphors for God are so multifaceted in the scriptures.

Among the multifaceted images of God that scripture writers have used are inanimate forms such as rock, sun, spring, shield, fortress, and fire.

Writers have compared God, whose voice is like thunder, whose spirit moves like the wind, and whose justice is like a deep ocean, with nonliving realities. Humans have enriched their image of God by calling on the human experience of animals, but some animal metaphors seem to clash when they try to show the various attributes of God. For instance, the raging lion, pouncing panther, fierce leopard, and powerful bear contrast strikingly with the image of a caring God who carries the followers on eagles' wings or protects them like nestlings. Hosea uses animal images as he quotes God lamenting over the ingratitude of the Israelites, whom he brought out of the land of Egypt. God speaks of punishing the Israelites:

> So now I will be like a panther to them,
> I will prowl like a leopard by the wayside,
> I will meet them like a she-bear robbed of her cubs
> and tear their ribs apart.
> Like a lioness I will devour them on the spot,
> I will rip them up like a wild beast.
>
> *Hosea 13:7–8*

God speaks of Godself in animal metaphors when describing the protection or punishment to be given the chosen people. Besides using metaphors from animal life, the scripture writers use metaphors and images from human life such as God as a potter, shepherd, farmer, hero, warrior, judge, midwife, king, husband, woman in labor, and father. God is none of these and yet all of them because God cannot be contained in language.

Even the emotions attributed to God reflect human experience. The scripture writers say that God shows anger, patience, jealousy, generosity, scorn, regret, hatred, and love—the same contradictory feelings that humans express. With such variety in metaphor and images for God, we wonder why most faith communities still address God in exclusively male terms. Female theologians have made creative efforts to devise metaphors for the sacred that would be more inclusive of women in society. They have found it difficult, however, to balance the paradox of immanence and transcendence as it intercepts the characteristics of the personal and impersonal, and yet make it fit the lived experience of humans.

In their search for suitable metaphors for God, Western theologians have identified love as a likely possibility, because men and women can relate to it out of their own experience. Biblical writers have acknowledged this term for their description of God. Writers of Hindu and other non-Western sacred works have included this aspect of love in identifying their deities. Saiva Siddhanta, a school of the South India Vaisnavisna sect, used the phrase "God is Love" before the time of Christian influence in India. Love is a necessary part of our immediate settings as well as in the larger areas of life. Universal principles of human dignity, beauty, peace, and truth challenge everyone to love without discrimination. Love can be both personal and impersonal, depending on the circumstances. Love's inclusiveness encourages the equality of all members of the faith community, in which justice can reign supreme and all people can live in harmony and partnership.

The Struggle for the Use of Inclusive Language in Religious Institutions

Language is considered inclusive when the words affirm the equality and dignity of each person regardless of race, gender, creed, age, or ability. The use of inclusive language was introduced into Western society by the contemporary women's movement. Traditional church members and leaders have often considered the move for inclusive language a cultural movement that should not influence the language of the synagogue or church, which they see as separate entities. Others who recognize the close connection between religion and culture wish to extend the gains made by the women's movement to their churches and synagogues.

Western democracies advocate the education of women. As women have entered educational and occupational fields that were formerly dominated by men, they have found that much of the language failed to recognize them as part of reality. Such designations as spokesman, councilman, upperclassman, and layman ignore the presence of women. The women's movement pressured government agencies to pass laws to ensure the recognition of women through the use of inclusive language. At their request, the U.S. Department of Labor revised its list of occupational classifications by eliminating sex-stereotyped job titles. The state of Connecticut passed a law in 1973 requiring that whenever the title for public office denotes gender, such as *chairman*, *alderman*, or *selectman*, the title should be appropriate to the sex of the person holding the office. Professional women from educational institutions have encouraged major textbook publishers to adopt nonsexist guidelines for their authors.

Women have encountered many problems in trying to transfer the principles of gender-inclusive language to their religious institutions. Church theologians and scripture translators have found it difficult to communicate the religious message in a way that is faithful to the original meaning and at the same time understandable to today's readers. Some of the translators were apprehensive about changing the masculine pronouns because they feared losing the beauty and clarity of the language while adapting it to the lived experience of men and women.

Western churches and synagogues found that they could make some necessary adaptations to the changing social times and began to issue documents that addressed the issue of language. The United Church of Christ voted in the 1973 General Synod to eliminate sex and race discrimination in every area of its practice. The Call to Action Conference, organized by a group of Roman Catholics in 1976, recommended to the National

Conference of Catholic Bishops and Catholic publishing houses that sexist language and imagery be eliminated from all official church documents, catechisms, liturgical books, rites, and hymnals.

Religious institutions have been willing to adapt in what they refer to as horizontal language. When language refers to humans, more gender-inclusive language can easily be substituted for the male terms. For example, in the Nicene creed recited by most Protestants, Roman Catholics, and Eastern Orthodox Catholics, the word *men* has simply been eliminated. It now reads, "For us [men] and for our salvation, he came down from heaven." Most Christian mainline denominations have also adapted the letters from Paul. Letters in which he addresses his audience as "brothers" now address "brothers and sisters." Plural forms of words, such as *theirs*, *ours*, and *them*, have replaced the male pronouns of *his* and *him* when they refer to humans.

However, the language that refers to God, which is often called vertical, is more difficult to adapt. The new Revised Standard Version of the Bible (1991), which is used by all Christian denominations, uses inclusive language for humanity but retains male images for God. Traditional members of religious institutions fear that changing the language for God would change the religious beliefs. Many people consider prayers such as the "Our Father" to be the words of Jesus and do not want to tamper with the words of God. Many believers object to the rendition of the Lord's Prayer from the United Church of Christ, which begins "God, our Father and Mother, who is in the heavens, may your name be made holy." They contend that not only does the prayer lose its majesty and tradition, which has been shared across generations, but the terms *mother* and *father* make God appear dualistic.

Yet history shows that language can be adapted to reflect the changing social needs. Christian language for God had inclusive features from the fifth century. Synesius, a spiritual writer, addresses God as Mother and Father:

> All the world is by Thy counsel . . . Thou art Father, Thou art Mother, Thou art Male and Thou are Female. Thou art Voice and Thou art Silence. Thou art Nature's inmost Nature. Thou art Lord, the Age of Ages.
>
> *Synesius of Cyrene, fifth century, in Gardner, 173*

Julian of Norwich, a renowned mystic, lived in a hermitage outside of a church in England in the fourteenth century. She often referred to God in the gender-inclusive language of mother and father: "As truly as God is our Father, so truly is God our Mother" (295).

In spite of the objections of traditionalists, the National Council of Churches has sought to change the words of scripture without changing the meaning. It is sometimes difficult to keep the natural flow of the language without diminishing its majesty. The original form of the following passage uses the personal pronouns *he* and *him*; in the revision the flow of the language is somewhat impeded.

Original version

> He was in the world, and the world was made through him,
> yet the world knew him not.
> He came to his own home, and his own people received him
> not.
>   *John 1:10–11, Revised Standard Version Bible*

Revision

The Word was in the world, and the world was made through the Word, yet the world did not know the Word. The Word came to the Word's own home, but those to whom the Word came did not receive the Word.
John 1:10–11, National Council of Churches inclusive language version, 1983

The United Church of Christ includes Mother and Father for God and refers to Jesus Christ as child rather than son in its attempt at inclusive language.

Original version

Go therefore and make disciples of all nations, baptizing them in the name of the Father and of the Son and of the Holy Spirit.
Matthew 28:19, New Revised Standard Version Bible 1991

Revision

Go therefore and make disciples of all nations, baptizing them in the name of God the Father and Mother and of Jesus Christ the beloved Child and of the Holy Spirit.
The Gospels and the Letters of Paul

In its *Guidelines for Inclusive Language* for the prayer of the faithful, which Catholics say at the daily liturgies, the Roman Catholic Church has suggested this adaptation for its invitation to prayer:

Original version

Let us Pray to the Father, who, through the Holy Spirit, has given life to Jesus, his Son, and has made him a source of life for us.

Revision

Let us pray to our Loving Creator, who, through the Holy Spirit, has given life to Jesus the Christ, the source of life for us.

Jews have changed the wording in psalms and prayers to avoid gender insensitivity by using impersonal pronouns that can reflect both sexes. The Central Conference of American Rabbis in 1988 adapted Psalm 15:

Original

> God, which man may abide in your house?
> What men may dwell in your holy mountain?

The man who is upright, the man who acts
justly and the men who speak truth within
their hearts.

Revision

God, who may abide in your house,
Who may dwell on your holy mountain?
Those who are upright; who do justly; who
speak the truth within their hearts.

Religious hymns, which occupy much of Christian church ritual, have also been adapted in their use of pronouns for God:

Original

God moves in a mysterious way, His wonders to perform;
He plants his footsteps in the sea, And rides upon the storm.

William Cowper, 1774

Revision

O God, in a mysterious way Great wonders You perform;
You plant Your footsteps in the sea, And ride upon the storm.

Presbyterian Hymnal, 1990

The *People's Mass Book* (World Library of Sacred Music, 1984) used by Roman Catholics has changed the hymn "Good Christian Men, Rejoice" to "Good Christian Friends, Rejoice."

Adaptation in rituals, prayers, hymns, blessing, and readings that are being made by the responsible church bodies accommodate the interests of all people. Women's groups have asked official church bodies to remove sexist language and have written to publishers of song books requesting nonsexist songs. The women's movement has helped to raise the consciousness of many religious groups to the harm of sexist language, which divides and alienates groups of the population. Contemporary women have been instrumental in changing the exclusive language in their Western religious traditions to include all of their members and to recognize all members' presence and gifts.

Summary

Language is crucial to the development of a person's self concept because it has the power to affirm or alienate the individual's relations with others in the community. In a patriarchal society that uses dualistic categories for building concepts, women are usually portrayed in an inferior position. It is an easy step for women to internalize this subordinate position when the exclusive use of male images for the deity makes maleness appear normative. If all religious myths and metaphors emphasize the attributes of a male deity, women feel devalued because they are forced to use language that represents a reality that excludes them and their experience.

The challenge to find words that adequately describe the deity is difficult because the sacred encompasses the opposing characteristics of transcendence and immanence with impersonal and personal aspects. The transcendent characteristic gives the deity or the sacred an identity in itself, whereas the immanent dimension designates its relation to humanity. The deity also has an impersonal aspect—similar to a force or energy—that gives it power to create and sustain. The personal quality allows members of the faith community to describe the sacred in human language suitable to their own experience. Women, who often seem to emphasize relationships, find the personal mode of communication more compatible with their life experience.

Human language does not contain the words necessary to encompass these opposing characteristics, forcing the use of metaphors and images to name the sacred. Metaphors for God have been so multifaceted that subsequently to reserve only male images to depict the deity is alienating to many women. The variety and plurality of metaphors for God in the Judeo-Christian traditions challenge the assumption that God is male and that patriarchy should be the exclusive model for Western society.

The women's movement has influenced many religious denominations to adapt their language to be more gender inclusive. Although church officials have made many efforts to accommodate the changes to horizontal language, which relates to humanity, they have been more resistant to attempts to change the vertical language, the language for God. Female scholars and theologians as well as women in their congregations continue their search for more inclusive language that will recognize the dignity of all people.

Questions for Discussion

1. Why can language shape our attitudes and behavior?
2. How do religious myths affect the attitudes of their followers toward the sacred, the environment, and gender relations?
3. How can metaphors for the deity arise from the culture's myths? Give examples.
4. Why do women and minorities suffer when metaphors for God are taken literally?
5. What metaphors for the sacred can you create?
6. What is your attitude toward gender-inclusive language? How have cultural, personal, and religious factors shaped your attitude?
7. Are you content with the solution given concerning the issue of gender-inclusive language in your faith community? What alterations might you consider?

Works Cited

Ali, Yusaf. *The Holy Quran*, trans. Muhammed Ashraf. Lahore, 1959.

Avila, St. Teresa of. *Interior Castle*. Trans. E. Allison Peers. Garden City, N.Y.: Image Books, 1961.

Berger, Peter. *A Rumor of Angels*. Garden City, N.Y., Doubleday, 1969.

Central Conference of American Rabbis. *Rabbis' Manual*. Columbus, Ohio: Special Edition, 1988.

Chodorow, Nancy. "Family Structure and Feminine Personality." In *Women, Culture and Society*, ed. M. Rosaldo and L. Lamphere. Stanford, Calif.: Stanford University Press, 1974.

Cowper, William. "Providence." In *World's Great Religious Poetry*. New York: Macmillan, 1946.

Daly, Mary. *Beyond God the Father: Toward a Philosophy of Women's Liberation*. Boston: Beacon Press, 1973.

Gardner, Alice. *Synesius of Cyrene: Philosophy and Bishop*. London: Society for Promoting Knowledge, 1886.

Gilkey, Langdon. *Naming the Whirlwind: The Renewal of God-Language*. Indianapolis, Ind.: Bobbs–Merrill, 1969.

Gilligan, Carol. *In a Different Voice*. Cambridge, Mass.: Harvard University Press, 1982.

The Gospels and the Letters of Paul. United Church of Christ Press, 1992.

Greeley, Andrew. *Angry Catholic Women*. Chicago: St. Thomas Moore, 1984.

Groome, Thomas. *Language for a "Catholic" Church*. New York: Sheed and Word, 1991.

Hammarskjold, Dag. *Markings*. New York: Knopf, 1968.

Julian of Norwich. *Showings*. Trans. Edmund Colledge and James Walsh. New York: Paulist Press, 1978.

Leeming, David Adams. *The World of Myth*. New York: Oxford University Press, 1990.

Lonergan, Anne, and Caroline Richards, eds. *Thomas Berry and the New Cosmology*. Mystic, Conn.: Twenty Third Publications, 1988.

People's Mass Book. Cincinnati: World Library of Sacred Music, 1984.

Ruether, Rosemary Radford. *Sexism and God Talk*. Boston: Beacon Press, 1983.

Schmidt, Roger. *Exploring Religion*. Belmont, Calif.: Wadsworth, 1988.

Stanton, Elizabeth Cady, ed. *The Woman's Bible* (1895). New York, Arno, 1972 (reprint).

Tennis, Diane. *Is God the Only Reliable Father?* Philadelphia: Westminister, 1985.

Wheelwright, Philip. *Metaphor and Reality*. Bloomington: Indiana University Press, 1975.

Suggested Readings

Bauman, Richard, and Joel Sherzer, eds. *Explorations in the Ethnography of Speaking*. New York: Cambridge University Press, 1974.

Bolen, Jean Shinoda. *Goddesses in Everywoman: A New Psychology of Women*. New York: Harper & Row, 1985.

Broner, Esther. *A Weave of Women*. New York: Bantam Books, 1978.

Chomsky, Noam. "A Review of Verbal Behavior," *Language* 35 (1959): 26–58. Reprinted in *Language and Mind*. New York: Harcourt Brace Jovanovich, 1972.

Greeley, Andrew M. *The Mary Myth: On the Feminity of God*. New York: Seabury Press, 1977.

Horowitz, Maryanne Cline. "The Image of God in Man—Is Woman Included?" *Harvard Theological Review* 72, nos. 3,4 (July–October l979): 175–206.

Jennings, Gary. *Personalities of Language*. New York: T. Y. Crowell, 1965.

Labov, William. *Language in the Inner City*. Philadelphia: University of Pennsylvania Press, 1972.

———. *Sociolinguistic Patterns*. Philadelphia: University of Pennsylvania Press, 1972.

Lakoff, Robin. *Language and Woman's Place*. New York: Harper & Row, 1975.

Lauter, Estelle. *Women as Myth Makers*. Bloomington: Indiana University Press, 1984.

Lloyd, Genevieve. *The Man of Reason: "Male" and "Female" in Western Philosophy*. London: Methuen, 1984.

Perera, Sylvia Brinton. *Descent to the Goddess: A Way of Initiation for Women*. Toronto: Inner City, 1981.

Preston, James J., ed. *Mother Worship: Themes and Variations*. Chapel Hill: University of North Carolina Press, 1982.

Robinson, W. P. *Language and Social Behavior*. Baltimore: Penguin, 1972.

Ruether, Rosemary Radford, ed. *Religion and Sexism: Images of Woman in the Jewish and Christian Traditions*. New York: Simon & Schuster, 1974.

———. *Sexism and God-Talk*. London: SCM Press, 1983.

Samarin, William. *Tongues of Men and Angels*. New York: Macmillan, 1972.

Sebeok, Thomas A., ed. *Style in Language*. Cambridge, Mass.: MIT Press, 1971.

Steiner, George. *After Babel*. New York: Oxford University Press, 1975.

Thorne, Barrie, Cheris Kramarae, and Nancy Henley, eds. *Language, Gender and Society*. Rowley: Newbury House, 1983.

William, Frederick, ed. *Language and Poverty*. Chicago: Markham, 1971.

Woolger, Jennifer, and Robert J. Barker. *The Goddess Within*. New York, Fawcett–Columbine, 1989.

CHAPTER 7

Contemporary Feminist Religious Movements

Religious women in today's Western societies have made tremendous strides in the last 30 years toward equal treatment in the secular arena. Women have entered facilities for higher learning in the same number as men. Managerial positions in business are now held by an equal number of women and men ("Men and Women in the Work Force," 16). Access to positions of leadership in local, state, and national government has been granted to women. Women have secured positions on the Supreme Court. Although discrimination toward women still exists, many of the old social barriers are crumbling. Still, women receive lower wages than men do for positions similar to men's (73 cents on the dollar), but they have watched the gap decrease. Better treatment of women has enhanced their self-image, a result of increased self-confidence.

Western religious institutions have not progressed toward women's equality as quickly as educational, political, and economic institutions have. Change does not come readily to patriarchal traditions entrenched by male-focused scriptures. The inherent conservatism of most faith communities impedes the progress desired by those members who do not profit from the status quo. Roman and Orthodox Catholics will not ordain women as priests, let alone bishops, nor will Orthodox Jews consider women rabbis. Often Protestant women in leadership roles find their efforts blunted by male-dominated governing bodies.

Thus women find themselves challenged to make their spiritual lives both relate to and support their growing equality and positive self-image. How best can they do this? We find a continuum of strategies in the various feminist movements that have developed recently in Western religious traditions.

Some argue that women should completely discard the male-dominated religious traditions of the West and replace them with a new goddess-centered spirituality. These radical feminists doubt that sexism can be elimi-

173

nated from Western religious traditions. In contrast, more conservative reconstructionist feminists want to stay within their traditions but mitigate its patriarchal tendencies (with the help of modern scholarship) by discovering, highlighting, and affirming the spiritual contribution and participation of women throughout the ages within their tradition. In a similar vein, other feminists have sought to unite around the struggle against oppression, which they find to be a fundamental, recurring theme in all Western religious traditions. Inspired by liberation theology's fight against oppression of the poor by the rich in developing countries, these reformers broaden that aim to include sexist oppression throughout the world. Other feminists who are inclined, like the radicals, to reject patriarchal Western traditions have sought to replace it not by inventing a new goddess religion but by reviving an old one: the ancient traditions of European goddess worship and witchcraft, called the wiccan movement.

Radical, Reconstructionist, and Reformist Feminist Scholars

Radical Feminist Scholars

The word *radical* is derived from the Latin word *radix*, meaning root. To go back to the roots of things means to examine the earliest aspects of a tradition. Radical feminists return to the earliest religious traditions, which they believe worshipped the goddess. They believe that they must disregard the male gods created by patriarchal cultures and worship the goddesses who directed an egalitarian culture. Some radical feminists want to replace the patriarchal culture of male domination with a goddess-centered culture in which women dominate. Other radical feminists reject the premise of the ascendancy of women over men but would include both sexes in rituals and ceremonies. A third segment would include men but give most prominent roles in rituals to women. The religious rituals from all three groups would center on the goddess and number more women than men in their groups.

Perhaps theologian Mary Daly best explains the stance of the radical feminists. She says that the women's movement has made women aware of the injustices aimed at women by contemporary patriarchal religions. Not only do the religious institutions betray women, but they "use their male God" to legitimate oppression, particularly that of women. Patriarchal religions are irredeemably antifeminine, she says, and therefore antihuman (57). She advises women to leave behind institutional religions because they are only instruments of their betrayal.

Criticisms of the father God extend to the male image of Christ because he has been established as the norm for humanity. Because God became human in male form, men have become the model for both men and women. The hierarchy of the Roman Catholic church has used this argument to prohibit women from full participation in the church as priests. Because Christ is the model for God, God must be male, they argue, and because Christ is the icon of God only a man can mirror or be an icon of Christ. The role of high priest and intercessor to God has been attributed to Christ by the church, so women, who do not mirror his gender, cannot exercise the role of priesthood. Mary Daly thinks that women should return to the goddess, where the image of the deity reflects their sex and establishes a norm that women can relate to naturally.

Both Jewish and Christian radical feminists believe that there is no place for the Bible in women's religious literature. Their prime reason is that the Hebrew Bible and the New Testament ignore the experience of women by erasing them from its history. God is always addressed in male language, ignoring the presence and feelings of one half of the population. The Bible justifies the oppression of women and the dominance of men, who have been encouraged to act violently toward the physically weaker sex. Elisabeth Schussler Fiorenza sums up the attitude of radical feminists toward the Judeo-Christian scriptures: "Therefore it is argued that feminists must leave behind biblical religion and reject the authority of the Bible because of its androcentric [male biased] patriarchal character" (150). Furthermore, radicals argue that contemporary scholarship, placing the Bible alongside of other mythologies, has relativized the authority of the Bible. It is impossible to attribute absolute authority to one set of scriptures when so many other sacred writings depict similar episodes in a different manner. With so many creation myths, any one of them could be called the "right" one. By exposing the degrading practices aimed at women in many religions, general patterns emerge that overshadow individual traditions. When one relativizes the Bible, one questions seriously the divine authority behind it. Perhaps if the scriptures are no longer sacred, the deity who is revealed in them is not either. Radical feminists do not regard the Judeo-Christian scriptures to be the word of God, but rather the words of men that were written from and for the experience of men.

A psychologist of religion, Naomi Goldenberg, identifies the problem of Judaism for women in its reverence of law and tradition. The law defines the role of women in society, the home, and the synagogue—a role always subordinate to men. "The nature of the religion lies in interplay between a father-god and His sons. In such a religion women will always be on the periphery" (Goldenberg, 7). Although Jewish law is supposed to make women separate yet equal, men perform the most important acts of religious duty. She says that women are expected to stay at home to prepare food and watch children so that men may be free to worship and study the Torah, which instructs women to be content with their subordinate roles in the Jewish society. Goldenberg claims that if women try to upset this role designation by assuming leadership roles, they will no longer be practicing Judaism.

Many radical feminists have little regard for the transcendent dimension of the divine. They argue that by constantly stressing the otherness of God—his power, infinity, perfection, knowledge, and eternity—one separates this God from the human condition. Humans, whose experience contains the opposite characteristics of dependence, limitedness, imperfection, ignorance, and mortality, find themselves to have very little in common with the deity. As the distance grows between this awesome God and these lowly mortals, a dichotomy arises, with the less desirable qualities assigned to humans. This dichotomy evolves to dualistic thinking that separates the categories of God/human, soul/body, intellect/emotions, spirit/matter, and man/woman. Women find themselves assigned to the least desirable traits, and thus the distance between them and the transcendent God is magnified.

Radical feminists would like to replace this transcendent God with an immanent presence of the deity who is so close to humans that it dwells within the person. If the person is female, the inner presence of the deity is likewise female. Women would replace the transcendent God with the immanent presence of the goddess within. The goddess would always be available to her bearer, so she could be approached in an intimate manner at the desire of the devotee. Women could identify with the goddess, who would understand their lived experience. Women could also identify with the nurturing qualities of the goddess in their role as physical or spiritual mothers. Recognizing the quality of creativity in art, music, and literature or the need for creative ability in dealing with life's problems, women could petition the creative power of the goddess. Carrying the spirit of the goddess within their bodies, women would feel empowered to overcome the dialectic that makes them feel inferior in the dualistic thinking of patriarchal religions.

Naomi Goldenberg suggests that the women's movement will influence the attitude of women toward male transcendent gods. They will increasingly come to favor the goddess, who overcomes this dualistic thinking that degrades women.

> The distinction between mind and body will begin to wane in Western culture as the women's movement continues to advance. More and more theorists will realize the futility of efforts to reform Judaism and Christianity. Gods who prefer men to women and spirit to body will no longer command respect.
>
> It is likely that as we watch Christ and Yahweh tumble to the ground, we will completely outgrow the need for an external god.
>
> *Goldenberg, 25*

This immanence of the goddess that fills the human person stresses the priority of the individual conscience over codified laws of patriarchal religions. Proponents of goddess religion point out that the priority of individual conscience would not lead to crime or anarchy because the worshipper of the goddess sees her in all of humanity and nature. She must be served well in all human relationships, be they political, familial, religious, or environmental. Recognizing the immanent presence of the goddess in the world, the cycles of nature, the mind, the body, the spirit, and the emotions within each person, Starhawk, an advocate of the goddess religion, says, "Thou art Goddess. I am Goddess. All that lives, all that serves life is Goddess" (263).

Aware of the identification of the woman with the goddess, Zsuzsanna Budapest, a Dianic high priestess, describes a religious ritual that honors the divinity within herself. She calls it a self-blessing ritual and says it has been passed down orally in her native Hungary and not written down until recently. "It is a woman's own blessing on herself; her own divinity is honored in a ritual with herself. It is a self-affirmation, a very private, and a very powerful ritual" (269). Standing before her altar on salt, which symbolizes wisdom, the woman dips her finger in a chalice of water and wine, which symbolizes the life force. She touches her dipped fingers to her forehead, saying, "Bless me mother for I am your child" to connect herself to the spirit she is addressing in herself. Next, she touches her nose, to remind herself of the nearness of the essence of the goddess to nature. When touching her lips, the devotee says, "Bless my lips to think of you," all the while meditating in the power of words.

> Then dip your fingers again, and touch your breasts, and say, "Bless my breasts, formed in strength and beauty." In matriarchies, the beauty standard was strength and beauty combined. Weakness was not rewarded. Weakness was not considered beautiful.
>
> And then again, dip your fingers, touch your genitals, and say, "Bless my genitals that bring forth life as you have brought forth the universe." Touching genitals and speaking of bringing forth life does not mean that all women must give birth to children. It is simply a recognition of our connection with all that is female. The biological destiny that was used against us actually is the basis of our divinity.
>
> *Zsuzsanna Budapest, 271*

Budapest thinks that women should try to overcome the body/soul dichotomy by reveling in their bodies, which are inhabited and penetrated by the spirit of the goddess. The devotee experiences the joy of having her full sexual identity affirmed as being made in the image and likeness of the godhead, who is female. She experiences the power and creativity of the goddess, which in turn empowers and affirms her.

Most radical feminists are connected with the monotheistic religions of Judaism and Christianity. But as feminine scholars investigate other cultures, they find rituals that these cultures have long used to glorify the power of women. The Apaches from New Mexico conduct a religious ceremony to the goddess Isanaklesh, who prescribes a ritual for young girls upon their first flow of menstrual blood. The goddess transforms the young girl into herself during the ceremony and empowers her with her own healing ability. In describing the ceremony, Ines Talamantez, a professor of religious studies, says, "Not only is the girl temporarily transformed into the goddess during this rite of passage; she is also permanently transformed into a mature Apache woman by the end of the ritual" (250). Friends and relatives are invited to a feast celebrating the girl's menarche, and young men from the tribe build her a temporary dwelling for the ceremony. Guests offer gifts, and music and dancing honor the girl in whom the goddess dwells. Both men and women profit from the coming of the goddess Isanaklesh. The women feel their empowerment, and the men honor women, whose life experience is connected so closely to the goddess. Radical feminists see the benefit in creating positive rituals and rites of passage like this for women today.

Radical religious feminists who have departed from their traditional Western religious denominations have found both solace and challenge in goddess-centered religions. Other feminists have moved into the social feminist movements and diverted their energies to improving the social, economic, and political conditions that affect women. Some create religious rituals that affirm women, and some join other religious movements that are more conducive to their interests. Wherever they go, radical feminists challenge thinking women to investigate the causes and possible solutions to the dilemmas that face women in institutional religions.

Elizabeth Gould Davis describes the ideas promoted by the return to the goddess movement. In her book she summarizes the history of the goddess culture, its replacement by patriarchy, and the ways patriarchy changed attitudes toward women. Her hope for the future is to restore women to their original place of prominence.

> In original myth, . . . there is an original Great Goddess who creates the universe, the earth, and the heavens, and finally creates the gods and mankind. Eventually she bears, parthenogenetically, a son who later becomes her lover, then her consort, next her surrogate and finally, in patriarchal ages, the usurper of her power. In the measureless eons of her exclusive reign, however, she inaugurates civilization in all its aspects. Under her rule the earth enjoys a long period of peaceful progress during which time cities are built, law and justice are instituted, crops are planted and harvested, cattle are domesticated for their milk and wool, fire is discovered and utilized, the wheel is invented, ships are first constructed, and the arts, from ceramics and weaving to painting and sculpture, are begun.
>
> Then suddenly all is ended. Paradise is lost. A dark age overtakes the world—a dark age brought on by cataclysm accompanied by a patriarchal revolution. Nomads, barbaric and uncivilized, roving bands of ejected, womanless men, destroy the civilized city states, depose the queens, and attempt to rule in their stead. The result is chaos. War and violence make their appearance, justice and law fly out the window, might replaces right, the Great Goddess is replaced by a stern and vengeful God, man becomes carnivorous, property rights become paramount over human rights, woman is degraded and exploited, and civilization starts on the downward path it still pursues.

Such is the theme of all myth—from the Golden Age of the Greeks and Romans to the Garden of Eden of Jew and Christian, and Happy Hunting Ground of the American Indian, and the Avaiki of the Polynesians—all ending in a fall from paradise and in utter failure.

When man first resolved to exalt the peculiarities of his own sex, muscularity and spiritual immaturity, he adopted the policy that reality meant tangibility and that what could not be seen or touched did not exist. . . . By discrediting the mystic power of woman, man cut himself off from the higher things, the "eternal verities," the sense of which had distinguished him from the lower animals. By crushing every manifestation of supersensory or extrasensory truth and worshipping only sensate matter, man made of himself a mere biological organism and denied to himself the divine ray that once upon a time woman had revealed to him. . . .

Her animal body, however, remained a necessary adjunct to the new physical man, and he set about to remold her from his own base material into a mere biological organism like himself—a fit mate, a help "meet" for him—his biological complement. Through the long centuries he succeeded in brainwashing her to the belief that she was indeed made from his rib, that she was formed to be a comfort to him, the receptacle of his seed, and the incubator of *his* heirs, who were the perpetuators of *his* name.

Thus the sacred flame of her primordial and divine authority was banked and dampened and finally smothered almost to extinction. Throughout the Arian and Piscean ages of strife and materialism, man's denser nature held sway while woman's etheric light lay hidden under the bushel of masculine domination.

We are on the threshold of the new Age of Aquarius, whom the Greeks called Hydrochoos, the water-bearer, the renewer, the reviver, the quencher of raging fire and of thirst. . . .

Today, as then, women are in the vanguard of the aborning civilization; and it is to the women that we look for salvation in the healing and restorative waters of Aquarius.

It is to such a new age that we look now with hope as the present age of masculism succeeds in destroying itself, as have all its predecessors in the incredibly long history of civilizations. . . .

The rot of masculist materialism has indeed permeated all spheres of twentieth-century life and now attacks its very core. The only remedy for the invading and consuming rot is a return to the values of the matriarchates. . . .

The ages of masculism are now drawing to a close. Their dying days are lit up by a final flare of universal violence and despair such as the world has seldom before seen. Men of goodwill turn in every direction seeking cures for their perishing society, but to no avail. Any and all social reforms superimposed upon our sick civilization can be no more effective than a bandage on a gaping and putrefying wound. Only the complete and total demolition of the social body will cure the fatal sickness. Only the overthrow of the three-thousand-year-old beast of masculist materialism will save the race.

In the new science of the twenty-first century, not physical force but spiritual force will lead the way. Mental and spiritual gifts will be more in demand than gifts of a physical nature. Extrasensory perception will make precedence over sensory perception. And in this sphere woman will again predominate. She who was revered and worshiped by early man because of her power to

see the unseen will once again be the pivot—not as sex but as divine woman—about whom the next civilization will, as of old, revolve.
Elizabeth Gould Davis, 68–69, 331–339

Radical religious feminists have met with criticism from other Western feminist theologians. Paula Fredriksen Landes, a reformist theologian, finds it difficult to understand the stance where "in their efforts to repudiate male religiosity these women paradoxically recapitulate patterns they condemn in men" (333). In desiring only female and goddesses rituals, critics say, the radical feminists deny any opportunity for the full participation of men. Other critics point out that when failing to consider the transcendent dimension of the divine, radical feminists lean toward psychology rather than religion. The radicals refuse to allow the divine to have an existence within itself, which is a characteristic of transcendence. These critics argue that if one considers the divine only in relation to oneself, as in the characteristic of immanence, one is in danger of constructing one's own gods and goddesses to comply with one's own needs and desires.

Reconstructionist Feminist Scholars

Rather than disregarding their religious traditions and turning to new forms, reconstructionist feminine scholars try to examine their traditions and scriptures from the experience of women. If they are religious historians, they try to recover the history of women from their faith communities. Because women's actions are omitted from the history written by men, feminist scholars must examine closely the few references made to women and try to draw from them women's presence and role in their faith community. Biblical scholars try to uncover the meaning of women's experience as recorded by their sacred scriptures. Female archaeologists add to the treasure of this knowledge by adding their perspective to the excavations. Each group tries to uncover the information that will help them reconstruct the role and experience of women at the time the traditions and scriptures were written.

Admitting that their attempts are challenging because of the lack of information regarding women, Jewish and Christian scholars are nevertheless making new discoveries. Elisabeth Schussler Fiorenza, a theologian as well as a religious historian, says, "I attempt to reconstruct early Christian history as women's history in order not only to restore women's stories to early Christian history but also to reclaim this history as the history of women and men" (30). She admits that biblical texts are a product of one androcentric patriarchal culture, but still reveres them as sacred documents that inform the theology and religious commitment of contemporary Jewish and Christian women.

One must understand the culture in which the documents were written in order to understand the position of women in the faith community and society. Sociologists, anthropologists, and historians pool their efforts to uncover the role of women that has been overlooked or neglected by male authors. Male writers of history, scripture, and theology have portrayed humanity as essentially male, so it is necessary for feminist scholars from all disciplines to uncover the contributions of women in each area. Fiorenza does not deny the patriarchal bias of Christian recorded history, but she says we must "reconstruct the history of women in early Christianity as a challenge to historical religious patriarchy" (35). Both Jewish and Christian reconstructionist scholars try to expose the oppressive patriarchal structures while empowering women in their struggle against such forms. By restoring women's religious history, scholars hope to make women more secure in fulfilling their historic roles in the present.

The challenge to reconstruct women's religious history seems difficult to Jewish theologians because so much of the religion is based on a concept of history that is considered a living memory. It is difficult for women to be active participants in a memory that keeps them marginal. Gloria Anzaldua, a Chicana writer, goes back to the years before the sixteenth century to illustrate the devotion to a goddess who was replaced by the Virgin Mary. She had to reconstruct from the memories and stories of her ancestors the role of the goddess in Mexico before the Spanish conquistadors.

Patriarchal interpretation of the New Testament tells Roman and Eastern Orthodox Catholic women that they cannot be priests because Jesus had only male apostles, whom he ordained priests. Some Roman Catholics teach that Jesus ordained the apostles as priests at the Last Supper. Feminist biblical scholars have pointed out that Jesus did not ordain anyone a priest because at that time the Christian priesthood was nonexistent. They also argue that women were indeed numbered among the apostles: Paul in Romans 16 refers to Junia as an apostle, and Mary Magdalene was an apostle to the apostles in that she gave them the message of the resurrection. She was instructed by the risen Christ to "preach the first Easter Sermon to the men" (Prohl, 69). At Pentecost both men and women were filled with the Holy Spirit (Acts 2). Women played a prominent role in the early Apostolic church. Priscilla instructed Apollo for the Christian ministry (Acts 18), and the four daughters of Philip served as prophetesses (Acts 21:9). Perhaps the example of Phoebe has been best reconstructed by the feminist linguist scholars. She has been referred to as *servant of the church* in Rom. 16:1 by male translators of the Greek word *diakonos*. Russell Prohl, a theologian, admits that *diakonos* can mean "full fledged pastors, preachers and evangelists" (69). Paul uses the term *diakonos* 22 times. Translators interpreted it 18 times as *minister*, 3 times as *deacon*, and only here as *servant* (Prohl, 70). Paul also refers to Phoebe as *prostatis*, which means "one who presides, a ruler, foreman or leader." In reconstructing the role of Phoebe in the early church, scholars have found that she was in charge of the church of Cenchrae, not just a servant.

Art historians have also helped to reconstruct the role of women in the early Christian church. They have found pictures in the catacombs that date back to the first century CE that portray seven women seated around a table, sharing the Eucharist. The researchers had to search hard for their evidence because someone had painted beards on the women and painted over their clothes to make them resemble men. Joan Morris, an art historian, tells us that women even served as bishops. A mosaic from the early church, perhaps even the first century, in the church of St. Praxedes in Rome, depicts a woman with the inscription *Theodora, Episcopa*. Someone had removed the last letter in the mosaic and changed her name to the male *Theodor* and *Episcopa* to *Episcopus*, but "the title Theodora Episcopa is repeated on columns outside the chapel" (Morris, 66).

The Roman Catholic church has ordained men as deacons in recent years but refuses to discuss the ordination of women as deaconesses. Religious historians have uncovered evidence that the order of deaconess, which began in the first century, continued well into the fifth century. A list of the clergy who ministered in the fifth century at the church of St. Sophia in Constantinople included 80 deacons and 40 deaconesses. In her study of the household codes or role assignments and characteristics of church leaders and deacons in the pastoral epistle of Timothy and Titus, Elisabeth Schussler Fiorenza says that they reflect the patriarchal tendencies of the second century church. The writer of late first or early second century letter to Timothy assigns qualities to the various positions of authority that have arisen in hierarchal form. He describes the qualities necessary for the presiding elder, deacon, wives, and children. Titus gives instruction to the church officials and then, in order, to their wives, older women, and children on how to conduct themselves appropriately in the newly organized hierarchical church. Fiorenza says Paul was more egalitarian in his inclusion of women as part of his formula "in Christ there are no Jews or Greeks, male or female slave nor free—but all are one in Christ Jesus" (Gal. 3:28). By going behind the second century writings, Fiorenza could reconstruct the environment of the earlier church where Paul had recognized the gifts of women in a more egalitarian organization.

Through the collaborative efforts of scholars from many disciplines, Christian women can find precedents for women to participate more fully in their institutional churches. They can find no reasons from either scripture or the first century church tradition to bar women from ordination to the priesthood. Rather, by studying the environment in which these scriptures were written and including the practices of the early church, they find that women had a prominent role in its functions. With the aid of linguists, art historians, and archaeologists, women theologians have found evidence to support their claims that women's gifts were recognized and rewarded before the effects of the patriarchal culture caused them to be ignored.

Judith Plaskow has done much reconstructionist work in the Jewish community. She underscores the difficulty in retrieving women's history in Judaism because of the significance of the Torah. She says that the Torah is not just history, but also a living memory. "The Torah reading, as a central part of the Sabbath and holiday liturgy, calls to mind and recreates the past for succeeding generations" (39). Women must listen to these readings that appear to ignore their presence. For instance, the reading from Exodus 19, which is read annually, remembers the giving of the Sinai covenant by Yahweh to the Jewish population. This covenant is most important because, in contrast to the covenant with the individual Abraham, this covenant is intended to bind the whole nation. However, Yahweh seems to direct his conversation and thus his contract to only the male members of Israel. Among the instructions given by Moses at the command of Yahweh was "Be ready for the day after tomorrow, do not touch a woman" (Exod. 19:15). The Jewish reconstructionist must try to find out where the women were in this scene. She must ask questions: Why were they not addressed by Moses? Were they not members of the nation of Israel? If a child must be born of a Jewish woman to be considered Jewish, did not women have some position among God's chosen people? It is unlikely that they were absent at this momentous occasion in Jewish history. Just because the male chroniclers failed to mention their presence, it does not mean they were absent or excluded from the covenant with Yahweh. One must look at the reconstructive work of the rabbis after the fall of Jerusalem in 70 CE to determine their interpretation of the Hebrew Bible. The rabbis could justify their own contemporary experiences if they could claim their presence in the earlier scriptures.

> So deeply is the Jewish present rooted in Jewish history, that after 70 CE when the rabbis profoundly transformed Jewish life, the changes they wrought in Jewish reality were also read back into the past so they could be read out of the past as a foundation for the present. Again and again in rabbinic interpretations, we find contemporary practice projected back into earlier periods so that the chain of tradition can remain unbroken.
>
> *Judith Plaskow, 41*

Feminists can perform a similar action by considering the present-day participation of women in Judaism. Women are active in most areas of reformed and conservative Jewish cultic and intellectual life. If they are active now, they must have participated in the past. By projecting back the present practices that acknowledge the active presence of women in the Jewish community, they argue that they were always present in the community. Therefore, women must have been present to receive the Sinai covenant along with the men of Israel. By reclaiming the history of women in the Torah, the entire Jewish community of men and women will profit from the more complete picture of their heritage.

Archaeologists often collaborate with Jewish theologians to do this. Carol Meyers, in studying the archaeological remains before the monarchy period in Israel, found that women played an important role in the Hebrew agricultural settlements by planting, gathering, weaving, and making pottery. If they were so essential to the economic community, must they not have been as integral to the religious community? Often what is taken for granted is omitted by the writers of sacred traditions who are trying to document the unusual and outstanding so it will not be lost to memory. The usual day-to-day activity is expected to live on in daily experience, so the male writers saw no need to record it. Although the routine experience of women was omitted, it does not mean that it did not exist. Jewish reconstructionists are trying to regain that experience so that women's history may be better appreciated.

Marcia Falk, a professor of religious studies, reports that many Jewish women's groups are making serious attempts at adding inclusive language to their religious rituals. They have even introduced the feminine pronoun *she* when referring to divinity. Falk does not want to replace a male metaphor with a female one, however, but would rather introduce a variety of metaphors for Yahweh. She incorporates this diversity of metaphors into her blessings. "When I compose my blessings, I draw my metaphors from all aspects of creation—as did the biblical poets who created the metaphors 'rock of Israel' and 'tree of life'" (132). The traditional Jewish blessing before eating addresses God as Lord and King. Falk searched the scriptures until she found the image of fountains, wells, and source, then composed the blessing "Let us bless the source of life that brings forth bread from the earth" (133). She thought that the traditional blessing "Blessed are you, Lord our God, king of the world, who brings forth bread from the earth" was less appropriate for the nurturing role of the deity because of its male emphasis.

When a culture has no written scriptures to reconstruct, scholars must examine the oral traditions. Gloria Anzaldua interviewed elders of her own Mexican Indian community who pray to the Virgin of Guadalupe. She found that before her identification with the Virgin Mary, the Virgin of Guadalupe was originally considered to be a Mesomerican fertility and earth goddess named Coatlopeuk. She was also considered to be a creator goddess and mother of gods and goddesses. The Aztecs, a male-dominated people who defeated the goddess-worshipping tribes, drove the goddesses underground, gave them hideous and evil characteristics, and prayed only to their gods. In 1531 at the site of one of the goddess's temples, a woman appeared dressed in the typical attire of the goddess, Coatlopeuk, to a poor Indian man, Juan Diego. She gave her name as Maria Coatlopeuk, which in Spanish sounds like Guadalupe. The Spanish conquistadors identified her with the dark virgin, Guadalupe, the patroness of west central Spain. She left her image on the cloak worn by Juan Diego, and the Roman Catholic church in 1660 named her mother of God, or the Virgin Mary. She was assigned to Mexico as their patroness and is venerated by Mexicans and Chicanos dotted over Mexico and the southwest United States. Our Lady of Guadalupe shrines are famous for healings and other miracles. Anzaldua says that today she is "the single most potent religious, political and cultural image of the Chicano/Mexicano. She, like my race, is a synthesis of the old world and the new, of the religion and culture of the two races in our psyche, the conquerors and the conquered" (79). By reconstructing the tradition behind the Virgin of Guadalupe, Anzaldua uncovered the original devotion to her native goddesses. By examining the roots of their present devotion to Mary as residing in the earlier goddesses of the Indian culture, Mexicans can make the connections that allow them to keep their identity as Indians and Spanish or American at the same time. Rather than totally taking on the saints of their conquerors, they can retain remnants of their native religion through devotion to Our Lady of Guadalupe.

Riffat Hassan, a Muslim woman theologian, has applied the reconstructionists' research to Islam. She admits that many of the misogynist practices against women in Pakistan are rooted in military dictatorship and religious autocracy. Efforts to change the laws that allow injustice and brutality toward women will be ineffective until change comes to the theology that supports these practices. Otherwise, she says that Muslim women will continue to be brutalized and discriminated against, despite the statistics that say that women's opportunities for education, employment, social, and political rights are improving. "No matter how many sociopolitical rights are granted to women, as long as these women are conditioned to accept the myths used by theologians or religious hierarchs to shackle their bodies, hearts, minds and souls, they will never become fully developed or whole human beings, free of fear and guilt, able to stand equal to men in the sight of God" (Hassan, 43). Since the injustice is rooted in the Quran, she suggests that a study of it should be made from a reconstructionist point of view.

Hassan says that Muslims base their negative view of women on the creation story in the Hebrew Bible that says woman was created second from a "crooked" rib and therefore can never be straightened out. She is held responsible for the fall and expulsion from the garden, and "so all daughters of Eve are to be regarded with suspicion, contempt and hatred and [reminded] that women were created not only from man but for man" (Hassan, 44). However, this story does not appear in the most sacred book of Islam, the Quran. These ideas appear in the *Hadith*, a collection of anecdotes about the prophet and sayings by the prophet and his companions, which was edited after his death by one of his companions. This story runs contrary to the Quran, which says that men and women were created simultaneously. By going back to the Quran rather than the later hadiths, or stories, that have been influenced by a patriarchal society, researchers find a truer picture of the intent of the prophet. Muslim women must challenge the authenticity of the hadith that justifies male domination and oppression of women because the Quran creation statements are more egalitarian. The Quranic legend that corresponds to the fall story in the Hebrew Bible does not blame woman for the introduction of evil. It focuses on the moral choice individuals must make when confronted by God and Shaitan (the Islamic word for Satan). Later commentaries on the story pointed to women as the cause of indecency and sexual sins. "Even to the day, Satan and his disciples are adopting the same scheme of depriving the woman of the feelings of modesty and shyness and they cannot think of any scheme of progress unless they expose and exhibit woman to all and sundry" (Maududi, 16 n. 13). The idea that woman was created for man is also left unsubstantiated in the Quran, which stress that all humans were made to serve God and humankind. Salvation is promised to both sexes if they do righteous deeds that are pleasing to God.

> If any do deeds of righteousness
> be they male or female
> And have faith
> They will enter Heaven
> And not the least injustice
> Will be done to them.
>
> *Surah 4: 124*

Islamic feminine theologians would like to reconstruct the original tradition of equality between the sexes that was perverted by later patriarchal commentaries. They feel that the Quran has been misinterpreted either intentionally or unintentionally by most Muslim societies. If only the theologians would go back to the Quran, they would understand that men and women are not only created equal in God's sight, but both have equal access to salvation. A correct theological interpretation would improve the condition of women and would be more faithful to the original intent of the founder, Mohammed.

Reconstructionists in all traditions have been criticized by radical feminists because they still hold onto the scriptures, even though the words and concepts are blatantly sexist. Radicals think the reconstructionists spend too much time and energy on outdated documents that were written by men in a patriarchal culture. As a result, they say, these documents have nothing to say to contemporary women. To investigate the traditions behind these scriptures is only a Band-Aid approach to an illness that needs radical surgery.

Reformist Feminist Scholars

Like the reconstructionists, reformers hold that the scriptures, traditions, and history of religions have something valuable to say today. They are unique in that the reformers focus on the theme of liberation that runs through the Jewish and Christian Bibles, looking for examples of God's concern for the poor and oppressed. Feminist theologians use the model of the liberation theologians who emerged from South America to protest the oppression of the poor and powerless by the rich and powerful. Liberation theology stresses freedom from economic, racial, and cultural oppression and decries the sins of capitalism, racism, and imperialism that cause the injustice. Feminist reformers add the sin of sexism to the list of injustices while at the same time recognizing the connections among all forms of oppression. When examining the strands of liberation that reach through scriptures and early histories of their religious traditions, feminist theologians realize that they can reject the attitude that "we must accept things the way they are." Because God liberates the followers from the effects and bondage of sin, they say, God also frees the oppressed from the bondage of racial, cultural, economic, and sexual exploitation.

The book of Amos from the Hebrew Bible has often been called the book of social justice and liberation for the poor. The prophet Amos tried to call the Israelites back to the great commandment to love God and their neighbors as themselves. Rather than allowing them to oppress the poor, Amos warned the wealthy in society to treat the poor kindly and with justice. In the same tradition, Jesus in the New Testament treated the poor, sick, outsiders, and women with respect and concern. Because of Jesus' concern for the powerless in his society, who were usually economically deprived, the liberation theologians speak of a preferential option for the poor. Jews, Christians, and Muslims believe that God revealed Godself through the scriptures, which speak of the need of liberation from evil. Therefore the followers of these religions should accept God's summons to participate more fully in this historical struggle for release from bondage.

Liberation theologians distinguish between personal and social sins. Personal sin usually resides with the individual, who harms someone through a selfish act such as theft, sexual misconduct, or gossip. Social sins usually reside in institutions or structures that have the power to influence many people at once. They are often called systemic sins because they reside in a system such as patriarchy, capitalism, and imperialism. These systemic sins include discrimination against persons who belong to a group, such as discrimination based on race, gender, ethnicity, poverty, and work. Such sins are more difficult to overcome because their perpetuators usually recommend a maintenance of the status quo. Since the powerful in society usually benefit from keeping things the way they are, they are not eager to make changes that would decrease their profit or status. Liberation theologians suggest a collaboration effort of large groups of workers, women, and other oppressed groups to reform the structures that cause the sin of injustice.

Reformist feminist theologians—Christian, Jewish, and Muslim—see the need to transform governmental, economic, and religious structures that alienate and oppress women. For inspiration, they look to the prophets of their religion who attempted to reform their religious traditions. Christian women point to Jesus, who reformed his traditional faith community by preaching that the reign of God was to begin on earth and continue into the future heavenly plane. He taught that heaven was a place of happiness, bliss, beauty, justice, and truth for everyone. He made efforts to transform the present earthly part of the reign of God to include the characteristics of the future life by alleviating the hardships of the poor, suffering, hungry, and women. In the gospel of Luke, Mary, the mother of Jesus, with her memorable prayer of the Magnificat, sides with the poor and oppressed against the wealthy and powerful of her time. In praising God, she says

> He has stretched out his mighty arm and scattered the proud in the conceit of their heart. He has brought down mighty kings from their thrones and lifted up the lowly.
> He has filled the hungry with good things and sent the rich away with empty hands.
>
> *Luke 1:51–53*

Mary, like her son, wished to liberate the people of God from the structures that bound them to subservience and oppression. The Jewish prophet Isaiah praises God for delivering God's people, who had been oppressed by their enemies.

> For you have broken the yoke that burdened them and the rod that beat their shoulders.
> You have defeated the nation that oppressed and exploited your people just as you defeated the army of Median long ago.
>
> *Isaiah 9:4*

Isaiah was trying to make his people aware of their need to trust in God instead of human kings. He said that instead of making alliances with the powerful of earth, they should return to the tradition of faith in God. The institutional structure of kingship must be reformed to fulfill the function assigned to it by God. In calling the structures back to their original purpose, Isaiah was fulfilling his prophet's mission of reform.

Muslims emphasize that Mohammed attempted to reform the barbaric social customs of the Arab tribes such as female infanticide. Mohammed demanded that girl babies be allowed to live and forbade the practice of female infanticide in his new formulation of Islam. Muslim reformist thinkers point out that in calling Muslims to reflect on the dignity of human life, Mohammed reformed the religious traditions of the Arab tribes.

Each of these prophets preached a message of salvation that points both to a supernatural future happiness and to a present society in which unjust practices and relations are overcome.

Feminist liberation theologians refuse to close their eyes to the discrimination against women in their various religious traditions. Professor of religious studies Denise Carmody says that liberation feminists "admit that Christianity has abused women in the past, but the essence of Christianity, its core love of God and neighbor, is an unparalleled liberation" (188). This liberation must be practiced by the church hierarchies that deprive women of their full participation in the institutional religions. "Until women get strict equality of right and opportunity, reformist feminists will call the Church guilty of sexist injustice (Carmody, 230). Rosemary Ruether claims that women are among those that God came to liberate. She tells women to pay special attention to the words of the prophets, who seemed to denounce the actions of institutional Judaism.

> Woe to those who make unjust laws that oppress my people. That is how you
> keep the poor from having their rights and from receiving justice. That is how
> you take the property that belongs to widows and orphans.
>
> *Isaiah 12:1,2*

Ruether notices that in the New Testament Paul points to a time when there
will be no separation into ethnic class, racial categories, or gender groups.
"There is no difference between Jews and Gentiles, slaves and free, men
and women: you are all one in union with Christ Jesus" (Gal. 3:28).
Reformist theologians take Paul's words seriously and try to implement
them here and now.

Women reformers must be careful to include all women in their plea for
equality. There is a danger that white, middle-class, educated women will
overlook the plight of their third world sisters whose economic oppression
prohibits their attempts at religious liberation. The necessity of women to
bond together in order to explore the "structural sin of patriarchal sexism"
has led some women to form their own church, called Womenchurch.
Elisabeth Schussler Fiorenza describes it: "As the church of women we celebrate our religious powers and ritualize our visions for change and liberation. We bond together in struggling with all women for liberation and we
share our strength in nurturing each other in the full awareness that the
church of women is always the ecclesia reformanda" (7).

One of the activities of Womenchurch is to devise rituals that are appealing to and affirming of the experience of women. An example of the bonding that is possible between women from different backgrounds is taken
from a ritual developed by Dian Neu. The ritual demonstrates the need for
liberation for all women suffering from political, economic, and sexist
oppression. The author incorporates the usual ingredients of a religious ritual: prayer, song, readings, symbols, and a community of support. The participants in the ritual hope to reform their community, which has caused
pain by raising the consciousness of the evils perpetrated by their patriarchal cultures. The following ritual is taken from *Waterwheel*, the publica-
tion for WATER, the Women's Alliance for Theology, Ritual, and Ethics. It
tries to show the concern of women for all women throughout the world.

Women Crossing Worlds: In Solidarity and Friendship

by Diann Neu

BACKGROUND: *Women Crossing Worlds is a project of WATER that invites
women of the Americas to accompany one another on our journey toward
liberation. Patriarchy has taught us to separate from one another. Rejecting
this division, we promise to work together to re-create society.*

This liturgy celebrates the friendship and solidarity of women of the Americas. It has been celebrated, shaped, and re-shaped by women's groups of Central, South, and North America.

PREPARATION: *Gather a large white handkerchief, a Guatemalan sash, a letter and/or a slide of the Mothers of the Plaza de Mayo or the Co-Madres marching, a slide of a Guatemalan child, and a slide of Salvadoran people. Bake or buy four different kinds of bread: tortillas, matzah, rye bread, wheat bread. Place in the center a small table covered with a colorful cloth.*

Call to Celebration

Today we gather to celebrate our friendship and solidarity with women of the Americas, especially women of Latin America. As Women Crossing Worlds, we promise to accompany one another as we work for justice.

Let us stand and begin our celebration with a litany of solidarity and friendship.

Litany of Solidarity and Friendship

Your response to each line is "We stand in solidarity and friendship."

Let us stand in solidarity as we struggle
R: **We stand in solidarity and friendship**.
From many different journeys. R:
From countryside and city center. R:
Crawling, walking, running. R:
Discovering many dances of life. R:
Affirming differences and similarities. R:
Working to overcome racism, sexism, heterosexism, classism. R:
Crossing worlds as friends. R:
Working for justice with hands joined. R:
(The leader gestures for all to join hands, pause, then drop hands and be seated.)

Song

"Voices" by Holly Near (words adapted by Diann Neu)

Listen to the voices of suffering women.
Listen to the voices of suffering women.
Calling out the messages of the moon and sea
Telling us what we need to know in order to be free.
Listen to the voices of suffering women.

Reading 1

INTRODUCTION: The Co-Madres of El Salvador and the Mothers of the Plaza de Mayo in Argentina provide strong examples of how women in the most difficult of circumstances remain vigilant. With white handkerchiefs on their heads, they march demanding the return of their "disappeared" loved ones. On the handkerchiefs are written the names of their disappeared loved ones, date of birth, date of disappearance. Often a picture is also attached. One of the mothers wrote these words: "Panuelo Blanco" from Cantos de Vida, Amor y Libertad, Madres de la Plaza de Mayo, Buenos Aires, 1982.

(The reader folds a white handkerchief into a triangle and places it on her head or shows a slide of the Mothers of the Plaza de Mayo or the Co-Madres marching.)

White handkerchief, White handkerchief,
you go looking and walking.
White Handkerchief, like the dove of peace
you represent the dignity of a woman
injured but not overcome . . .
You are the woman worker, the employee,
the woman student.
You are the one who struggles day and night
the one who laughs and cries.
You are the history of my people who
struggle, who struggled and who will
continue to struggle until love will be true,
until there is liberty for all.

Song

Listen to the voices of the young children.
Listen to the voices of the young children.
Calling out the messages of the earth and sky.
Telling us what we need to know in order to survive.
Listen to the voices of the young children.

Reading 2

INTRODUCTION: Julia Esquivel is an exiled Guatemalan poet. In this poem, "The Wounded Quetzal" from *Threatened with Resurrection*, she speaks of the children, the hope of the future.

(The reader places a Guatemalan sash around her head or shows a slide of a Guatemalan child.)

Small Indian child, bearing a thousand crosses
on your back, bent from your birth.
Teacher of the earth, of the forest,
of weeping and of laughter.
A fiery coal burns in my heart,
a cry I cannot stifle strikes it.
I hear the flapping wings of the quetzal
struggling to free itself from the bloody claws
of the condor, from the bald eagle.
Indian Guatemala (Nicaragua, Chile, Brazil,
South Africa, Argentina, El Salvador . . .),
always alive, struggles to break into flight
toward a land of wide horizon,
a land without owners . . .
Run, run, Indian child,
run like a deer on the mountains;
there, where the quetzal soars to new flights.

Prayer

O God, Creator and Artist, Mother and Father.
You fill the eyes and hearts of children
with laughter and love,
twinkling mischief and abounding curiosity.
We see them brimming with hope
secure in an unspoken promise
that life is a blessing;
that your world and your people are good.
Forgive us for all the ways in which we have
betrayed the children.
Too many babies die before they are five,
experience hunger, weakness,
avoidable disease and death.
Too many soon look out on the world
with the round bewildered eyes of fear and disappointment.
Forgive us that we have cared more
about profits than about people,
about gaining gold than guarding the children.
Enable us all to know and use our power;
give us guidance and understanding
to see clearly what we can do to ensure
that no child is hungry or thirsty,
and that fathers and mothers are not forced
to abandon their children
in order to earn their daily bread.
O God, Creator and Artist, Mother and Father,
bless all children with food, shelter, clothing
and love. Amen. Blessed be. So it is.

Reading 3

INTRODUCTION: Karen Jensen, a North American pastor, reflects on her experience in El Salvador. This reflection, excerpted from *Probe*, Vol. xvii, No. 3,1989, is based on Esther 4:14.
"And who knows whether you have not come to the place where you are for such a moment as this?"

(The reader picks up a letter or shows a slide of Salvadoran people.)

I saw Esther today.
I saw Esther in El Salvador.

A child in a refugee camp, swollen stomach from lack of food, infested with parasites. He stood there by my side with love in his eyes, and held out his hand to share all he had, a ripe, old banana. For me! I have enough to eat. My belly is full. He is empty. This is his food for the day. But how could I refuse? He wanted to give to me. We sat on a rock, side by side, amid the mud and dirt. His smile was our Thanksgiving to God. He carefully broke the banana in half, and with his hand said, "Take and eat." I ate my half more quickly than he did his. He noticed. And carefully he broke his remaining piece of banana and gave once again unto me. . . .

I met Esther today.
I met Esther today in El Salvador.

A young mother, frail and weak. She walked with a limp. The woman beside me saw my gaze. "There was a bomb attack. Everybody ran. She was pregnant. She had to run, too. The baby came. She gave birth on the run. She had to pick up her baby and keep running. She still isn't well." My eyes met with Esther's. She brought me her child.

I held Esther today.
I held Esther in El Salvador.

A baby. A baby born on the run. Her body long. Her bones bare. Her face alight with love. She gave me all she had. A smile and the joy of holding her. Of feeling her gentle life against my body.

I danced with Esther today.
I danced with Esther in El Salvador.

It was a despedida. A good-bye celebration. Gifts were given. A gourd which serves as a cup. A circle of rope. A petate for sleeping. The music played in that bamboo hut, and I held in my arms the child, Esther, born on the run, as we danced on the dirt floor.

I saw Esther today.
I saw Esther in El Salvador.

Full of laughter and joy. A song in her heart. A commitment on her lips. Singing of the goodness of God.

> She opened her arms and said unto me.
> "Come! Believe! Build a new society with us.
> We have all we need. God with us.
> God's Word. One another.
> And our hands and our feet!
> Come! Believe! Build a new society with me!"

Meditative Song

Play the tape of "Sing to Me the Dream" by Holly Near from Sing to Me the Dream.

Reflection

The Co-Madres, the Mothers of the Plaza de Mayo, the children, the young mothers, the babies of every country are our friends. From them we hear, "Come! Believe! Build a new society with me!"

How can we build a new society together?

What do we want to create? How will we do it? Whose voices will guide us?

Let's take a few minutes to think about these questions and then share our reflections.

Circle of Solidarity

To rebuild society we need to implement all of these ideas and more. The work is endless, everlasting, and life-giving. We need to feel the support of one another to keep us empowered.

So, stand up. Form a circle. Put your arms around one another. Lean back. Feel the strength and support of this community. Remember this feeling when times are tougher.

Blessing of Bread

Remember this feeling as we take, bless, break, and eat bread together.

(Four people speak a sentence similar to the following as they each bring bread to the table.)

Voice 1: Daily bread in every land is the bread of necessity, the bread of life.

Voice 2: Women bake bread daily: tortillas, wheat bread, rye bread, matzah.

Voice 3: Women are as common as these common, daily breads.

Voice 4: When you see bread, bake bread, eat bread, remember the women of the world.

Let us extend our hands, palms up, and bless these breads (*silent blessing*). Let us pass these breads around, take pieces of them, and eat as we listen.

Bread-Sharing Reading

"New Dawn," by Escqario Sosa Rodriguez from *Companera* (Nov.–Dec. 1987), Caracas, Venezuela

> *Woman*, lovely name charged with hope.
> *Sister*, word that instills dignity.
> *Comrade, mother, friend, beloved.*
> So many names for a being
> with such creative hands,
> a heart full of solidarity,
> a beautiful voice silenced for so many years
> but now willing to shout out against injustice,
> willing to sing of hope.
> Woman, good friend,
> together we dream of a new dawn.
> With your experienced hand in my new one,
> let us sweep away oppression;
> let us lovingly wash our children's hungry faces.
> Women, sister, comrade,
> let us together weave a huge coat
> to warm our old people.
> Together let us weave a patchwork quilt
> of love and kindness.
> Together, woman, let us, you and me, cook
> a huge dinner for all the hungry of the world.
> Woman, good friend,
> let us dream together of a new tomorrow.

GREETING OF PEACE: Put your arms around one another again. Lean back in the circle. Feel the strength and support of this community as we dream of a new tomorrow. Embrace one another with this power. Filled with this power, let us bless one another by speaking aloud a word or phrase of solidarity and friendship.

CLOSING SONG: "Yo Soy Mujer" by Maria Del Valle and Mildred Bonilla from *The Best of Struggle*, Womancenter at Plainville.

> I am a woman in search of equality.
> I will not stand for any abuse or malice.
> I am a woman and I have dignity
> and soon justice will become a reality.

Marian Henriques Neudel describes an innovative approach to include women in a conservative Jewish congregation. The group calls itself the Upstairs Minyan and is based at the Hillel Foundation at the University of Chicago. A minyan is the quorum of ten men required for a Jewish service, but women and men are included in the Upstairs Minyan. Women do readings at the ceremonies of this minyan they call their own. In the earlier stages of the group they used English, but now that they have sufficiently mastered the language, they read in Hebrew as the usual Jewish service prescribes. They lead the Saturday morning services along with the men and on some high holidays recite the blessings for reading the Torah. They also read from the Hebrew Torah scroll, which is a role usually assigned to men. Some of these women have taken to wearing the prayer shawl and even the skull cap, which are traditionally reserved for men.

The members of the Upstairs Minyan have changed the liturgical text of the Jewish prayerbook to reflect their sensitivity to inclusive language. Because of the importance of the covenant to Jews, some women had expressed concern about the use of only the male names of Abraham, Isaac, and Jacob in prayer. The women of the minyan noticed that the female counterparts of the recipients of the covenant—Sarah, Rebecca, Leah, and Rachel—were mentioned in Genesis. Neudel says, "A tradition is defined and laid out by its remembered beginnings; this element of Jewish origins had been tragically, but unnecessarily, lost" (182). Therefore, the women inserted the names of both partners, men and women, into the prayer book to be used by minyan members and nonmembers alike.

Women have brought to the group the results of their collaborative efforts. "Status in the group derives almost entirely from ability and willingness to lead services, read Torah, teach skills and share Jewish knowledge" (Neudel, 184). Although the rabbi is present, his authority is not supreme. Women are even called to be cantors at the ceremonies. Respect for the gifts of women and support for their continued development has been a hallmark of the Upstairs Minyan. Women have been encouraged to study the Hebrew language Bible, rituals, and traditions in order to gain equal involvement in the organizational and liturgical leadership of their congregation.

Another attempt to incorporate the liberating experience of women is recorded in a 1987 group effort at composing an interreligious worship service. The service was planned, executed, and celebrated complete with prayers, music, dance, and readings of the ritual. Members of the planning group—Protestant, Catholic, Jewish, and Muslim women—who met at

Marymount College in New York City in 1987 believed that the "hours spent together by the small planning committee had built mutual acceptance of individual differences and each person's rich spiritual resources" (Levitt, 183). The following is a portion of the service.

Gathering: An Interreligious Worship Service

Prepared by Virginia Baron; Carla De Sola (dance); Norma Levitt; Joan Ronayne, R.S.H.M.; Catherine Vincie, R.S.H.M. (music)

Musical Prelude

Lighting of the Candles (liturgical dance)

Opening Prayer:

Eternal Spirit, we believe in your limitless fidelity to us; deepen our faith within us. We believe in your absolute trust; enliven our hope. We believe in the certainty of your love; infuse new love into us.

We come before you as women of faith; look on our impoverished spirit and empower us to fullness of faith. Look on the gifts you have given us and inspire us in the creative use of them. Look on the oppressed and unfree areas of our lives; call us into new freedom. Look on those issues which unite us; let the unity of your life flow through us to one another.

God of all creation, we believe that you have an eternal care for all of your people; guide us as women of faith to promote your love wherever it is overshadowed or destroyed by divisiveness, destruction, war, or oppression of any kind. You are a God of peace; open our minds and hearts and help us to be peacemakers. You are the source of our inspiration, you are our strength, you are our light and our hope; may we always remember to call on you, especially in times of powerlessness, weakness, and uncertainty. We praise and thank you for your eternal goodness and for the abundance of life you continue to give us.

We love you especially for the gentle ways in which you constantly re-create us, and we beg you to bring about the true recognition of women everywhere as daughters of God, called to the fullness of life in you, and sharers in the building of your sovereignty on earth.

Accept our prayer, Adonai, which comes from hearts hungry for you and for your justice; hearts also humbled by our own many infidelities, yet confident in your goodness and compassion which are beyond all human understanding. Amen.

Period of Silence

Music of the Spirit

Responsive Reading:

Reader:	Grant us power, O God, to right the wrongs which we inherit.
All:	The sins we perpetuate, the oppression we endure.
Reader:	For the prejudice of race against race,
All:	And for distorting facts to fit our theories;
Reader:	For the deception of sexes against each other,
All:	And for denying responsibility for our own and others' misfortunes;

Reader:	For the disdain against those whose age disturbs us,
All:	And for pretending to emotions we do not feel;
Reader:	For the aggression of religious prejudice and the denial of religious freedom,
All:	And for deceiving ourselves and others with half truths;
Reader:	For keeping the poor in chains of poverty,
All:	And turning a deaf ear to the cry of the oppressed;
Reader:	For waging war and supporting violence,
All:	And for appeasing aggressors;
Reader:	For poisoning by cynicism,
All:	And for withholding trust and love; forgive us, O God.
Reader:	You, O God, have fashioned us in your image, to be co-creators with you in a world where we can help to make a better life.
All:	Teach us to right the wrongs we inherit, the sins we perpetuate,
Reader:	The oppression we endure.
All:	Give us the assurance that each one of us matters and that every action counts.
Reader:	Grant us hope, to lift us out of a sense of powerlessness.
All:	Hope sustains us when we rise each morning, when we undertake every task, when we turn to our neighbor in trust.
Reader:	As we consider our concerns, O God,
All:	Grant us hope, grant us power, grant us peace.

Hymn to be sung during the Roll Call of Women:

Gather Us In

Here in this place, new light is streaming,
Now is the darkness vanished away.
See, in this space, our fears and our dreamings
Brought here to you in the light of this day.
Gather us in, the lost and forsaken,
Gather us in, the blind and the lame,
Call to us now, and we shall awaken,
We shall arise at the sound of our name.

We are the young, our lives are a mystery,
We are the old, who yearn for your face.
We have been sung throughout all of history,
Called to be light to the whole human race.
Gather us in, the rich and the haughty,
Gather us in, the proud and the strong,
Give us a heart so meek and so lowly,
Give us the courage to enter the song.

Not in the dark of buildings confining,
Not in some heaven light years away.
But here in this space, the new light is shining
Now is the kingdom, now is the day.
Gather us in, and hold us forever,
Gather us in, and make us your own.
Gather us in, all peoples together,
Fire of life in our flesh and our bone.

Roll Call of Women:
As women of faith, we stop to remember women who have
gone before:

> women who have left their mark on our lives, on the
> lives of others in society, and on history. . .
> women whose lives give us courage when our spirits
> are burnt out . . .
> women who would not accept definitions assigned to them
> by tradition when it meant confining their aspirations . . .
> women who were willing to clear new paths in unfamiliar
> territory for the sake of their families or their communities . . .
> women who walked in the light of their own energy and
> enthusiasm to create institutions of hope for the lost,
> the sick, and the forgotten . . .
> women who have dared to be all they could be, in the
> dark times and in the bright times.

All: "Gather Us In" (first verse)
We pause to remember women we never knew whose lives
have inspired us:

Naming of Names
Silence

All: "Gather Us In" (second verse)
We pause to remember women we have known whose encouragement and
example have pushed us to the limits of ourselves:

Naming of Names
Silence

All: "Gather Us In" (third verse)
We pause to remember women we know who may be unknown to the
world but who have poured their power and love blessings on us:

Naming of Names
Silence

As women of faith, we give thanks for the lives of all the women we have
named. We ask the God of creation to dwell in us so that we may be a light for
those who come after us.
All: "Gather Us In" (all verses)

Benediction (liturgical dance)

Reformist feminist theologians have been criticized for ignoring some
traditional doctrines and practices of their churches and synagogues. In
their emphasis on the liberating texts of their scriptures, they disregard
other references that maintain the status quo. Their critics accuse them of
sifting and sorting traditional doctrine to pick certain ones instead of
accepting all of the revelation as God-given. They argue that whenever one
element of a whole, such as liberation, is chosen for the model to achieve
reform, other elements may be obscured. It seems to some of the critics
that reformist theologians make their central focus the issue of woman's

rights rather than emphasis on the divine. When social causes appear to overshadow the focus of religion, critics claim that relation to the divinity can disappear. Radical feminists wonder why the reformers want to bother with scriptures and traditions that are so blatantly discriminatory against them. Reconstructionist are more sympathetic to their venture because they value the need of women to bond together to achieve a rightful place in their religious traditions.

Contemporary Goddess-Centered Religions

The History of Witchcraft

Advocates of goddess worship say that the goddess has continued to be venerated through the ages even though such worship has been denounced by patriarchal societies. Christianity initially forced the goddess religion underground, where it remained in the form of witchcraft. Witchcraft has a long history as a form of goddess worship, spanning from the early folk religions to the present. Supporters of goddess worship refer to it as wicca.

In the preliterate traditional African, Native American, and European folk religions (whose remnants exist today), shamans and shamanesses were considered religious leaders whose wisdom was highly venerated. Because they understood the healing power of herbs, plants, and potions, they were often considered to have powers that other members of society did not possess. The druid priests and priestesses of Ireland, medicine men and women of Native American religions, and shamans and shamanesses still practicing in traditional African religions combine their knowledge of natural forces with psychological insights for effective healing.

The sand paintings of the Navajo Indians are an example of these combined forces. The patient sits on the sand in a middle of a painting and tries to absorb the thoughts of the picture into his or her own psyche. These paintings are designed to put the sick person in harmony with the universe as he or she relaxes on it, feeling the heat and peace of solitude. The patients internalize these feelings of health and harmony and then can integrate them into their own experience. While in this peaceful, relaxed posture, the patients can separate themselves from the confusion and emotions that might cloud their self-knowledge and impede their physical recovery and psychological harmony.

A shamaness from the Baganda tribe in Uganda still uses a milk stone to deter illness and subsequent death from poisonous snake bites. The special stone is soaked in milk and applied to the wound, which draws the poison out, leaving the victim healthy and strong. Other illnesses, however, were difficult to cure in the past. Realizing that some natural forces were out of their control, the shamans resorted to magic in an attempt to assert control over them. The magic developed into rituals in which natural objects such as sticks, trees, and flowers were used to secure protection from evil.

Sometimes the pollen, leaves, or seeds were ground into powders to be consumed by individuals who desire fertility, safe childbirth, or a successful hunt. Shamanesses and shamans developed love potions to attract desirable marriages.

These superhuman abilities to bend nature to their will brought shamans esteem from their beneficiaries but suspicion from their enemies. Sometimes those who exhibited the powers of magic, whether they were considered healing and helpful or evil and destructive, were labeled sorcerers, magicians, or witches—terms that have a negative connotation. The Hebrew Bible mentions the punishment given to a sorceress: "You will not allow a sorceress to live" (Exod. 22:18). Yahweh says to his people, "If anyone has recourse to the spirits of the dead, or to magicians . . . I shall set my face against him and outlaw him from his people" (Lev. 20:6). The Egyptians in the thirteenth century BCE denounced magicians and conjurers who claimed to secure their power from alien gods. They concluded that the Hebrew prophet Moses and his followers were servants of an alien god and must be witches. Roman laws against magicians and practitioners of witchcraft were also dramatic. The Twelve Tables, a collection of the earliest known laws of the Roman people, ordained that a man should not remove his neighbor's crops to another field by incantations or conjure away his corn. The penalty was death for practicing incantations or administering poisonous drugs.

During the Middle Ages, Christian churches joined forces with the secular governments of Europe to seek out and persecute persons who held the dubious powers of magic. Christians tied witchcraft to the powers of evil, assuming that if the powers could not be determined as coming from God, then they must have their origin in God's enemy, the devil. It was thought that it would only be right for the Christian church and the Christian state to fight the demonic powers so that God's kingdom, not the devil's, would be established on earth. Two Dominican clergymen, James Sprenger and Henrich Kramer, were sent as inquisitors to Germany to investigate the claims of witchcraft in the fifteenth century CE. They found that most witches were women who disobeyed God's laws: Acting as midwives, these women gave the expectant mother herbs to curb their labor pains. The inquisitors viewed this as complete disrespect to God, who had punished Eve by telling her she would bring forth her children in pain. Kramer and Sprenger wrote *Malleus Malificarum*, or *Hammer of Witches*, which was promulgated by the Roman Catholic church in 1486.

> All witchcraft comes from carnal lust, which is in women insatiable. . . .There are three things that are never satisfied, yea, a fourth thing which says not, it is enough: that is, the mouth of the womb. Wherefore for the sake of fulfilling their lusts they consort even with devils. . . . And blessed be the Highest Who has so far preserved the male sex from so great a crime: for since He was willing to [be] born and to suffer for us, therefore he has granted to men this privilege.
>
> *Summers, 47*

The crimes of accused witches were reportedly casting spells on humans, animals, and cultivated fields; transforming themselves into animals; having intercourse with the devil, who usually appeared in the form of he-goat; and holding a ritual called witches sabbath. The witches apparently had control over men's sexual organs, which they severed and hid from them. The Dominican friars, Sprenger and Kramer, asked the following question:

> What is to be thought of those witches who in this way sometimes collect male organs in great numbers, as many as twenty or thirty members together, and put them in a bird's nest, or shut them up in a box, where they move themselves like living members?
>
> *Summers, 121*

The surgery did not seem to seriously afflict the male victims, because they would come looking for their missing parts. One man reached out to retrieve his organ from a nest in the tree and, taking the largest one there, was told to put it back because "it belonged to the parish priest" (*Malleus Malificarum*, 121).

One of the cases documented in the *Malleus* gives some indication of how little recourse the accused person had to justice. As the story goes, one elderly woman was annoyed because she was not invited to a neighbor's wedding, so she asked the devil to rain hailstones on the celebration at the height of the party. The devil obliged her by carrying her through the air to a mountain where some shepherds witnessed her action. She dug a hole, urinated in it, and stirred the liquid with her finger. Then the devil carried the liquid to a cloud, which showered hailstones on the dancing guests. Testimony from the suspicious guests and the shepherds was enough to convict the woman of witchcraft, for which she was burned (*Malleus*, 175).

Most of the persons accused of witchcraft in Europe and America were women. Usually they were women unprotected by men, such as widows or single women not under the domination of their fathers. Often these women had become recent recipients of property or wealth that a neighbor or magistrate wanted to secure. After a bitter disagreement, a neighbor would accuse the woman of cursing his cattle or causing some ailments to the family. The accused would be thrown in prison, and the neighbor would graze his cattle on her land or plow it for himself.

Anyone could bring the accusation against the women—sometimes children, sometimes hysterical young girls in questionable trances, or sometimes someone who would profit by her death. Rumors were sufficient cause for an arrest. Even statements made by the accused's personal enemies were ample evidence to bring claim against the defendant. The suspected witch would then be tortured until she confessed to relieve the pain. If she tried to recant the confession made under such duress, the judge would decide that the devil was really behind her lies and that she must be guilty because good people would never give in to the devil. She was condemned to death, usually by hanging or being burnt at the stake.

One method employed to determine an accused witch's guilt or innocence was an ordeal of water. Townspeople stripped the suspect, tied her
hands and feet together, and then dragged her through a river or lake. If
she drowned, she was considered innocent; if she did not, she was judged
guilty and deserving of death.

The craze to seek out and punish witches spread with the English
colonists to New England. The Protestant ministers and their congregations
believed that witches entered into a covenant with the devil, who gave them
supernatural powers. It was reported that they were more than threats to
their neighbor's well-being. They were heretics as well and thus enemies of
God and society. The witches were accused of causing illness and death to
infants and young children. The accuser would speak of a "thriving child"
who suddenly gave out a great screech as if it "were gravely hurt," after
which it did "pine away," continuing in a "sad condition" until it "died"
(Boyer and Nessenbaum, 1:94). Other injuries such as temporary blindness,
accidents, or loss of memory were blamed on the witch, who was accused
of performing the devil's evil deeds. Her accuser could bring charges of hin-
dering the reproductive abilities of both humans and cattle by preventing
conceptions, causing miscarriages or abortions, and causing "monstrous" or
deformed births. It was thought that a witch's evil abilities extended to the
ruination of food. She could cause a tub of butter suddenly to go rancid
and could spoil beer in the making, causing it to "jump out of the barrel,"
or disappear altogether (Boyer and Nessenbaum, 1:94).

The witch did not always act alone. She was believed to be helped by
imps, or animal familiars, who were supernatural fiends and friends of the
devil. The imps sucked on her body and left their marks in the form of an
outgrowth, referred to by her adversaries as the witches teat. A suspected
witch was stripped naked and her body searched for the tell-tale marks,
which would be most commonly found on the breasts or around the genitals. About 80 percent of the witches were women and were believed to
encourage younger women, at the devils bidding, to join with them in their
evil pact. The group of witches was said to meet at a "sabbat" celebration in
a field, usually around midnight, to revel and celebrate by dancing with the
imps and with the devil himself. They would all renounce their baptismal
commitment to God and sign a pact with the devil. Usually the witches
were said to be carried to their celebration by a he-goat, which they would
kiss under his tail. Sometimes their accusers saw them flying through the air
on brooms or rakes to reach their sabbat celebration with the devil and his
fiendish friends.

The Puritans of New England were strict about the sexual roles of men
and women in society. Most of the accused witches were women who challenged the gender roles by outspokenness or aggressive behavior. Puritan
ministers insisted that they also challenged the supernatural order created
by God. "Neighbors testifying against the accused often cited hostility to the
Puritan God, church, or clergy as evidence of witchcraft" (Karlsen, 121).
Women belonging to more egalitarian or minor sects, such as the Quakers,

were especially suspect because they violated Paul's injunction "not to speak in church." When accusation of heresy was combined with witchcraft, convictions were easily arranged.

The medical profession had something to gain in New England by ridding itself of the competition of midwives and healers. Women were barred from becoming doctors in seventeenth century America but often had esteemed home remedies that had been passed from generations of mothers to daughters. These remedies became suspect. If the remedies contradicted the scientific wisdom of the male doctors, the doctors believed the source to be the devil, claiming that only through pacts with the devil could these stubborn women maintain their knowledge.

Statistics from the Salem, Massachusetts, witch trials indicate that most of the victims were women without husbands, brothers, or sons. Many of them had inherited property: "These women were aberrations in a society with an inheritance system designed to keep property in the hands of men" (Karlsen, 101). Religious and economic motives that revolved around the accepted sex roles of women in church and society prompted the arrest, conviction, and execution of hundreds of women accused as witches in New England in the seventeenth and eighteenth centuries.

The persecution of witches began to wane as the influence of the Puritan religion diminished. The rational aspects of the Enlightenment (an eighteenth century philosophical movement) also helped to overcome the superstitious claims of people ignorant of the scientific principles of cause and effect. Finally, a religious phenomenon known as the Awakening gained prominence in the United States in the nineteenth century and appeared to endorse emotional states like those attributed to witches. Women began to use the gifts of healing again, and midwives were allowed to pick the herbs that they used to deaden pain, to assist in childbirth, and to aid the digestive process. Present-day members of the craft, however, wish to remind us of the many people executed from the eleventh to eighteenth centuries. Estimates of the number of victims range from hundreds of thousands to millions.

> The people accused of witchcraft were victims of the fears and superstitions of society. In the history of witchcraft the accused were often thought to have committed evil and murderous deeds, but innocent people suffered in vain. A thought may be spared for the victims.
>
> *Newall, 127*

Witchcraft lay nearly dormant until the twentieth century, when witchcraft covens in England began to emerge with the goddess as the object of worship. Interest in ecology also brought an interest in folk magic and natural healing substances. Feminists who saw no future for women in patriarchal religions began to look for alternative religious experiences. They began to explore the newly rediscovered goddess cultures of old and saw some connections to the earth magic of healing. These women decided to create a new variety of religious experience using some of the ingredients of witchcraft and the goddess religions. They called their creation wicca.

Modern Wicca

The word *wicca* is derived from the Old English word *wic*, which means "to bend or twist." The image of a wicker basket constructed from bent reeds illustrates the power of bending to create something useful. The old English word for weaving also relates to the craft of wicca. The artist envisions a finished cloth or picture and then brings the vision to a reality. The word *wicca* relates well to the modern version of witchcraft, because today's witches see themselves as trying to construct a reality that will lend itself to more productive and satisfied individuals and society. The word *craft* is also used because it reflects the attempts of women to vitalize and bring to birth the gifts of both men and women.

Starhawk, a recognized witch and leader of a practicing coven, says wicca "is not a religion with a dogma, a doctrine, or a sacred book. It is a religion of experience, of ritual, of practices that change consciousness and awaken power from within" (1979, 24). Naomi Goldenberg says that scholars from Western patriarchal religions that emphasize doctrines, rigid laws of discipline, and sacred books point out that wicca is not really a religion because those ingredients are missing (113). Members of wicca argue, however, that the patriarchal doctrines and scriptures ignore the experience of women and that a new religion must therefore be established to incorporate their interests. Starhawk calls wicca a reawakening of the goddess religion of old, not a new religion. Modern wiccans see their connection to the ancient herbalists, healers, and counselors who were considered the wise men and women of medieval European, traditional African, and Native American societies.

The deity for wicca is a goddess because a goddess is connected to nature as the source of life, but especially because she can be perceived as the power within each individual. The goddess is believed to inhabit each person intimately, empowering the individual to thought and action. The immanence of the goddess is stressed in her relation to nature in the form of earth, water, wind, fire, the moon, milk, plants, and trees. This immanent presence of the goddess in all things serves to connect her to them and to connect them to one another. According to Starhawk, the witch who is conscious of these connections can use her psychic power to extract the healing powers from nature in the form of herbs. She can also use her psychic power to help others recognize the healing powers within themselves (both physical and psychological). The immanent goddess shows these supernatural powers to her followers, who use them to awaken these powers in others. Starhawk describes the attributes of the goddess that make her attractive to the followers of wicca.

> The goddess can be seen as the symbol, the normative image of immanence. She represents the divine embodied in nature, in human beings, in the flesh. The goddess is not one image but many—a constellation of forms and associations—earth, air, fire, water, moon and star, sun, flower and seed, willow and apple, black, red, white, Maiden, Mother, and Crone. She includes the male in her aspects: He becomes child and consort, stag and bull, grain and reaper, light and dark. Yet the femaleness of the Goddess is primary not to denigrate the male, but because it represents bringing life into the world, valuing the world.
>
> *Starhawk, 1988*

Women in wicca find much challenge and comfort in the goddess. She liberates them from their fears and lack of self-esteem. She restores a sense of dignity to the female body, which changes through aging. Rather than allowing men to dictate the attributes of attractiveness, which constrains beauty to youth, mature women appreciate the beauty of maturity and old age. They can identify with the phases of the moon, which represent the phases of the goddess. Her youth and independent virginity give way to the full moon, which typifies motherhood and abundance. The waning moon represents the crone, or wise old woman, who willingly shares her wisdom with all members of wicca. The three phases of the moon illustrate the connection of the goddess with nature, but also with the inspiration of culture. She is the one who inspires women to create by their weaving, poetry, literature, art, and scientific endeavors. However, the goddess is not neglectful of men or their power.

> The female image of divinity does not . . . provide a justification for the oppression of men. The female, who gives birth to the male, includes the male in a way that male divinities cannot include the female. The Goddess gives birth to a pantheon that is inclusive rather than exclusive. She is not a jealous God. She is often seen with a male aspect—child or consort. In Witchcraft, the male aspect is seen as the Horned God of animal life, feeling, and vital energy. Manifesting within human beings and nature, the Goddess and God restore content and value to human nature, drives, desires, and emotions.
>
> *Starhawk, 1988*

Rather than emphasize the transcendence of the divinity, Starhawk says that the wiccan craft is an earth religion with a basic orientation to earth, life, and nature. Divine authority is not mediated through priestesses or anyone else in the egalitarian covens, which recognize the self-worth of each member.

The coven is the basic structure of wicca, a group of about 13 members of one or both sexes. Covens usually meet during the full moon, and the 13 members commemorate the 13 full moons of the year. The number stays small in order to engender an atmosphere of love and trust. The members pool their energy in order to empower each other. They form a circle to perform their rituals so they can contain the power that is raised. By chanting, dancing, and concentrating their will, the coven members raise this power in the symbolic form of a cone. At its peak, the power is released to the goddess so she can reenergize the members or perform a specific action such as comforting or healing. After the peak is reached, the members fall to the ground, relax, and return to a calm and quiet period. The quiet is the fruitful part of the coven's ritual in which, in silent meditation or trance, members can put to good use the psychic power that they have released. Usually food and socializing follow until they bid the goddess farewell and formally open the circle. The members part with the salutation "merry meet, merry part, and blessed be."

The egalitarian aspect of witchcraft stresses that all women are priestesses and goddesses. They are encouraged to build altars and keep a mirror there in order to remind themselves that each time they see their reflection, they see the goddess. When they meditate at their altar, they are encouraged to use their power to bend or invigorate their will. The strong will that can be developed through this discipline has given them powers that sometimes resemble magic. Witches are seriously enjoined to use this power for good because they believe that if they curse someone, the evil will rebound on them threefold. The only time a witch can wish people evil is if they are attacking her in word or deed. The motto of wicca is "Do what thou wilt, as long as it harms none."

When wiccans worship the male god, they often refer to him as the horned god. The horns represent his fertility and link him to the changing seasons. He dies symbolically every autumn in order to rise again during the winter solstice. He appears as the consort or son of the goddess, and he is called by names that indicate his characteristics such as Apollo, the sun; Osiris, the dying god; or Pan, the changeable one. Men wiccans are referred to as gods or sometimes as warlocks.

There are a variety of wiccan ritual tools. As with most other aspects of wicca, the tools may be created by the practitioner or given to him or her. They may also be purchased at a wiccan store. A wand is a tool of invocation used to call upon the god or the goddess, and a broom is used to clean and purify the area of worship. The athane is a ritual knife used for the casting of magic spheres and directing of energy, never for cutting or wounding.

Naomi Goldenberg says that "to witches, magic is the ability to bring about change in the world" (110). The change must begin with an attitude or image formed in the imagination. Props such as candles, crystal balls, crystals, incense, and jewelry help to focus the imagination in order to accomplish the change. Witches use tarot cards to reveal possibilities in the future life of the person having the cards read, by examining their present situation. Tarot decks contain 78 brightly colored cards that depict a moment in one's life. It might be an event, a person, a mood, an attitude, or a behavior.

"Because Tarot cards are explicit in their portraits of matters relating to love, death, joy and work, they immediately affect the ideas and emotions of anyone who concentrates on them" (Goldenberg, 101). By examining the emotions and feelings they have while studying the cards, wiccans gain greater self-knowledge. Through discussion with the witch reader, the person receiving the reading can better understand the situation he or she is presently enduring. The reader then can help the person to make decisions for the future that will be the most beneficial for that person and others.

Critique of Contemporary Goddess Religions

Although they recognize that wicca provides a satisfying religious experience to its followers, some theologians have serious reservations about its qualification as a religion. Scholars question the emphasis on a female deity. The male clergy of the Western religions of Judaism, Christianity, and Islam, which focus on a male deity, object to the devotion to a goddess. Western thinking since Aristotle has emphasized dualism that separates rational and emotional and matter and Spirit. Goddess religions do not make use of the technique of dualistic thinking. Wicca tries to integrate the body/soul, matter/spirit dichotomies into one unit. Goddess religion sees no need for the ascetic practices patriarchal religions endorse to overcome the temptation of the world or flesh. This principle runs contrary to the principle that mind, spirit, and soul are superior to emotion, matter, and body. If the goddess permeates all, there is no need to separate this unity into categories in which one group dominates another.

Members of wicca try to develop their wills: They wish to bend natural and psychic forces to their individual wills. Patriarchal religions are concerned about the sin of pride or human will that might threaten submission to God's will. They see wicca as threatening the authority of institutional religion as well as God himself. Wicca does not discuss any sins against a covenant or law that stands outside the immediate human condition. There is no original sin from which its members must be reclaimed by baptism. This situation in turn does not require a savior to deliver the followers from the evil effects of sin. In fact, there is no need for a sacramental system. Without the emphasis on a transcendent god, there is not a future salvation for which one must strive.

All world religions have sacred scriptures or sacred texts. Without sacred writings, wicca appears to be classified as a preliterate religion. Those interested in the evolution of religion from polytheism to monotheism place wicca in the prehistoric era of nonliterate people. Intellectuals admire the documentation that is supported by the authority of the written word, so many academics and theologians do not take seriously the efforts of a religious group that does not own a standardized or revealed text.

There are not many laws in wicca. Morality is not judged in the manner of most world religions. There is no code of laws to measure the goodness or badness of an act because one's moral actions may become so relativized that one cannot make accurate moral decisions based on an objective moral code. Rather than considering sexual behavior as something to be controlled, wicca members take sex for granted and consider it something to be enjoyed. Rituals are often conducted in the nude, not anticipatory to sexual activity but as honest appreciation of the powers of the body. Patriarchal religions that seek to control the sexual behavior of their female members find it difficult to reconcile this relaxed attitude toward sex with their rigid laws concerning sexual behavior.

Other women hold reservations concerning the beliefs and practices of wicca as well. Reconstructionist and reformist feminists prefer to work within their own traditions for recognition of their gifts as women. But many groups of women, especially the radical feminists, admire the wiccan members for their attempts to find an alternative to patriarchal religion that can provide some women with challenge and satisfaction.

Summary

Most of the recent writing concerned with the rectification of patriarchal churches has been done by women in the Western traditions. Radical feminists representing Jewish and Christian women advocate the abandonment of God and Christ in order to return the goddess. They reject the scriptures of the Hebrew and Christian Bibles because these texts justify the oppression of women and the dominance of men. Radical feminists prefer the immanent presence of the goddess over the transcendent presence of God, who they perceive as a distant god with whom they have little in common. Radical feminists devise rituals to the goddess, whom they perceive as preceding the patriarchal religions and their gods.

The reconstructionist feminist scholars try to work within the scriptures and history of their religious communities to expose the roles, concerns, and experiences of women. By collaborating with feminist scholars in related fields, reconstructionists can uncover evidence that supports the role of women in the early phases of their religious traditions. If there is evidence to support the full participation of women in their historical religious communities, there is reason to repeat that precedent today. Jewish and Muslim scholars must bypass the commentaries made by later patriarchal writers to get to the original documents that show the intent of the founders.

Reformist feminist theologians ally themselves with the methods of the liberation theologians, who decry all forms of injustice and discrimination. These theologians examine the prophetic traditions of their religious communities, which called their members to view each person with dignity and equality. Reformers are concerned with the social dimensions of sin that reside in the structures of society. They list sexism along with racism, classi-

cism, imperialism, and colonialism as social sins that call for the transformation of the structures that caused them. Feminist reformers attribute the
social sin of sexism to patriarchal churches that deny women full participation in their structures. In order to compensate for their injustice, reformers construct their own rituals when they meet together in groups such as
Womenchurch, Upstairs Minyan, or other interreligious groups.

Contemporary goddess religions in Western society trace their origin to
the mother goddess through the route of European witchcraft. Although
innocent people were killed as devil-worshipping witches and the craft was
forced underground, belief in the healing, nurturing characteristics of the
mother goddess survived for centuries and continues today. The persecution of witches, who were mostly women, became especially vicious in
Puritan New England because the charge was tied to heresy. Many of the
women accused of witchcraft and heresy had dared to challenge the teachings of their patriarchal churches. Witchcraft has reappeared today, however, in the form of wicca, which fosters worship of the goddess. Female
members of covens relate to the presence of the goddess within themselves, and men relate to the horned god. Wicca structures are egalitarian,
as are their rituals.

Women in these movements justify their beliefs and actions as ways to
discover a satisfying alternative to patriarchal religions, which fail to utilize
the experience of women.

Questions for Discussion

1. How do radical feminists justify their position? What are some criticisms of their beliefs and practices?
2. What is the aim of the reconstructionist feminists? Why do they need
   the collaboration of experts from allied fields?
3. How do the reformist theologians aim to accomplish their purpose of
   liberating women?
4. Create your own religious ritual to commemorate a rite of passage for
   a woman. You may construct your ritual for her birth, puberty, marriage, death, or other life event.
5. Why was Christianity so opposed to the practice of witchcraft?
6. How were economic factors connected to the witchcraft persecutions?
7. Why do modern wiccans emphasize the immanent qualities of the
   goddess?
8. What arguments may arise against the practice of wicca?

Works Cited

Anzaldua, Gloria. "Entering into the Serpent." In *Weaving the Visions*, ed. Judith
    Plaskow and Carol Christ. New York: Harper & Row, 1989.

Boyer, Paul, and Stephen Nessenbaum, eds. *The Salem Witchcraft Papers: Verbatim Transcripts of the Legal Documents of the Salem Witchcraft Outbreak of 1692.* 3 vols. New York: Da Capo, 1977.

Brown, Virginia, Carla De Sola, Norma Levitt, Joan Ronayne, and Catherine Vincie. "Gathering: An Interreligious Worship Service." In *Women of Faith in Dialogue*, ed. Virginia Ramey Mollenkott. New York: Crossroads, 1987.

Budapest, Zsuzsanna. "Self Blessing Ritual." In *Womanspirit Rising*, ed. Carol Christ and Judith Plaskow. New York: Harper & Row, 1979.

Carmody, Denice, and John Carmody. *Christianity: An Introduction*. Belmont, Calif.: Wadsworth, 1983.

Cunningham, S. *Wicca: A Guide for the Solitary Practitioner*. Boston: Beacon Press, 1992.

Daly, Mary. "After the Death of God the Father: Women's Liberation and the Transformation of Christian Consciousness." In *Womanspirit Rising*, ed. Carol Christ and Judith Plaskow. New York: Harper & Row, 1979.

Davis, Elizabeth Gould. *The First Sex*. Baltimore: Penguin, 1971.

Falk, Marcia. "Notes on Composing New Blessings." In *Weaving the Visions*, ed . Judith Plaskow and Carol Christ. New York: Harper & Row, 1989.

Fiorenza, Elisabeth Schussler. *Bread Not Stone*. Boston: Beacon Press, 1984.

———. "Discipleship and Patriarchy." In *Women's Consciousness, Women's Conscience*, ed. Barbara Andolsen, Christine Gudorf, and Mary Pellauer. New York: Harper & Row, 1985.

———. "In Search of Women's Heritage." In *Weaving the Visions*, ed. Judith Plaskow and Carol Christ. New York: Harper & Row, 1989.

Goldenberg, Naomi. *Changing of the Gods*. Boston: Beacon Press, 1979.

Hassan, Riffat. "Muslim Women and Post-Patriarchal Islam." In *After Patriarchy*, ed. Paula Covey, William Eakin, and Jay McDaniel. Maryknoll, N.Y.: Orbis, 1991.

Karlsen, Carol. *The Devil in the Shape of a Woman*. New York: Vintage, 1989.

Landes, Paula Fredricksen. *Signs* 6, no. 2 (Winter l980): 328–34.

Levitt, Narma. "Preparing an Interreligious Service." In *Women of Faith in Dialogue*, ed. Virginia Mollenkott. New York: Crossroads, 1987.

Maududi, A. A. *The Meaning of the Quran*, vol. 2. Lahore: Islamic Publications, 1971.

"Men and Women in the Work Force," *Time* 140, no. 8 (August 24, 1992): 16.

Meyers, Carol. *Discovering Eve*. New York: Oxford University Press, 1988.

Mollenkott, Virginia Ramey. *Women, Men and the Bible*. New York: Crossroads, 1980.

Morris, Joan. *The Lady Was a Bishop*. New York: Macmillan, 1973.

Neu, Diane. "Women Crossing Worlds In Solidarity and Friendship," *Waterwheel* (Winter 1989–90).

Neudel, Marian Henriquez. "Innovation and Tradition in a Contemporary Midwestern Jewish Congregation." In *Unspoken Worlds*, ed. Nancy Auer Falk and Rita Gross. Belmont, Calif.: Wadsworth, 1989.

Newall, Venetia. *The Witch Figure*. London: Routledge & Kegan Paul, 1973.

Plaskow, Judith. "Jewish Memory from a Feminine Perspective." In *Weaving New Visions*, ed. Judith Plaskow and Carol Christ. New York: Harper & Row, 1989.

Prohl, Russell. *Women in the Church*. Michigan: Eerdmann,1957.

Starhawk. *Dreaming in the Dark*. Boston: Beacon Press, 1988.

———. "Witchcraft and Women's Culture." In *Womanspirit Rising*, ed. Carol Christ and Judith Plaskow. New York: Harper & Row, 1979.

Summers, Montague. *Maleficarum of Henrich Kramer and James Sprenger*. New York: Dover, 1971.

Talamantez, Ines. "The Presence of Isanaklesh: A Native American Goddess and the Path of Pollen." In *Unspoken Worlds*, ed. Nancy Auer Falk and Rita Gross. Belmont, Calif.: Wadsworth, 1989.

Suggested Readings

Bolen, Jean Shinoda. *Goddesses in Everywoman: A New Psychology of Women*. New York: Harper & Row, 1984.

Carroll, Bernice. *Liberating Women's History: Theoretical and Critical Essays in Women's History*. Urbana: University of Illinois Press, 1976.

Christ, Carol P. *Laughter of Aphrodite: Reflections on a Journey to the Goddess*. New York: Harper & Row, 1987.

————. "Why Women Need the Goddess: Phenomenological, Psychological and Political Reflections." In *Womanspirit Rising*, ed. Carol Christ and Judith Plaskow. New York: Harper & Row, 1979.

Delmar, Rosalind. "What is Feminism?" In *What Is Feminism? A Reexamination*, ed. Juliet Mitchell and Ann Oakley. New York: Pantheon, 1986.

Ehrenreich, Barbara, and Dierdre English. *Witches, Midwives and Nurses: A History of Women Healers*. New York: The Feminist Press, 1973.

Firestone, Shulamith. *The Dialectic of Sex: The Case for Feminist Revolution*. New York: Bantam, 1970.

Griffin, Susan. *Woman and Nature*. New York: Harper & Row, 1978.

Grimshaw, Jean. *Philosophy and Feminist Thinking*. Minneapolis: University of Minnesota Press, 1986.

Heilbrun, Carolyn. "On Reinventing Womanhood," *Columbia* (Fall 1979): 31–32.

————. *Toward a Recognition of Androgyny*. New York: Harper & Row, 1973.

Hunt, Mary. "Sharing Feminism: Empowerment or Imperialism?" *Journal of Women in Religion* 1 (Fall 1981): 33–46.

King, Ursula. "Goddesses, Witches, Androgyny and Beyond: Feminism and the Transformation of Religious Consciousness." In *Women in the World's Religions*, ed. Ursula King. New York: Paragon House, 1987.

Matter, E. Ann. "The Virgin Mary: A Goddess?" In *The Book of the Goddess Past and Present: An Introduction to Her Religion*, ed. Carl Olson. New York: Crossroads, 1983.

Morgan, Robin. "Introduction." *Sisterhood Is Powerful: An Anthology of Writings From the Women's Liberation Movement*. New York: Random House, 1970.

Murray, Margaret Alice. *The Genesis of Religion*. London: Routledge & Kegan Paul, 1963.

Ochshorn, Judith. *The Female Experience and the Nature of the Divine*. Bloomington: Indiana University Press, 1981.

Olson, Carl, ed. *The Book of the Goddess Past and Present: An Introduction to Her Religion*. New York: Crossroads, 1983.

Orenstein, Gloria. *The Reflowering of the Goddess*. Oxford: Pergamon Press Athene Series, 1990.

Perera, Sylvia Brinton. *Descent to the Goddess: A Way of Initiation for Women*. Toronto: Inner City Books, 1988.

Puhvel, Jaan. *Comparative Mythology*. Baltimore: Johns Hopkins University Press, 1987.

Rich, Adrienne. "Prepatriarchal Female/Goddess Images." In *The Politics of Women's Spirituality: Essays on the Rise of Spiritual Power within the Feminist Movement*, ed. Charlene Spretnak. New York: Doubleday, 1982.

Rohrolich, Ruby. "State Formation in Sumer and the Subjugation of Women," *Feminist Studies* 6, no. 1 (Spring 1980): 76–102.

Schur, Edwin M. *Labeling Women Deviant: Gender, Stigma and Social Control*. New York: Random House, 1984.

Sjoo, Monica, and Barbara Mor. *The Great Cosmic Mother: Rediscovering the Religion of the Earth*. New York: Harper & Row, 1987.

Starhawk. *The Spiral Dance: A Rebirth of the Ancient Religion of the Great Goddess*. New York: Harper & Row, 1979.

———. *Truth or Dare*. New York: Harper & Row, 1987.

———. "Witchcraft as Goddess Religion." In *The Politics of Women's Spirituality*, ed. Charlene Spretnak. Garden City, N.Y.: Anchor, 1982.

Teubal, Savina. *Sarah, the Priestess: The First Matriarch of Genesis*. Athens, Ohio: Swallow Press, 1984.

Tiffany, Sharon. "The Power of Matriarchal Ideas," *International Journal of Women's Studies* 5, no. 2 (1982): 138–47.

Tillion, Germaine. "Prehistoric Origins of the Condition of Women in 'Civilized' Societies," *International Social Science Journal* 69, no. 4 (1977): 671–81.

Weinbaum, Batya. *The Curious Courtship of Women's Liberation and Socialism*. Boston: South End Press, 1978.

Reasons for Women to Value Religion

Although women have been mistreated by their patriarchal faith communities, many choose to remain in religious traditions. They must find some satisfaction, challenge, and solace from their traditional religious communities that compensate for the hardships assigned to them by these same institutions. We examine some of the reasons in this final chapter.

Meaning and Belonging Dimensions of Religion

Human beings appear to have a need to invest their existence with meaning. Humans are not satisfied with the answers of science that give the *how* of things: They seem to desire to know the *why* as well. Viktor Frankl, a psychologist and survivor of Nazi death camps, argues that humans are as motivated by a desire for meaning in life as they are by the will to live. "There is nothing in this world, I venture to say, that would so effectively help one to survive even the worst conditions, as the knowledge that there is meaning in one's life" (Frankl, 164).

One of the benefits of all religions is that they provide a means to cope with the evil, sin, frustrations, and sufferings in this world. All religions admit to the presence of evil, but they reassure their followers that they need not succumb to that evil. The experience of pain and pleasure is common to all humans, but as people reflect on the causes and results, they try to derive meaning from the diversity of their encounters. As members of religious communities reflect on the puzzling discrepancies of justice in this world, they are pressed toward a satisfying resolution through their religious beliefs and practices. Members of various religions derive meaning

213

from the effects of evil as well as good. For instance, in the face of death, the experience of grief and loss can be muted by the hope of seeing a loved one in a future life. The hope of a pleasant rebirth will carry many who believe in reincarnation through a lifetime of oppression and suffering. The meaning dimension of religion represents an ambitious attempt to give the entire cosmos significance. Religion provides solace in times of grief and offers courage in the face of deprivation and danger. When providing guidance and strength for the achievement of goals, religion can establish moral codes to regulate the behavior of its members.

Religions also satisfy the need of humans to belong to a community. The various traditions of faith give humans a sense of social stability, role clarification, and group and individual identity. It is difficult to be either human or religious in isolation. We need others to bestow upon us a sense of identity as we gradually assume our roles in a stable community. Humans can better exercise their religious beliefs in communities of faith, whether they are Hindu ashrams, Buddhist sanghas, Jewish minyans, Catholic or Protestant congregations, or Islamic ummahs. Roger Schmidt, a professor of religion, points out the belonging function of religions.

> The social nature of religion, and, in particular, of holy rites, provides a context in which the crises of individual and group life can be resolved. In binding humans together, religion serves as a form of social control. As a source of stability and identity, religious institutions are sometimes reactionary and repressive, but they can also be instruments of reform and change. Holy communities are no strangers to conflict, but, as an integrative social force, they aim at the preservation and celebration of group life, particularly through their ritual practices, taboos, and moral teachings.
>
> *Schmidt, 13*

The meaning and belonging dimensions of religions fulfill such basic needs for all humans that women and men will remain in their faith communities in spite of frustration, disappointment, or oppression. Many of the village women in Asia, Africa, and the Middle East have no option but to remain in their religious traditions, which are also their social communities, because these traditions offer the critical values of meaning and belonging. Even if sexism is rampant and women are told that they are inferior to men, women are wary of cutting themselves off from all possible sources of meaning and belonging. Many village women of Hindu, Buddhist, and Chinese and Japanese religions as well as Jewish, Christian, and Muslim women would rather be second-class members of a sexist society than be alienated social outcasts with no community, worldview, or system of values.

Most Western-educated women in Western societies can choose whether to belong to a church or synagogue or to assume a completely secular lifestyle without the recrimination assigned to their third world sisters.

They may choose to stay with their denomination because they find the belonging dimension of religion very satisfying and because they gain emotional support from like-minded members. Speaking to other women in a community of women who share the same goals, problems, and disappointments can be reassuring, and sharing reflections on scriptural or sacred writing can be intellectually stimulating. Realizing that other members of the faith community share the same pleasures and frustrations can support and console each person. The satisfaction possible from the fulfillment of meaning and belonging needs directs many women to remain in their faith communities in spite of the discrimination and injustice that occur.

Human relations among members of faith communities are regulated by laws that define the rights and duties of its members. A system of values that govern human behavior is usually referred to as morality. When members deviate from the accepted code of behavior, their sense of belonging is threatened by religious sanctions that may isolate them from the community. For example, the Arapaho, Sioux, and other Plains tribes of North America developed a severe form of punishment known as shunning to discipline errant tribal members. Offenders were expelled from the tribe for a period of time, knowing that they could die from hunger because no one was allowed to come to their aid.

The Nature of the Ethical Task from the Experiences of Men and Women

"Ethics can be defined as the critical study of the moral life of society. The ethicist does not simply catalogue moral behavior, but investigates the values and principles and rules by which people live" (Jersild and Johnson, xvii). The values and principles often differ between men and women because of their different life experiences. Regardless of the arguments of *why* women's experience differs from men's—whether it is environment or heredity—researchers today agree that the inclinations of women (Gilligan 1979), their socialization process (Chodorow 1978; Messer-Davidow 1985), priorities, learning modes (Miller 1986; Ferguson 1992), and approaches to problem solving (Belenky et al. 1986) are different from men's. It is realistic to expect that men and women approach ethical or moral decisions in a different manner. Studies have shown that even if women and men reach the same conclusion to a moral decision, they will have used different approaches to reach that decision.

Because the scriptures for existing religions were written by men and implemented by patriarchal societies (Fiorenza 1985; Lerner 1979; Eisler 1988; Bennett 1989; Ruether 1983), it is reasonable to expect that norms for behavior and morality would be articulated and refined by men. Because women's contribution were minimal, their experience was usually ignored in the creation of codes to regulate the behavior of both sexes. Men's and women's daily life experience differ considerably in most religious societies.

Ideas of Good and Evil

Moral decisions that make use of ethical systems are based on ideas of good and evil. Studies conducted in the West have shown that men and women differ in their concepts of good, upon which desirable behavior is based, and evil, which is to be avoided. Men's ideas of the good tend to focus on rights—to property, person, freedom, liberty, and the pursuit of these rights. Abstract truths about these unalienable rights typify male writings on the subject. Carol Gilligan (1982) claims that a morality of rights is characteristic of men's moral reasoning and that a morality of responsibility is more characteristic of women. Part of men's psychosocial development is marked by separation from the parenting one, whereas women emphasize the quality of attachment, especially to the mother (Chodorow, 1978). Rights are more likely to be stressed in the separation process because the emphasis is on the autonomous individual. Men consider the violation of these individual or human rights more evil than women do.

Women appear to be more relational in that they place their emphasis and value on their relationships. Nancy Chodorow (1974) suggests that the egos and personalities of women are constructed in terms of their relationships to others. Carol Gilligan stresses the importance of relationships for women:

> Women not only define themselves in a context of human relationship, but also judge themselves in terms of their ability to care. Woman's place in man's life cycle has been that of nurturer, caretaker and helpmate, the weaver of those relationships on which she in turn relies.
>
> *Gilligan, 1979, 440*

Women tend to see themselves at the center of a web of multiple relationships, each of which carries a responsibility. Multiple responsibilities pull the bearer of these burdens in many directions, causing uneasiness and stress. Because women see themselves carrying the responsibilities for these numerous relationships, they often feel overburdened. Yet women tend to see the good in their continued efforts toward the welfare of those to whom they minister. Their responsibilities toward their family, friends, and society in general challenge them to provide for their needs. Western studies show that women's sense of the good involves loving care for others to the point of sacrificing their own needs and aspirations. Whereas men tend to concern themselves with principles and the arrangement of priorities for good among the principles, women are more interested in the concrete situation that calls for an immediate response. Nel Noddings, an ethicist, describes the concern of women regarding caring.

> But women, as ones-caring, are not so much concerned with the rearrangement of priories among principles; they are concerned, rather, with maintaining and enhancing caring. They do not abstract away from the concrete situa-

tion those elements that allow a formulation of deductive argument; rather, they remain in the situation as sensitive, receptive, and responsible agents.

Noddings, 42

Because women see themselves as trying to respond to their multiple responsibilities in each concrete situation, they are aware that there are times when they cannot fulfill all those obligations that they perceive as necessary and good. Their failure to fulfill satisfactorily their sense of the good leaves them saying things like "What more should I have done?" The woman's sense of evil is usually not the violation of rights or abstract principles that so often characterizes that of the man in patriarchal religions; instead, it is a failure to respond adequately to the demands made upon her in a specific situation.

Ideas Concerning Sin

The differences in male and female attitudes toward good and evil are related to the differences in attitudes toward sin. For most men in patriarchal Western religions, the worst sin is pride because the all-powerful, all-good, all-knowing God is so superior in the hierarchy of relationships that his subjects must show submission and deference. Islam, one of the most patriarchal religions, directs its followers to submit to the great Allah in all things.

> In the name of God, the Compassionate, the Merciful, Say: God is One, the Eternal God. He begot none, nor was He begotten. None is equal to Him.
>
> *Quran Surah 112*

It is not surprising that such an awesome God should expect obedience from his subjects. Anything that would deny submission would be labeled as pride. Even the physical posture of prayer in Islam, in which the Muslim kneels with his forehead touching the floor, denies any proud stance before God.

One of the interpretations of the fall story in Judaism and Christianity attributes the sin of pride to the disobedience of Adam and Eve. They were forbidden by God to eat of the fruit of the tree in the middle of the garden under pain of death.

> Then the snake said to the woman, "No you will not die. God knows in fact that the day you eat it your eyes will be opened and you will be like gods, knowing good from evil."
>
> *Genesis 3:4–6*

The temptation to be like gods, especially in their quest for immortality, has led some men to use children to perpetuate their name and lineage, to construct buildings as monuments to their memory, and to wage wars to leave their imprint on the world. Realizing the negative effects of such grandiose endeavors, most men disdain pride and extol the virtues of self-sacrifice and service to others. They define sin as a form of pride, as in self-assertion, self-love, self-centeredness, the desire to be as God, and the will to possess.

John Calvin, one of the founders of the sixteenth century Christian reform movement, warned his followers of the evils of pride. In a reference to the Genesis story, he said

> Man's mind, full as it is of pride and boldness, dares to imagine a God according to its own capacity. . . .Man tries to express in his work the sort of God he has inwardly conceived. Therefore, he conceives an idol.
>
> *Calvin, X18*

When promulgating the capital sins as written by male theologians, the Catholic church places the sin of pride at the head of the list. Even Saint Paul suggests that Christians should follow the example of Christ.

> The attitude you should have is the one that Christ Jesus had: He always had the nature of God, but he did not think that by force he should try to become equal to God.
>
> Instead, he emptied himself of all that he had and took the nature of a servant. . . .
>
> He was humble and walked the path of obedience to death, death on the cross.
>
> *Phil. 2:5–8*

Paul urged men to die to their pride and to unite their sacrifice to that of Christ, who spent his life in service to others. From the Christian standpoint, pride is to be remedied by self-sacrifice and loving service performed for the good of others.

A woman who grows up in a patriarchal society may not relate well to the concept of pride as evil because pride appears foreign to her lived experience. Seeing herself as the nexus of multiple relationships, she has spent her life adapting to others' needs. She needs no reminder of the worth of self-sacrifice and service because she has been in a series of other-focused relations in which the tendency is not to self-assertion, but to self-denial and loss of self-identity. The constant outpouring of herself often leaves little upon which to build her own self-esteem. Her lack of self-confidence is exacerbated by societal attitudes and institutions that have treated women as inferior persons. Therefore, sin for women is not pride, but the helplessness that results from an internalized depreciation of self. Persons with such feelings of worthlessness begin to actually believe that they deserve the unjust treatment they receive. Many battered women will remain with their tormentors because they feel that they do not merit better treatment. Some women lack the self-confidence to take charge of their own lives, and so the notion of sin as arrogant pride does not seem relevant to them.

> The temptations of woman as woman are not the same as the temptation of man as man, and the specifically feminine forms of sin . . . have a quality which can never be encompassed by such terms as *pride* and *will to power*. They are better suggested by such items as triviality, distractibility, and diffuseness; lack of an organizing center or focus; dependence on others for one's own self-definition, . . . in short, underdevelopment or negation of the self.
>
> *Saiving, 37*

There may be a sin similar to pride, however, in women's experience: manipulation. When one has spent oneself in the repetitive service of others at the loss of one's own growth opportunities and identity, one normally expects expressions of gratitude. If their continued efforts appear unappreciated, women may inflict guilt on the ungrateful recipients of their generosity. Because most women are not afforded all the opportunities that men receive, they experience a helplessness, self-pity, and frustration that leads them to manipulate others in order to gain their ends.

Men and women in Western patriarchal societies therefore differ on the idea of the good and evil, which is part of the meaning dimension of religion. As a result they differ in their ideas of sin. The belonging dimension of religion seems especially pertinent to women who see themselves as a hub in a web of relationships. A woman often make moral decisions from the concrete situation that she and others are experiencing. Men in patriarchal societies tend to base their moral judgments on abstract principles that define the good and which in turn act as a rational guide for their actions.

Rights and Relationships

Although the ethical task of bringing discernment and sensitivity to moral judgment may be the same for both genders in Western patriarchal religions, the routes to the task often differ for men and women. Men often resolve moral decisions by analyzing the abstract truths in the forms of rules or rights. Even as children playing informal games on the sand lot, boys spend much time arguing over the rules. Sayings such as, "It is not fair" and "cheater's proof" emerge from the games frequently. Pushing and shoving can escalate to fights that can rupture relationships (Gilligan, 1982, 10). In studies by Jean Piaget and Jane Lever, the behavior of girls in childhood games tend less to be bound by abstract rules. Girls appear more tolerant of intrusions, more accommodating to changing situations, and more willing to innovate their play than boys do. "Rather than elaborating a system of rules for resolving disputes, girls subordinated the continuation of the game to the continuation of relationships" (Lever, 481). These patterns that young girls exhibit seem to continue in adulthood, where the sense of belonging takes precedence.

Women analyze the facts of the situation in a context of multiple relationships. If a woman finds herself with an unwanted pregnancy, she generally will consider her multiple responsibilities. These include responsibilities to other children, the child's father, her parents, her friends, or her work.

Arguments appealing to the "rights of the unborn" may not carry the weight with her that her responsibilities toward others do.

A study of college presidents to discern the moral reasoning process used by both genders (Mennuti and Creamer) found that all the presidents used the elements of justice, care, and self in solving moral dilemmas. The authors designated justice as a concern for rights of others or the concern for competing rights. It showed itself in the presidents' use of rules, standards, duties, and obligation as their orientation in making ethical decisions. Care was the orientation applied to concern for others, seen especially in the presidents' attempts to consider the effects of the moral decision on the people involved and to maintain harmonious relationships. Self had to do with the concern for one's own principles and for the good of self, as manifested in self-appraisal and the appraisal of others. Women in the sample coupled their concern for justice with their concern for care more often than men. Men were more likely than women to appeal to the principle of justice alone in their moral reasoning process. Women considered more heavily their relationship with the people in the moral dilemmas, whereas men were oriented more toward the abstract truth of justice.

TABLE 8.1   Patterns of Orientation Use by Sex (in percent)

Orientation Pattern	Women	Men
Justice	0	15
Justice/self	28	47
Justice/care	39	0
Justice/care/self	33	37

Source: Rosemary B. Mennuti and Don G. Creamer, "Role of Orientation, Gender, and Dilemma Content in Moral Reasoning," *Journal of Student Development* 32.4 (1991): 246.

Psychologists such as Freud and Erikson depict men's maturation and development as commensurate with the establishment of autonomy and independence. They say that the male child realizes his own identity in separation from the mother and therefore can make his moral choices in a dispassionate and objective manner. Freud and Erikson feel that he is no longer influenced by his connection to the relationship that might inhibit his objectivity in the pursuit of the ethical task.

Women's attempts at autonomy are often hindered by economic dependence upon the family, lack of child care, inequality of pay and promotion in the labor force, and closer ties to the mother. Freud and Erikson say that women do not have to sever their relations with their mother in order to identify with the opposite sex as men do. Rather than finding their identity in separation, women find it in connection. Carol Gilligan describes a morality of responsibility based on connection as opposed to the masculine morality of rights based on separation. In analyzing a characteristic response of women, Gilligan claims that "morality and the preservation of life are contingent on sustaining connections, seeing the consequences of action by keeping the web of relationships intact" (1982, 50). Gilligan illustrates her point with the Abraham story from the Hebrew Bible in which the patriarch is ready to sacrifice his son for an abstract principle. She contrasts with it the story of Solomon, where a woman is ready to sacrifice the truth of her motherhood for the life of her child (1982, 104).

The Judgment of Solomon

Later two prostitutes came to the king and stood before him. "If it please you, my lord," one of the women said, "this woman and I live in the same house, and while she was in the house I gave birth to a child. Now it happened on the third day after my delivery that this woman also gave birth to a child. We were alone together, there was no one else in the house with us; just the two of us in the house. Now one night this woman's son died; she overlaid him. And in the middle of the night she got up and took my son from beside me while your servant was asleep; she took him in her arms and put her own dead son in mine. When I got up to suckle my child, there he was, dead. But in the morning I looked at him carefully, and he was not the child I had borne at all. Then the other woman spoke. "That is not true! My son is the live one, yours is the dead one"; and the first retorted, "That is not true! Your son is the dead one, mine is the live one." And so they wrangled before the king. "This one says," the king observed, "'My son is the one who is alive; your son is dead,' while the other says, 'That is not true! Your son is the dead one, mine is the live one.' Bring me a sword," said the king; and a sword was brought into the king's presence. "Cut the living child in two," the king said, "and give half to one, half to the other." At this the woman who was the mother of the living child addressed the king, for she felt acutely for her son. "I beg you, my lord," she said, "let them give her the live child; on no account let them kill him!" But the other said, "He shall belong to neither of us. Cut him in half!" Then the king gave his decision. "Give the live child to the first woman," he said, "and do not kill him. She is his mother."

All Israel came to hear of the judgment which the king had pronounced and held the king in awe, recognizing that he possessed divine wisdom for dispensing justice.

1 Kings 3:16–28

Nel Noddings gives another interpretation of the Abraham story that does not extol him for his obedience to God's command to kill his son Isaac. Nodding asserts that caring is so central to a woman's development of morality that she tends to define herself in terms of the capacity to care (42). She says a mother would never consent to kill her son, even at the direction of an all-powerful deity because "our natural relatedness gives birth to love" (43).

For us, then, Abraham's decision is not only ethically unjustified but it is in basest violation of the supraethic of caring. The one-caring can only describe his act—"You would kill your own son!"—and refuse him forgiveness.

> Abraham's obedience fled for protection under the skirts of an unseeable
> God. Under the gaze of an abstract and untouchable God, he would destroy
> *this* touchable child whose real eyes were turned upon him in trust, and love,
> and fear. I suspect no woman could have written . . . *Genesis* . . . but per-
> haps I should speak only for myself on that. The one-caring, male or female,
> does not seek security in abstractions cast either as principles or entities. She
> remains responsible here and now for this cared-for and this situation and for
> the foreseeable futures projected by herself and the cared-for.
>
> *Noddings, 43*

Carol Gilligan stresses the need of women to react in concrete situations
by connecting themselves to the cared-for person. Rather than theorizing
about an abstract principle, which requires some separation from the concrete situation in order to lend objectivity to the discussion, women
immerse themselves in the concrete situation. It is in living out the challenge that the moral dilemma presents that women can use their ability to
care.

> Women not only define themselves in a context of human relationships but
> also judge themselves in terms of their ability to care. Women's place in man's
> life cycle has been that of nurturer, caretaker, and helpmate, the weaver of
> those networks of relationships on which she in turn relies.
>
> *Gilligan, 1979, 431*

Priorities Versus Communitarian Approaches

The alienation myths of some patriarchal societies stress the separation
that results in dualistic thinking. This dualism manifests itself in the following manner: Humans are separated from God, spirit from matter, man from
woman, persons from their environment, reason from emotion, objective
from subjective, and earth from heaven. Unfortunately, in patriarchal societies, this separation does not portray an egalitarian relationship between
the opposite elements. Rather, patriarchies establish a priority in which one
element of the dyad is considered better than the other. The Judeo-
Christian myth of the fall story tells the woman that her husband will rule
over her. Adam renames woman Eve (Gen. 3:20), emphasizing his power
over her by his ability to rename her in the same way that God renamed
Abraham and Sara. The power of men to rule women was advocated by
Aristotle, who attributed to men the characteristics of rationality, objectivity,
intellectual activity, initiative, and spirit. The philosopher assigned the
opposite, less desirable traits to women, such as passion, subjectivity, emotion, passivity, inertia, and body.

When men are presented with prioritized, dualistic thinking from their
philosophers and theologians, the weight of these experts' authority justifies ethical action. Many ethical dilemmas lack clear-cut answers between
good and evil or between the better of two goods or the lesser of two evils.

When the choice lies between the rights of a person and the rights of a
community, men often make the choices differently than women. In an

atmosphere of competing rights, men find it easier to prioritize some rights as superseding others. For instance, studies have shown that men find the lifeboat ethics game challenging and spend time setting priorities for the persons to be saved. In the game the players must choose people for a lifeboat after the capsize of an ocean liner. The number of persons that the lifeboat can hold is limited, so the choice involves picking the most valuable members who can help one another and the species to survive. Such persons as a doctor, a woman of reproduction age, and a scholar are usually chosen first. When women play this game, they change the rules, refusing to save only a chosen few. They find alternative ways to save everyone.

Women, aware of the need of relationships to form community, are more likely to focus on the egalitarian aspects over the prioritizing dimensions. Aware of the tension between the personal and communal goods, needs and aspirations, they attempt to resolve the dilemma without prioritizing rights and values. Women see themselves as part of the whole and therefore believe it necessary to improve themselves and those close to them in order to improve the community. Feminist ethicists perceive connections between women and other oppressed groups in society. They perceive numerous similarities between sexism and racism. Many women object to the value theories that rank persons and values according to priority. They prefer not to make ethical decisions in which some values are chosen at the expense of others. Neither do they adhere to the theory that some people should be chosen at the expense of others. In their concern for the good of all, educated Western women seek a commitment to social justice that raises their consciousness of the need to commit to racial, economic, religious, and political justice.

Men and women find comfort, solace, and hope in the meaning and belonging dimensions of religion. The moral guidance provided by religious belief systems is helpful to all religions' members in defining meaningful human relationships. Although men and women may approach moral decisions differently based on different criteria, both are capable of making sound moral decisions. Religious communities are bound together by these moral decisions that give meaning to life and enhance the sense of belonging. Mutual agreement on religious norms stabilizes the faith community, gives members an identity, and fulfills the need for belonging to the group.

Relation to the Deity

Male members of Hinduism tell women that they must be born again as men in order to achieve mosha, or the cessation of the endless round of rebirths. Yet many Hindu women feel that they too are beloved of the gods, such as Krishna and Rama. They believe that if they perform the actions of devotional worship, which include the reverence of images of deities as mediational aids, and offer food to the deities, they will gain the blessings of that god or goddess. Some women believe that pilgrimages to temples and sacred sites such as rivers and trees, along with the proper song and dance performed in the spirit of bhakti, or devotion, will ensure the proper and direct relationship between the devotee and the deity. A woman can experience this relationship by appealing directly to the deity of her choice through prayer of petition, thanksgiving, or praise. She need not request any priestly mediator but can approach the deity independently.

Women familiar with the Puranic stories of Krishna can identify with their heroine Radha, the favorite of the god Krishna. They imitate her relationship to Krishna in the manner of the soul seeking union with the god. They repeat the beautiful love poems said to each other by the lovers Radha and Krishna and approach the god in a loving manner similar to the example of Radha. David Kinsley says "there are rituals, festivals, customs and life cycle rituals that are distinctively female-oriented and provide women with a satisfying and meaningful context in which to express their Hindu spiritually" (138). Although the holy men are esteemed and brahmans and temple priests conduct the public service, women are active in popular religion.

Fieldwork by authors such as Susan Wadley and Kathleen Erndl have showed that Hindu women express their devotion through such practices as pilgrimages or processions. They can perform some austerities such as walking, fasting, circumambulating shrines and temples, or fulfilling personal vows. These vows are more than promises to do something: They involve a whole religious ritual. Women chant to invoke the deity, make drawings to depict the desired blessing or event, recite stories that give the mythical basis and justification for the ritual, and explain the purpose of the vows. Usually a woman will perform these rites in company with other women, independent of priestly or male sanction. Many of these rituals demonstrate the creativity of women because the stories are passed down from mother to daughter, each offering her own unique interpretations. Sandra Robinson, a religious studies professor, says that the vows are usually made to a deity to obtain favors for others, such as a happy marriage for a daughter, health of a family member, or success in schooling or business for a relative (201). Because these vows do not directly benefit the woman performing the ritual, but someone else, the idealistic dimension blends with the practical because the woman who makes the vow knows that she is the efficient cause of the desired result. She is the one whose generosity and skill in story telling and visualizing can effectively bring to fruition the blessing she desires.

Some Buddhist women have been able to achieve the notable spiritual heights of a bodhisattva. Usually only men can be bodhisattvas, but some women can achieve that status in some Mahayana branches in China and Japan. Through meditation and correct religious practices, women can reach a stage of enlightenment equal to men's. Although these men and women attain the perfect enlightenment that will free them from the endless round of rebirths, in their generosity they elect to stay on earth in order to share their great learning with others. The bodhisattva, through her instruction regarding the ultimate goal of meditation, which is enlightenment, helps to free others from their earthly sufferings. When the possibility of a woman becoming a bodhisattva was challenged in Mahayana Buddhism, sutras were written that reached the conclusion that "so far as living the spiritual life and attaining its highest goals are concerned, a distinction between male and female is made only by the enlightened worldling, and not by a truly wise bodhisattva" (Schuster, 91). Some Buddhist women believed that they are able to pursue their spiritual journey outside the structure of the male-dominated sangha of monks. Although access to the role of bodhisattva is limited, at least some women can achieve that position of leadership in the Mahayana Buddhist community.

Most Jewish and Christian women engage in religious rituals conducted by men, but some women choose to bypass the cultic roles in order to reach God directly. Their personal prayers of petition, gratitude, or praise seem to connect them to their personal God. They can approach God directly without the assistance of a male cultic mediator such as priest, minister, or rabbi. Literate religious women can study their scriptures, utilizing their own experience, and find experiences written there that mirror their own. They may rejoice at the good news spread by the righteous of God or find solace from the words of comfort directed to the innocent victim. They can praise God with words that are relevant to their own lives or find appropriate words in the scriptures that speak to them. Through study, they can use their own intelligence to complete their spiritual journey. They can, through prayer and discussion, arrive at deeper insights regarding their relationship to God. Christian women with access to the sacramental system can utilize that avenue to intensify their personal relationship with God. Reformed and conservative Jewish women can use this route of study to improve their knowledge and understanding of their religious tradition and their God.

Just as Christians remember the words of Paul, that "in Christ there is neither male nor female" (Gal. 3:28), members of the Islamic community can point to some words of the Quran that uphold the value of women. Some members of Islam wish that the prophet would have developed further this recognition of women, but he, like Paul, was a product of his times. Theodora Foster Carroll, an international development specialist, defends the prophet Muhammad for his recognition of women in his newly formed society of believers.

> It also has been said that he was not consistent enough in applying his principles uniformly to men and women, being like Paul, a product of a traditionally conservative society and a man caught up in the political ramifications of establishing a new liberal religion. If he had been, he might not have encouraged patriarchy to supersede the existing matriarchy so totally, nor might he

have instituted the veiling of women and the seclusion of wives and concubines. Nevertheless, considering the age in which he was preaching, his limited but concerned recognition of women and some of their specific problems was quite remarkable.

Carroll, 203

Carroll points out that Muhammad was especially conscious of the need to liberate girl infants from infanticide and female orphans, widows, and slaves from neglect.

Kill not your children for fear of want, for them and for you will we provide. Verily, the killing of them is a great wickedness.

And touch not the substance [inheritance] of the orphan, unless in an upright way, till he attain the age of strength. And perform your covenant.

Quran 17:33, 36

The Quran shows equal regard for both parents in surah 17, which again stresses the opportunity for women to see themselves equal before Allah even though some other Quranic surahs seem to contradict this view.

Thy Lord hath ordained that ye worship none but him; and kindness to your parents, whether one or both of them attain to old age with thee: and say not to them "Fie!," neither reproach them; but speak to them with respectful speech; and defer humbly to them out of tenderness; and say, "Lord have compassion on them both, even as they reared me when I was little."

Quran 17:23–24

Muslim women can take great consolation and accept a challenge when they reflect upon their acceptance by Allah. They have constructed rituals that acknowledge this acceptance not only by their deity but also by one another, who are equal before Allah.

Women can communicate their direct experience of life to their god or goddess, who knows no barriers regarding sex. They can present their everyday concerns and expect to be heard by a deity who accepts them as creations of love. Their relationship with their God depends not on their class, race, or sex, but on an awareness of their access to the source of their spiritual strength. A woman can approach this benevolent God with the confidence of a friend with whom she can share her aspirations, sorrows, hopes, and griefs, confident that she will be heard.

Access to Salvation

Religions offer their adherents a promise of salvation either in this life or the next or both. Some members of religious traditions see the need to transform this world into a more peaceful, equitable, and just habitat.

Others perceive salvation as deliverance from the sufferings of this world into happiness and bliss in the next. Some religions combine both elements: a desire to better this world and the hope of a new world of rest and contentment. Whatever form their promise of salvation takes, the members of each religious community look forward to something worthwhile and beneficial.

Part of any religion's attempt to cope with the problem of evil in the world is acceptance of the fact that evil exists and confidence that this evil can be overcome, either in this world or the next. This liberation from the world's evil, often referred to as salvation in Western religion, is called nirvana in Buddhism and mosha in Hinduism. The hope of a happy future helps some members to cope with the evil and sufferings in the present. Those who wish to change the evil in the present world examine the causes and strive to transform the persons or structures that cause the wrongdoing. Whatever emphasis the religion chooses, women and all people are likely to benefit from the emphases on love, justice, and truth that accompany the quest for salvation.

The Brahmanic system of Hinduism claims that women cannot achieve salvation (mosha) until they return in another life as a man. However, some scriptures, such as the *Bhagavad Gita* and *Bhagavad Purana*, say that holy persons who engage in devotional Hinduism can attain salvation in this lifetime through their religious practices of bhakti. Women can engage in devotional practices with their gods and goddesses, perform austerities, and live good lives according to their religious customs and laws. To believe that women do not have immediate access to salvation seems contradictory to many adherents of Hinduism who believe in the saving power of their gods and goddesses.

Theodora Foster Carroll says that the "affection of the masses for the *Gita* [*Bhagavad Gita*] largely springs from the poem's offering of universal salvation, opportunity, and hope to all, including shudras and women" (49).

> For if they take refuge in Me son of
> Prtha, even those who may be of base origin
> Women, men of the artisan caste, and serfs
> too even they can go to the highest god.
> *Bhagavad Gita 9:32 (Prabhavananda and Isherwood Translation)*

Carroll says that although the *Gita* opened the way to spiritual salvation which had been previously closed to women, it failed to really improve their status because it did not exhort better treatment of women and lower classes. Even recent reformers "have conveniently ignored the *Gita*'s assertion of equality in their determination to use the ancient laws of Manu to restrict modern women's freedom or equality" (50).

The *Bhagavata Purana* is a poem that describes the actions and love of the god Krishna for humans. It is so popular among the people that parts of it are acted out in a form of a play in many parts of India. Women often take prominent roles in the drama, which extols the women's love for the god.

Watching the production or listening to the poem assures women that they can assume responsibility for their own spiritual life free from the hindrances erected by the brahmins' structures of institutional religion. Women can also gain confidence from the *Bhagavata Purana,* which claims that the path of bhakti, or devotion, is open to people of any gender, class, or educational background.

Women in nearly all branches of Buddhism can achieve salvation in ways similar to men's—that is, by joining the sangha and devoting themselves to its meditative and moral disciplines. In branches such as the Mahayana Pure Land movement, laymen and -women both are believed able to achieve enlightenment right after death by their devotion to the savior figure Amida Buddha, with no need for monasticism or meditative practices. In Buddhism laywomen, like laymen, can perform merit-producing activities that gain them a better rebirth in their next life and prepare them to achieve nirvana: feeding the monks, adorning stupas (or shrines), or worshipping Buddha images. Women are allowed to join the sangha in the order of nuns and to use the techniques of meditation and discipline to gain enlightenment and nirvana, an end to the round of rebirths. In some modern Theravada lay movements and in Mahayana movements such as Zen, laywomen and laymen are encouraged to practice meditation in their daily lives, even if they are unwilling or unable to become full-time members of the sangha.

Jewish and Christian women believe that salvation is accessible, although they do not always agree on the time when this salvation will occur. Some Jewish and mainline Christians, both Catholic and Protestant, prefer to focus on the need for salvation in this world. Other more conservative groups look to a future world in which the soul will enjoy the happiness and peace of a heavenly existence. Some branches, such as Orthodox Judaism and Jehovah's Witnesses, believe that salvation will occur on earth in the future when a messiah figure establishes a paradise in this world. Those looking to salvation in the future use vocabulary that speaks of personal reward, justice, and lack of suffering in a heavenly realm. Many adherents from both groups—those expecting salvation in the present and those who expect it to occur in the future—will admit to the idea of salvation beginning in this world and culminating in the next.

Educated women from developed countries are conscious of the need to improve conditions in their areas and often work to change the structures that cause injustice. They see the classism that develops from exploitation of women in their own countries as well as the oppression of their sisters from the third world. Thinking women from all religious cultures perceive the subtle relationships among sexism, classism, and racism that result when oppression is rampant anywhere. Conscious that all humans should have access to salvation through freedom and justice in this world, many religious women seek to achieve that goal for all their sisters and brothers as well as themselves.

One of the ways to achieve this religious goal of equal access to salvation in this world is an effort to correct political, economic, and social injustices—the roots of sexism, racism, classism, and imperialism. Education helps women see the need for their involvement in the political arenas of their countries. Time-consuming ties to child care and menial jobs have barred women from the opportunities to campaign for political offices. Attachments to the domestic sphere have prohibited women from entering the arena of international affairs. But now women are encouraging one another to get involved in local politics, with the future possibilities of national and international offices. Having been marginal to political institutions for so many years, women are now using their involvement to change the structures that cause the political inequalities. Such organizations as League of Women Voters, Bread for the World, and Network (a group of Christian women lobbyists) try to influence legislation. From their positions within the political and legal systems, women can become empowered to change the educational, housing, health, salary, and economic limitations that affect all oppressed or minority groups. Particularly in the United States, many women are using political pressure—letters and phone calls to government representatives, lobbying, and letters to newspapers—along with other means to change the structures that cause injustice and oppression and hinder salvation in this world.

When political access is not available to them, creative women have used other means. Energetic women have learned how to cross international borders in order to improve conditions for other women and children who are suffering economic deprivation. An example of this sisterly concern is the group called Los Niños, meaning *the children*, which operates on the border of southern California and Mexico. The group was organized by American Catholic families, mostly mothers, who were concerned about the poor nutrition and high infant mortality rate in the colonies or poor villages across the border. In the beginning the parishes gave direct aid of food and clothing to mothers and children from low-income areas of Tijuana, Mexico. Recently, however, the Los Niños program has changed emphasis from direct aid to actions that foster self-reliance and independence in Mexican mothers. Members teach them efficient agricultural methods and proper nutrition. The Los Niños program describes its projects as follows.

> This valuable program offered to women in the low-income areas of Tijuana and Mexicali (colonies) focuses on the important relationship between nutrition and good health.
>
> Over a six-month time period, the women learn about the basic food groups, the nutritional content of various foods, and the importance of a balanced diet to physical and emotional well-being. During the course, the participants join together to prepare nutritious and economical dishes.
>
> The women in the group are encouraged to talk about individual interests and concerns, providing an open forum for discussion of health-related issues. Information is shared about relevant subjects such as child development, family relations, and breast-feeding.

Classes are taught by "promotoras," Mexican women from the community who have been trained by a "coordinatora," a licensed nutritionist and health-care worker.

Upon graduation, the students are encouraged to assume the new role of "promotoras," and remain with the program on a new level. They help perpetuate the program for the benefit of others in the community.

Los Niños, 3.

American college students from all over the country in an internship program teach children how to plant their own gardens, using techniques to preserve their natural resources such as recycling and forming compost piles. The group from Los Niños has persuaded the Mexican government to plant trees and is working with city officials to implement the program that calls for the planting of one million trees in five years in Tijuana. It is hoped that the change from the sterile desert area to a fertile, abundant one will reflect the changes of the attitudes and energies of the people, who can live fuller more satisfying lives. A movement started by Catholic religious women to help other women has burgeoned to a national program involving persons of all religious backgrounds.

Before structures can change, the attitudes of individuals must change. By scanning the scriptures of most religions, one can discover the words of the prophet or prophetess that call followers to concern for social justice, alleviation of suffering, and empowerment of the poor and oppressed. Islam instructs its adherents to care for orphans. Buddhists try to extinguish their cravings for material goods and consumerism, and Christians point to Jesus as the example of the Messiah who came to cure the sick, heal the lame, and give sight to those who are blind to the social inequalities in society. Even the Hindu scriptures that prioritize social classes offer a means of salvation that involves compassionate actions toward others. By trying to change the attitude of the people close to them, women hope to spread the ideas of a more equal society to the world.

Economic injustice toward women has been documented in many studies. According to a 1992 U.S. government report, salaried women receive $0.73 for each dollar that men are paid. Welfare rolls are heavily laden with women and children. Maternity leaves and day care opportunities are still lacking, which cause working women severe difficulties. Opportunities for advancement into high-status positions are denied to women, not because of their lack of competence, but because of the discrimination exercised toward them in political, religious, and social institutions. Many Christian and Jewish faith communities make it difficult for their members to divorce and remarry in their institutions, which contributes to the economic deprivation of women. Because of illegitimacy and divorce, and the poverty they engender for women, the term *feminization of poverty* has become an appropriate description in America. Katherine Kersten, director of the Center of the American Experiment in Minneapolis, reports that one quarter of American children are born out of wedlock and that most of these children endure lives of deprivation as a result. She quotes the findings of sociologist Lenore Weitzman, who reports that divorced men experience an average of 42 percent rise in their standard of living in the first year after the divorce, whereas divorced women and children experience a 73 percent decline. Yet institutional religions in America have had little to say about this injustice except to sympathize with the situation called feminization of poverty, rather than listening to the women who have had firsthand experience.

One might expect that religions dedicated to the principle of justice might exercise that principle in behalf of women. Women worldwide have suffered economic injustice at the hands of their religious traditions. The laws of primogeniture in many developing countries leave women economically tied to husband, father, or son. The systems of both dowry and bride price in some Hindu, Chinese, and African traditional religions relegate the woman to the position of chattel. In denying educational opportunities to girls, orthodox Judaism keeps women economically dependent on their male relatives. When a Hindu husband decides to leave his home to enter the life of a hermit or wandering ascetic, his wife must depend on sons for economic support. The Islamic wife often must share her husband and his resources with three other wives and their children. In the United States women and nonwhite Americans suffer the most from economic deprivation.

Women in both developing and developed countries share a special concern for the religious issue of social and economic justice and have made some attempts at raising the consciousness of others on these issues. A group of women called Women of Faith—including women of various religions from all over the world—met at a conference in Stony Point, New York, in 1980 and at Marymount College, Virginia, in 1984. They called their conferences *Women of Faith in Dialogue* and identified the challenge presented by militarism, sexism, racism, and economic and social injustice as related to religious beliefs. The women attending the conference and writing their proceedings realized that their diversity of religious backgrounds did not divide them, but rather enabled them to see the connections uniting them. They succeeded in establishing a network that through further communication is expected to expand nationally and internationally. One of the participants of the conference, Eva Catafygiotu Topping, sums up the aim of Women of Faith. "Only by working together in ever increasing numbers will we be able to save our global village from nuclear madness and extinction. Inspired by faith, hope and love, willing hearts and hands can build a new, just, and peaceful world order. Women of faith must join hands for this task" (126).

Religion has served to keep women in economic subservience by failing to acknowledge their dignity. Women are victims of discrimination, which is considered unjust in most religions' principles of equality, dignity, and freedom. As feminist scholars study the doctrines and scriptures of various religions, they notice the discrepancies between the written word and the actual practices. By reminding both men and women of their commitment to justice and economic equality, these scholars promote more harmonious and satisfying relationships for all humankind.

Many women of faith have also seen the connection between justice for individuals and justice for the earth. Rather than taking the injunction of the Judeo-Christian Bible literally to "dominate the earth," many women would prefer to nurture the earth in the same manner that they might nurture their children. Mother earth has been a significant symbol for women, from the time of the mother goddesses and their association with the earth's fertility. Living so close to the natural cycle of birth and death, women have been intimately linked with its seasonal changes. The attitude of the North American Indians toward earth as mother, for example, can be seen in the words of Smoholla, a nineteenth-century leader of the Nez Perce (from the northwest United States).

> You asked me to plow the ground. Shall I take a knife and tear my mother's breast? Then when I die she will not take me to her bosom to rest.
>
> You asked me to dig for stone. Shall I dig under her skin for bones? Then when I die I cannot enter her body to be born again.
>
> You ask me to cut grass and make hay and sell it and be rich like the white man. But how dare I cut off my mother's hair?
>
> *Spindin, 150*

Because of their emphasis on the interconnectedness of relationships, many women understand the alliance of animals, plants, air, and water. Their attitude toward justice should include a concern for the ecological balance of the biosphere. It is natural for women to want to protect their children from birth defects caused by toxic chemicals and nuclear wastes. Defoliation of rain forests, eradication of animal sanctuaries, and deregulation of our nation's hazardous solid wastes are issues that many women seek to correct through lobbying and networking for legislation. These concerns have led some women of the developed countries to raise the moral and ethical challenge of changing lifestyles to provide more permanent solutions to problems of toxic wastes that pollute our air, land, and water. Women have been active participants in such religion-related groups as Bread for the World, Concern, and Care, which try to improve world conditions.

The Spiritual Life

Another reason that women tend to value religion is their attraction to the spiritual life. Anne Carr, a theologian, defines spirituality as our "'religious experience'; [our] beliefs, convictions, and patterns of thought; [our] emotions and behavior in respect to what is ultimate, or to God" (201). Spirituality embraces all of life because it is at the heart of our efforts to be fully human. It reflects our inner, honest, searching self that expresses itself in our style of judging, acting, and loving. It is the degree of our harmony with all that is within and without us—ourselves and others—and with the ultimate, whether we call it Goddess, Brahman, Allah, or God. Although spirituality has as its goal union or harmony with the holy or ultimate, it does not try to make us otherworldly; rather, it renders us more fully alive.

Spirituality is more than theology or the study of the divine. It is holistic in that it encompasses all the aspects of religion. Spirituality includes the intellectual dimension of religion because sacred writings, scriptures, and doctrines form its basis. It reaches into the emotional dimension of religion in that our human feelings and affections are prominent in the spiritual life. Our participation in rituals and mode of worship, whether alone or with others, is determined by the quality of our spiritual life. Our spirituality can reveal our deepest identity as we view ourselves in relation to the ultimate questions: Who am I? Why am I here? Where am I going?

The spiritual life is marked by a deepening relationship with the divine. Just as all human relationships are intensified or strengthened by communication, the relationship with the divine is strengthened by communication in the form of prayer. Prayer has been defined in Western traditions as the lifting up of one's heart and mind to God. It has also been said to be an expression of one's relationship to the deity. Just as we use thoughts and words to express our relationships with one another, thoughts and words of prayer express our relationship to the divine. These prayers can be words of praise, such as the Jewish psalms, or words of supplication or thanksgiving to a Hindu deity, the Christian God, or Muslim Allah. Prayer can take the form of meditation, especially in Buddhist and Hindu traditions, in which the devotee tries to arrive at greater knowledge of the ultimate or absolute reality by silent reflection on its principles.

A harmonious relationship with the divine is thought to overflow into our relationship with others. As the seekers of spirituality pursue spiritual growth, they notice an integration of their relationship with self, others, and their environment. They usually attribute this wholeness to a power beyond themselves as they feel lifted beyond their previous experiences of separation and disharmony. Christians call this power the grace of God; Muslims, the gift of Allah; Hindus, the love of a god or goddess; Jews, the help of God. In all cases the power is recognized as coming from outside oneself. The spiritual person grows in awareness of this power and is consciously motivated to the culmination of a lifestyle consistent with this life principle.

Just as our physical, emotional, intellectual, and social development is influenced by our family, friends, culture, race, sex, and society, so is our spiritual development informed by these factors. Religious myths, symbols, customs, images, and metaphors have the power to stimulate or impede spiritual growth. Reaction to these religious factors will be moderated by the historical and cultural settings of the individual receiving them. Because the social formation of women differs from that of men in most cultures, one would expect a different approach to spirituality for each gender. Women who have been socialized toward the values and roles of nurture and relatedness will likely approach their spiritual tasks differently than men, who have been socialized to the values and roles of autonomy and objectivity.

Differing Approaches of Women and Men to the Spiritual Life

Women, whose opportunities for public leadership in their faith communities have been severely limited, have often developed deeply intense lives of prayer. Although the secondary status of women in religion is unjust and needs to be righted, women have nevertheless contributed a great deal to the spiritual tradition of most religions. Separate studies by Carol Christ and Amanda Porterfield indicate that women's spirituality is different from men's in that it is more related to nature and natural processes and to the home and the domestic realm than to history making and culture. They describe women's spirituality as more diffuse, concrete, personal, emotional, and general and describe men's as more focused, universal, abstract, and intellectual.

John Carmody, a theologian, trying to explain the spiritual development of Christian men, downplays the differences between men and women. He thinks these differences are less important that the commonalities. He does believe that U.S. culture has a general social bias that hinders men from displaying emotion or revealing their inmost thoughts and feelings. This makes spiritual sharing difficult for men because they are not encouraged to display the emotions of fear, doubt, hurt, or confusion. "Today it takes great courage for a man to admit to any such vulnerability or negativity. He is bound to expect that any such admission will seem weak, womanly, wimpy" (19). He suggests that men have traditionally used their energy in athletics, workaholism, and a wide range of active commitments that have prevented the passive receptiveness so necessary for divine revelation.

> I am not sure what the optimal balance is between the drive that gets things done and brings one to that peculiar fatigue that is highly creative, and the drive that clearly is abusive and detrimental. Women, of course, have their drives, and perhaps more importantly the myriad ways they are put upon, but the paradigm of type A behavior I have in mind seems indebted to testosterone. With no wild boars and tigers to slay, no Visigoths to beat back, we men regularly displace our aggression onto our work, competing with nature, other workers, and ourselves for both the joy of it and the hell. Not only do we die younger than women, we take a longer time to gain subtlety, wholeness, and what the Taoists call *wu-wei*: creative inaction, not-doing that makes everything run better. Good government, Lao Tzu says, is like cooking fish: the less stirring the better. Intrusive testosterone does not learn this easily.
>
> *Carmody, 38*

Although Carmody's description may not fit all men from all religious traditions, it does underscore some of the physical and cultural conditions that shape men's spiritual behavior in Western society. Wilkie Au, a Jesuit priest, stresses the need for the virtue of self-denial for men because of their resistance to surrendering themselves to the transcendent. "Self denial is most accurately understood as being directed against any forms of selfishness that would make one unavailable for the service of [the deity]" (33). Au underscores the danger in self-denial when one tries to deny a self that one has not yet fully formed. If one has been denied the opportunities to develop a healthy self-concept, there is very little self to deny.

Women writers often use the term "transcending self" rather than "denying self" in their attempt to evoke the image of a person as a being capable of communicating with the ultimate mystery of reality. They recognize that in order to move beyond self, one must possess a healthy sense of self. Au says, "Because we cannot give what we do not have, self-donation presupposes self-possession. This issue is especially problematic for women, who have been socialized to place the needs of others before their own and thus repress awareness of their own rightful needs or feel guilty and selfish for having them" (34).

Prayer has long been associated with spirituality because it becomes an expression of one's relationship to the ultimate. Women, who relate to one another and to men differently than men do, would likewise possess an unique relationship to a God, Goddess, or Ultimate Reality. Because women tend to live in the concrete situation of everyday experience, their prayer often revolves around their lived experience. They live close to the earth in their daily basics of life and develop a healthy respect for the routine duties connected with it. Cooking, shopping, washing dishes, cleaning, doing laundry, and caring for others allow many women to find God in the humdrum and ordinary experiences of life, the concrete situations of the here and now.

Women often see the connecting patterns of prayer that help strengthen their own web of relationships. Praying seems to connect the various threads of their own lives. Through prayer and recollection, many women can discern the origin of the threads of light and darkness, power and paralysis, courage and fear, life and death. Tamar Frankiel, a Jewish writer on feminine spirituality, says "we yearn for . . . an inward connection with God that brings us serenity in the midst of our busy lives, a knowledge that God speaks to us and guides us, and a comfort that we can speak to God" (87). Out of this impulse to connect evolves a prayer that overflows into service for others. The relationship with God, Allah, god, or goddess overflows into relationships with others, connecting others to that same love. In the Christian tradition, male theologians stress the separation between the prayer of meditation and active participation in the mundane world. One goes apart to pray, fearful that the cares of this world will distract the focus of one's intentions. Male theologians say that one can better concentrate on the divine when concrete concerns do not interfere with one's involvement with the abstract. Many women find that this dichotomy fails to reflect their experience of connection. Rather, they see that action flows from their contemplative prayer and that in turn their active service toward others helps to nourish their prayer. Instead of separation, feminine spirituality stresses the connection between the phases of prayer and action.

Not only do women stress the connection between meditative prayer and action in the service for others, but they also see the need to balance solitude with opportunities for community. Out of their solitary prayer comes the awareness of the need of supportive relationships with women of all ages, races, and classes. By reflecting on the lives of model members or founders of their religious communities, many women see the need to practice cooperative and egalitarian relationships with each other and all the brothers and sisters of the larger faith community. Susan Muto, a theologian, visualizes some ingredients of a women's spiritual community.

> Women imagine what the world might look like if people learned to love one another, to remove diminishing stereotypes, and to propose ways of thinking that would foster reform in church and society. To listen without judging, to take risks without killing originality—these are essential starting points as we enter a new era of faith and creativity, of friendship and mutuality.
>
> *Muto, 12*

In this vision of community the energy flowing from solitary prayer is moved to soup kitchens, to orphanages, to shelters for the homeless, to camps that house migrant workers, to hospitals, and to schools. Aware of the needs of each of her sisters and brothers, a spiritual woman not only prays for their welfare, but actively involves herself and her male counterpart in trying to achieve their happiness because they too retain in their humanity a spark of the divine.

That women's spirituality is less focused, more emotional, and more personal and concrete than men's have some particular advantages. When working in partnership with men and their more focused, abstract, and intellectual spiritual characteristics, women can accomplish much good by directing this joint energy for the benefit of all.

Mysticism

Most spiritual writers consider the mystical state as the culmination of spiritual development. The mystical experience as defined by Robert Ellwood, a religious studies professor, consists of three elements. He says it must (1) be an experience in a religious context that (2) is interpreted as an encounter with ultimate divine reality (3) in a direct and nonrational way (129). The experience engenders a deep sense of unity or harmony with the divine, and self, others, and the universe. Evelyn Underhill, a twentieth-century British writer and Christian mystic, defines mysticism as the "direct intuition or experience of God: and a mystic is a person who has had such a direct experience—one whose religion and life are centered, not merely on accepted belief and practice but on that which he regards as personal first hand knowledge" (10). R. C. Zaehner, a religious writer, distinguishes between Eastern and Western mysticism. He says that in the mysticism typical of Vedantic Hinduism the self feels itself as identical with the absolute self, Brahman, the one reality beyond the natural world of mere appearance, and in which the individual self is totally merged with, absorbed in, the absolute (28).

People undergoing the mystical experience find it difficult to explain it in terms that are understandable to others. Saint Teresa of Avila complained that there were not words in the language capable of describing her mystical experience. She along with other mystics remind us that the holy is both immanent and transcendent at the same time. The Quakers teach that the holy is the small voice of God within us, but at the same time it transcends all that is finite and transitory. Dag Hammarskjold, the former secretary general of the United Nations, wrote of God dwelling within us but at the same time dwelling in others and the things in the world around us. Like other mystics from most traditions, Hammarskjold emphasizes that the transcendent is within us. Some Buddhists teach that the Buddha nature is in all of us and that the Pure Land is here in our immediate experience. The zen master Ha Kuin says

> All beings are primarily Buddha . . .
> Not knowing how close the truth is to them,
> Beings seek it far away—what a pity!
> The place where you stand is the Land of Purity,
> And your person, the body of the Buddha.
>
> *Shibayama, 67*

The experience of mysticism creates a oneness that abolishes the distinction between the transcendent and immanent, the sacred and the profane, the natural and supernatural, and the subject and object. Because union with God or ultimate reality is so difficult to express in human language, some mystics resort to analogies to describe their experience. Some Hindu mystics speak of the soul's absorption in ultimate reality as salt dissolving in water. Saint Teresa of Avila writes that the soul's union with God is like the joining of the flame of two candles or like a river entering the sea.

Both Eastern and Western traditions have a history of mysticism. The Hindus have holy men who travel around oblivious to the weather or lack of food, shelter, or clothing. These men seem to have one foot on this earth and the other in the beyond. The Buddhists who have achieved enlightenment find themselves in a state of bliss and peace. Zen masters use meditation to overcome the dualistic thinking that divides the world into good and bad, matter and spirit, dark and light, and death and life in order to find the harmony derived from the unitive experience. The sufi mystic in Islam approaches Allah in such an intimate manner during ecstasy that he is suspected of bridging the gap between the finite and the infinite. In the Jewish tradition, study of the Torah can become a mystical experience. Rabbi Steinsaltz says that "when a person is engaged in Torah without ulterior motive, he may be said to be united with the Divine Will. He is thinking God's thoughts concerning God's world. . . . The one who is engaged in Torah becomes part of the Shechinah itself . . . far beyond anything that is of this world" (148).

The knowledge of the ultimate or self that derives from the mystical experience appears to be immediately infused. Although study and self-discipline can prepare one for the mystical experience, they are not the main agents of this experiential knowledge. The knowledge appears to be given by the deity or derived from the sudden realization that comes from intense meditation. During the mystical experience, the devotee feels a suspension of ordinary time perception and a feeling of deep joy, which is usually followed by a period of deep intense spiritual journeying, involving more study and religious practices.

The mystical experience holds much attraction to contemporary Western women. Dorothee Soelle, a feminist theologian, says mysticism is attractive to women because it is based on experience, not authority, and because it refers to God as one whose essence is not patriarchal power, might, and domination (179). Soelle indicates that the mystical experience provides women who have been denied participation in the religious establishment an opportunity to find God beyond the official authoritarian structures of their religious traditions. The feminine mystic often looks on God as friend or lover whose joyful presence engenders a ever-deepening relationship of love and mutuality. She treasures the presence of God, with whom she communicates in an interdependent relationship of love.

Andal, who lived in the sixth century CE in Tamelvad, India, is an example of a mystic who sought union with the god Krishna through a spiritual marriage. As described in Chapter 4, her devotion to Krishna expressed itself in such terms of emotional, passionate longing for her beloved that she desired to marry him. Legend says that Andal, dressed as a bride, stood beside Krishna's shrine and then slowly disappeared. Her spiritual union with Krishna transcended the physical separation that divided mortality and immortality in a manner typical of the mystical experience.

Saint Teresa of Avila was a Christian mystic of the sixteenth century who described the process of her spiritual journey to the mystical state. In her book *The Interior Castle*, she depicts the path of the soul to mystical union with God as a series of seven rooms or mansions that one must travel through to finally arrive at the center one, which brings the seeker to the highest mystical state of union with God. The outside mansion she refers to as the place of conversion, where one moves from a purely self-centered attitude in life toward a greater realization of one's goal of union with God. The goals of materialism, consumerism, or exploitation of others are no longer appealing, nor is the motive for one's actions the pragmatic attitude of "what's in this for me."

The second mansion resembles the steps of most paths to religious perfection in that she urges the rigors of self-discipline: controlling oneself through fasting and curbing sensuality, greed, anger, and other tendencies that could hamper one's spiritual development. By attaining power over oneself, she says, one can transcend one's all consuming needs in order to be ready for the Lord.

Teresa designated the third stage, or mansion, to conform to "externals." She found herself in this stage for eighteen years because she felt herself confined to a boxlike structure. She knew there was something more outside her area of confinement, but she just could not seem to break out of it. She said that she was only conforming to the expectations of her role as a member of the Carmelite order of women religious. This outward conformance, without the interior love, made her realize that although the Lord had come into her life, she was bound by her own finiteness. She was still confined to her self-imposed box, but at times she was touched by the infinite. Through meditation she recognized three tasks that she must accomplish in order to escape the box. First, she realized that she would have to break her attachment to her own needs, which seemed to be devouring her. She was too attached to acceptance by others, her good name, her need to control, and her material comforts. She was too insecure to let go of her captivating needs until she realized, through prayer, her need to develop the virtue of detachment. Next, she had to work on her pride, which she derived from her satisfaction in knowing that she kept all the rules that led her to be in the right place at the right time. She was happy with herself that she always completed her round of duties, including attendance at all prayer functions. However, her pride prevented her from truly facing the Lord in prayer, and she remained content in her dishonesty. Finally, she had to accept the fact that she had no great love in her life- -neither for God nor for other people. She felt duty bound with the attitude that "I have to do this." Without much enthusiasm, she found herself so bored with life that she viewed it as a "mound of dirt to be moved shovelful by shovelful." She lived in mediocrity rather than enthusiasm because her love for others seemed to be based on her need of their affirmation. The Lord finally broke in to her prayer and allowed her to see that she was loved and that he would help her to accomplish her ability to love. When she let go of her own devouring needs and obsessions, she moved freely on to the next stages.

Teresa called the fourth stage Gustos, or consolations, that seemed to be infused by God. She reached an awareness that God really loved her and began to regard life and all that was in it as a gift. Her stance before God became one of gratitude for each person or event that came into her life.

In the fifth mansion, Teresa emphasized the need of affective prayer. Her intimate relationship with God led her to perceive the Lord as a friend. She liked to "waste time" with her divine friend, just contemplating God's goodness. She could laugh with and tease God in prayer just as she could relax with a good friend. One time when she was riding a horse to a very important meeting with her bishop, the horse stumbled and she fell into a mud puddle. Her remark to God was, "No wonder you have so few friends, look how you treat them." She could appreciate the playfulness in prayer that reflected the spontaneity and humor of good relationships.

She called the sixth mansion the place of a loving person in a loving community. As a member of a religious order, she lived close to her other sisters and sometimes aroused their ire with her attempts to reform the order. At the same time, she found herself receiving great consolations from God in the form of visions and trances. She realized that she must translate her love of God to love of others in order to justify the ecstasy of the mystical experiences. Sometimes she seemed to rise above the floor, and her sisters would detect a strong smell of roses or other flowers in the place of her vision long after she departed the room. Teresa herself would insist that she emerged from these peak moments of mystical experience to the normalcy of life that brought concern and love for others.

Teresa referred to the last stage of mystical experience as her spiritual nuptials. She envisioned her union with God as both sweet and painful at the same time. She seemed to overcome the dualities of pleasure and pain, spirit and body, and time and space. She described her experience in the *Interior Castle* as follows:

> It pleased the Lord that I should sometimes see the following vision. I would see beside me, on my left hand, an angel in bodily form—a type of vision which I am not in the habit of seeing, except very rarely. . . . It pleased the Lord that I should see this angel in the following way. He was not tall, but short, and very beautiful, his face so aflame that he appeared to be one of the highest types of angel who seem to be all afire. . . . In his hands I saw a long golden spear and at the end of the iron tip I seemed to see a point of fire. With this he seemed to pierce my heart several times so that it penetrated to my entrails. When he drew it out, I thought he was drawing them out with it and he left me completely afire with a great love for God. The pain was so sharp that it made me utter several moans; and so excessive was the sweetness caused me by this intense pain that one can never wish to lose it, nor will one's soul be content with anything less than God. It is not bodily pain, but spiritual, though the body has a share in it—indeed, a great share. So sweet are the colloquies of love which pass between the soul and God that if anyone thinks I am lying I beseech God, in His goodness, to give him the same experience.

After such experiences, Teresa returned from her experience of oneness to the requirements of social living. Most mystics do return from their experience to enter the practical everyday life with a new vitality and strength. Many mystics of the Western tradition renounce their attachment to worldly things in order to act in the world more efficiently. The mystical experience releases the most creative and integral aspects of humans as they strive to become one with self, their deity, others, and the universe. Most Western theologians claim that the mystical states of being can offer clues to more satisfying lives for the individual and society.

Andal and Saint Teresa are examples of women mystics whose approach to God bypassed the rules and regulations set up by their patriarchal religious traditions. They could experience the deity directly in an intimate manner of lover and beloved. In doing so, they were able to bridge the gap between mortality and immortality, immanence and transcendence, human and divine.

Summary

The meaning and belonging dimensions of religion continue to meet basic human needs. Some women from patriarchal traditions remain in their religious communities because they have no place else to go to fulfill these critical needs of meaning and belonging. Even if sexism is rampant and their religions tell them they are inferior to men, they will not cut themselves off from the group that, however poorly, meets some basic needs. Morality is a value offered by religious communities to regulate the behavior of its members. Because of the socialization process in most faith communities, women and men approach the moral decision-making process differently. Conscious of her multiple relationships and her need to consider the concrete situation in which she resides, a woman is less likely than a man to consider universal principles and abstract reasoning when making her ethical decisions. Men and women often differ on their concept of good, the basis on which they determine good and evil, which in turn affects their moral decisions. Although men and women may both arrive at the same moral decision to benefit the meaning and belonging needs of their faith communities, the routes they take to that decision may differ.

Some women find that they can enter into a personal relationship with their deity, which enables them to bypass the public rituals conducted by males. They find satisfaction and consolation from this relationship, which cannot be hampered by sexist rules or doctrines. Some women express this devotion through pilgrimages, processions, vow making, or rituals. Literate religious women can study their scriptures and, through discussion with other women, use their intelligence to pursue their spiritual journey.

The promise of salvation that religions hold out to their followers has a special attraction for women. If life on earth is miserable, women can hope for a better rebirth or a happier heavenly life. Some religions teach that salvation begins on earth and continues in the future. The adherents of these teachings see the need to improve the conditions of humans on earth. Many educated women band together to try to help their sisters affected by racism, classism, and sexism. Aware of the public nature of these evils, women work together to change the structures that cause the injustice.

Spiritual growth has a special attraction for women from all world religions. It allows them to approach the deity, unencumbered with regulations imposed by male authorities. They can enrich their lives by the experience of prayer. Women number with the men among the mystics whose experiential knowledge of God or the ultimate borders on direct union. Women can revel in the knowledge that their mystical union can have a transformative effect on themselves and others as they attempt to reach the harmony and union promised by the mystical states of spiritual development.

Questions for Discussion

1. How does religion enhance the sense of meaning and belonging in one's life?
2. Why do religions offer moral guidance for their followers?
3. Why is it helpful for women to see themselves in relationship with a deity as they embark upon their spiritual journey?
4. How can women work together to ensure the benefits of salvation in this world for one another?
5. What are some advantages of considering salvation as relief occurring in this world? In the future?
6. Why does the spiritual life hold such an attraction for women?
7. Is there anything in Saint Teresa of Avila's spiritual path to mysticism that you can apply to your life?

Works Cited

Au, Wilkie, S. J. *By Way of the Heart*. Mahwah, N.J.: Paulist Press, 1989.

Avila, St. Teresa of. *The Interior Castle, or the Mansions*. Rev. Prior Zimmerman, O.C.D. reviewer. London: Thomas Baker, 1930.

Belenky, Mary Field, Blythe McVicker Clinchy, Nancy Rule Goldberger, and Jill Mattuck Tarale. *Women's Way of Knowing: The Development of the Self, Voice and Mind*. New York: Basic Books, 1986.

Bennett, Anne McGrew. *From Women Pain to Women Vision*. Minneapolis: Fortress, 1989.

Calvin, John. *Institutes of Christian Religion*, vol. 1 (1654). Trans. Ford Lewis Battles. Philadelphia: Westminster Press, 1960.

Carmody, John. *Toward a Male Spirituality*. Mystic, Conn.: Twenty Third Publications, 1989.

Carr, Anne E. *Transforming Grace*. New York: Harper & Row, 1988.

Carroll, Theodora Foster. *Women, Religion and Development in the Third World*. New York: Praeger, 1983.

Chodorow, Nancy. "Family Structure and Feminine Personality." In *Women, Culture and Society*, ed. M. C. Rosalo and L. Lamphere. Stanford, Calif.: University of Stanford Press, 1974.

———. *The Reproduction of Mothering: Psychoanalysis and the Sociology of Gender*. Berkeley: University of California Press, 1978.

Christ, Carol. *Diving Deep and Surfacing: Women Writers in Spiritual Quest*. Boston: Beacon Press, 1980.

Eisler, Riane. *The Chalice and the Blade*. New York: Harper–Collins, 1988.

Ellwood, Robert. *Mysticism and Religions*. Englewood Cliffs, N.J.: Prentice Hall, 1980.

Ferguson, Marianne. "Is the Classroom Still a Chilly Place for Women?" _College Student Journal_ 26 (December 1992): 507–11.

Fiorenza, Elisabeth Schussler. "Discipleship and Patriarchy." In _Women's Conscience_, ed. Barbara Andolsen, Christine Gudorf, and Mary Pellauer. New York: Harper & Row, 1985.

Frankiel, Tamar. _The Voice of Sarah_. New York: Harper–Collins, 1990.

Frankl, Viktor. _Man's Search for Meaning_. Trans. Illse Lasch. New York: Washington Square Press, 1964.

Ghanananda, Swami, and Sir John Stewart-Wallace, eds. _Women Saints of East and West_. London: Ramakrishna Vedanta Centre, 1955.

Gilligan, Carol. _In a Different Voice: Psychological Theory and Women's Development_. Cambridge: Harvard University Press, 1982.

———. "Women's Place in a Man's Life Cycle." _Harvard Educational Review_ 49.4 (1979): 429–40.

Hammarskjold, Dag. _Markings_. New York: Knopf, 1964.

Jersild, Paul, and Dale Johnson, eds. _Moral Issues and Christian Response_. New York: Holt, Rinehart and Winston, 1988.

Kersten, Katherine. "What Do Women Want? A Conservative Feminist Manifest," _Policy Review_ (Spring 1991): 113–127.

Kinsley, David. _Hinduism, A Cultural Perspective_. Englewood Cliffs, N.J.: Prentice Hall, 1993.

Lerner, Gerda. _The Majority Finds Its Past: Placing Women in History_. New York: Oxford University Press, 1979.

Lever, Jane. "Sex Difference in the Games Children Play," _Social Problem_ 23 (1976): 478–87.

Los Niños. [Pamphlet.] San Ysidro, Calif., 1992.

Mennuti, Rosemary B., and Don G. Creamer. "Role of Orientation, Gender and Dilemma Content in Moral Reasoning," _Journal of College Student Development_ 32.4 (1991): 246.

Messer-Davidow, Ellen. "Knowers, Knowing, Knowledge: Feminist Theory and Education," _Journal of Higher Education_ 65 (1985): 8–24.

Miller, Jean Baker. _Toward a New Psychology of Women_. Boston: Beacon Press, 1976.

Miller, Jean Baker. _Toward a New Psychology of Women_, 2nd ed. Boston: Beacon Press, 1986.

Muto, Susan. _Womanspirit_. New York: Crossroads, 1992.

Noddings, Nel. _Caring_. Berkeley: University of California Press, 1984.

Porterfield, Amanda. _Feminine Spirituality in America from Sarah Edwards to Martha Graham_. Philadelphia: Temple University, 1980.

Prabhavananda and Isherwood, trans. _Bhagavad Gita_. New York: Mentor Books, 1964.

Robinson, Sandra. "Hindu Paradigms of Women: Images and Value." In _Women, Religion and Social Change_, ed. Yvonne Yasbeck Haddad and Ellison Banks Findley. Albany: State University of New York, 1985.

Ruether, Rosemary Radford. _Sexism and God Talk_. Boston: Beacon Press, 1983.

———. _Womenguides: Readings Toward a Feminist Theology_. Boston: Beacon Press, 1985.

Saiving, Valerie. "The Human Situation: A Feminine View." In _Womanspirit Rising_, ed. Carol Christ and Judith Plaskow. New York: Harper & Row, 1979.

Schmidt, Roger. _Exploring Religion_. Belmont, Calif.: Wadsworth, 1988.

Schuster, Nancy. "Striking a Balance." In _Women, Religion and Social Change_, ed.

Yvonne Yasbeck Haddad and Ellison Banks Findley. Albany: State University of New York Press, 1985.

Shibayama, Zenkai. *A Flower Does Not Talk*. Rutland, Vt.: Charles E. Tuttle, 1970.

Soelle, Dorothee. "Mysticism, Liberation and the Name of God," *Christianity and Crisis* 41:11 (June 22, 1981): 179.

Spindin, Herbert. "The Nez Perce Indians," *Memoirs, American Anthropological Association* 2 (1908).

Steinsaltz, Rabbi Adin. *The Long Shorter Way: Discourses on Chasidic Thought*. Ed. and trans. Yehuda Hanegbi. Northvale, N.J.: Jeson Aronson, 1988.

Topping, Eva Catafygiotu. "Working Together." In *Women of Faith in Dialogue*, ed. Virginia Ramey Mollenkott. New York: Crossroads, 1987.

Underhill, Evelyn. *The Mystics of the Church*. New York: Schocken, 1964.

Zaehner, R. C. *Mysticism, Sacred and Profane*. London: Oxford University Press, 1961.

Zenkai, Shibayama. *A Flower Does Not Talk*. Rutland, Vt.: Charles Tuttle, 1963.

Suggested Readings

Boulding, Elise. *The Underside of History: A View of Women Through Time*. Boulder, Colo.: Westview Press, 1976.

Brownmiller, Susan. *Against Our Will: Men, Women, and Rape*. New York: Simon & Schuster, 1975.

Chatterji, Jyotsna. "Editorial: Religions and the Status of Women," *Religion and Society: Quarterly Bulletin of the Christian Institute for the Study of Religion and Society* 32 (June 1985): 1–2.

Christ, Carol P., and Judith Plaskow, eds. *Womanspirit Rising: A Feminist Reader in Religion*. New York: Harper & Row, 1979.

Davis, Elizabeth Gould. *The First Sex*. New York: Putnam, 1971.

De Beauvoir, Simone. *The Second Sex*. New York: Knopf, 1953; reprint. New York: Vintage Books, 1974.

Dinnerstein, Dorothy. *The Mermaid and the Minotaur: Sexual Arrangements and Human Malaise*. New York: Harper & Row, 1977.

Dunfee, Susan Nelson. "The Sin of Hiding: A Feminist Critique of Reinhold Niebuhr's Account of the Sin of Pride," *Soundings* 65 (Fall 1982): 316–27.

Ellis, Marc H. *Toward a Jewish Theology of Liberation*. Maryknoll, N.Y.: Orbin Books, 1989.

Elshtain, Jean Bethke. *Public Man, Private Woman: Women in Social and Political Thought*. Princeton: Princeton University Press, 1981.

Erikson, Erik. *Childhood and Society*. New York: Norton, 1950.

Falk, Nancy. "Introduction." In *Women, Religion and Social Change*, ed. Yvonne Yasbeck Haddad and Ellison Banks Findley. Albany: State University of York Press, 1985.

Fisher, Elizabeth. *Woman's Creation: Sexual Evolution and the Shaping of Society*. Garden City, N.Y.: Doubleday, 1979.

Hammond, Dorothy, and Alta Jablow. *Women in Cultures of the World*. Menlo Park, Calif.: Cummings, 1976.

Hardy, Sarah Blaffer. *The Woman That Never Evolved*. Cambridge: Harvard University Press, 1981.

Hellwig, Monika K. "The Critical Function of Feminine Spirituality," *Commonweal* 112 (May 3, 1984): 264–68.

Iglehart, Hallie. *Womanspirit: A Guide to Woman's Wisdom*. New York: Harper & Row, 1983.

Jaggar, Alison M. "Human Biology in Feminist Theory: Sexual Equality Reconsidered." In *Beyond Domination: New Perspectives on Women and Philosophy*, ed. Carol Gould. Totowa: Rowan and Allanheld, 1983.

Janeway, Elizabeth. *Man's World, Woman's Place: A Study in Social Mythology*. New York: Morrow, 1971.

Keller, Evelyn Fox. *Reflections on Gender and Science*. New Haven, Conn.: Yale University Press, 1985.

Keohane, Nannerl O., Michelle Z. Rosaldo, and Barbara Gelpi, eds. *Feminist Theory: A Critique of Ideology*. Chicago: University of Chicago Press, 1982.

Kessler, Evelyn. *Women: An Anthropological View*. New York: Holt, Rinehart & Winston, 1976.

McMillan, Carol. *Women, Reason and Nature: Some Philosophical Problems with Feminism*. Princeton: Princeton University Press, 1982.

Massaud, Samar F. "The Development of Women's Movements in the Muslim World," *Hamdard Islamicus* 8 (Spring 1985): 81–86.

Mathiasson, Carolyn J. "Introduction." In *Many Sisters: Women in Cross-Cultural Perspective*, ed. Carolyn Mathiasson. New York: Free Press, 1974.

———. *Many Sisters: Women in Cross-Cultural Perspective*. New York: Macmillan, 1974.

Mernissi, Fatima. *Beyond the Veil: Male–Female Dynamics in a Modern Muslim Society*. Cambridge, Mass.: Schenkman, 1975.

Mollenkott, Virginia Ramey. *The Divine Feminine: The Biblical Imagery of God As Female*. New York: Crossroads, 1983.

Moore, Katharine. *She for God: Aspects of Women and Christianity*. London: Allison & Busby, 1978.

Ochs, Carol. *Behind the Sex of God: Toward a New Consciousness—Transcending Matriarchy and Patriarchy*. Boston: Beacon Press, 1977.

Ochshorn, Judith. *The Female Experience and the Nature of the Divine*. Bloomington: Indiana University Press, 1981.

Pearsall, Marilyn, ed. *Women and Values: Readings in Recent Feminist Philosophy*. Belmont, Calif.: Wadsworth, 1986.

Pomeroy, Sarah B. "A Classical Scholar's Perspective on Matriarchy." *In Liberating Women's History: Theoretical and Critical Essays*, ed. Bernice Carroll. Urbana: University of Illinois Press, 1976.

Rakow, Lana F. "Rethinking Gender Research in Communication," *Journal of Communication* 36 (Autumn 1986): 11–26.

Reiter, Rayna Rapp. *Toward an Anthropology of Women*. New York: Monthly Review, 1978.

Robb, Carol S. "A Framework for Feminist Ethics." In *Women's Consciousness, Women's Conscience: A Reader in Feminist Ethics*, ed. Barbara Andolsen, Christina Gudorf, and Mary Pellauer. New York: Harper & Row, 1985.

Rohrlich-Leavitt, Ruby, ed. *Women Cross-Culturally: Change and Challenge*. Chicago: Aldine, 1975.

Ruether, Rosemary Radford. "The Future of Feminist Theology in the Academy," *Journal of the American Academy of Religion* 53, no. 4 (December 1985): 703–13.

_____. *New Woman, New Earth: Sexist Ideologies and Human Liberation*. New
   York: Seabury Press, 1975.
Sacks, Karen. *Sisters and Wives: The Past and Future of Sexual Equality*. Urbana:
   University of Illinois Press, 1982.
Saunders, Lesley, ed. *Glancing Fires: An Investigation into Women's Creativity*.
   London: Women's Press, 1987.
Schimmel, Annemarie. *Mystical Dimension of Islam*. Chapel Hill: University of
   North Carolina Press, 1975.
Smith, Ruth L. "Feminism and the Mora Subject." In *Women's Consciousness,
   Women's Conscience: A Reader in Feminist Ethics*, ed. Barbara Andolsen,
   Christina Gudorf, and Mary Pellauer. New York: Harper & Row, 1985.
Spender, Dale. *For the Record: The Making and Meaning of Feminist Knowledge*.
   London: Women's Press, 1985.

Glossary

Androcentrism.   Views male as normative for humanity.

Androgynous.   Having both male and female characteristics.

Archaic States. City states that arose with kingship but no longer exist.

Aryans.   Nomadic pastoralists from Central Asia who swept down to Southern Europe and India and replaced the goddess culture with their own gods.

Bodhisattva.   One who has reached the highest stage of meditation in Buddhism but stays on earth to share his or her learnings with others.

Catacombs.   Underground passageways where early Christians met and hid the bodies of their martyrs during the Roman persecutions.

Catal Hüyük.   An archeological site in the present area of Turkey that dates from the sixth century BCE.

Chastity.   Abstention from sexual behavior.

Concubine.   A woman, often a slave, in a polygamous relationship with a man. She was not considered the wife.

Covenant.   An agreement such as that between Yahweh and Israel in which Yahweh said he would be Israel's god and they would be his people. Both partners assume mutual obligations.

Dorians.   A warlike group who invaded Greece and Crete with iron weapons and destroyed the more highly developed culture already in place there.

Dowry.   The amount of money and goods a bride brings to her marriage.

Ecclesiology.   The study of the church.

Feminism.   The belief that men and women are equal in dignity as human beings.

Guru.   An esteemed teacher in Hinduism who has already reached the state of samadi.

Harem.   An enclosure for women established by setting aside certain rooms in a house for women and their eunuchs; the group of women occupying a harem.

Immanence.   The closeness or near presence of the sacred that often is believed to dwell within humans.

Kurgans.   Pastoral people who invaded the Old European civilization and replaced the goddesses with their own gods.

Mantra.   A secret prayer bestowed on devotees by a guru to help them advance in meditation.

Martyrs. Early Christians who gave their lives for their beliefs in Christ.

Matrilinearity. Lineage traced through the mother.

Matrilocality. When the husband joined the wife in her area of residence, often with her family, clan, or tribe.

Metaphor. A literary device used to illuminate one concept in terms of another.

Mishnah. A code of Jewish law based upon the opinions of leading rabbis, promulgated in the second century CE.

Misogyny. Hatred of women.

Monogamy. Marriage between one man and one woman.

Monotheism. Belief in only one deity.

Mosha, Moksha, or Moksa. Hindu terms for salvation, the release from the eternal rounds of rebirth.

Mycenaeans. Indo-Europeans who invaded Greece and Crete and assimilated much of the culture of the earlier Minoans.

Mysticism. A religious experience that brings the devotee to a close union with God.

Myths. Stories that give explanations for the origin of the universe, the problem of evil, the identity of the group, and the purpose of life.

Neolithic Age. The name given to a time span covering the centuries between approximately 6500 BCE and 3500 BCE.

Paleolithic Age. The name assigned to a time span covering the centuries between approximately 30,000 BCE and 7,000 BCE.

Pantheon. A group of gods and goddesses who are usually organized in a hierarchy.

Parthenogensis. Birth given to the universe or humans without the need of the partner of the opposite sex.

Patriarchy. Institutional or structural domination of women by men, who claim natural superiority by divine intent.

Patrilinearity. Lineage traced through the father.

Patrilocality. When the wife moved to the residence of the husband.

Polygamy, or Polygyny. The practice in which men are allowed to have more than one wife at the same time.

Polytheism. Belief in many deities.

Quran. The Islamic sacred scriptures.

Radical Feminists. Feminists who reject the scriptures of Hebrew and Christian Bibles as well as the male deity and prefer to worship the presence of the goddess.

Reconstructionist Feminists.   Feminists who study their own scriptures, trying to uncover evidence that supports the role of women in their religious communities.

Reformist Feminists.   Feminists who use the methods of liberation theology to uncover injustice and discrimination in their religious traditions, hoping to reverse the policies to accommodate social justice.

Sacred Thread.   A rite of passage for Hindu boys of the upper-three castes that enables them to study the scriptures and participate in rites that will give them salvation.

Samadi.   A trancelike state of meditation that leads Hindus to mosha.

Sexism.   The functioning ideology that keeps the structures of patriarchy in place.

Sharia, or Shariah.   The code of law in Islam, which is based on the Quran and the life of Mohammed.

Surah.   A chapter in the Quran.

Talmud.   The main collection of Jewish law, comprised of the Mishnah and its commentaries.

Tapas.   Ascetic exercises such as fasting, exposure to the elements, and sleep deprivation that help one to gain the self-control necessary for the higher states of prayer in Hinduism.

Transcendence.   The mysterious "otherness" dimension of the sacred that goes beyond human categories.

Wicca.   The current practice of witchcraft; followers worship the goddess and trace their heritage to witchcraft in medieval Europe.